SPIDER WOMAN'S GRANDDAUGHTERS

SPIDER WOMAN'S GRANDDAUGHTERS

TRADITIONAL TALES AND
CONTEMPORARY WRITING BY
NATIVE AMERICAN WOMEN

EDITED AND WITH
AN INTRODUCTION BY
PAULA GUNN ALLEN

BEACON PRESS · BOSTON

Beacon Press
25 Beacon Street
Boston, Massachusetts 02108

Beacon Press books
are published under the auspices of
the Unitarian Universalist Association of Congregations.

96 95 94 93 92 91 90 89   2 3 4 5 6 7 8

Text design by Ann Schroeder

Library of Congress Cataloging-in-Publication Data
Spider Woman's granddaughters.
Bibliography: p. 233.
1. Indians of North America—Women—Literary collec-
tions.   2. Short stories, American—Indian authors.
3. Short stories, American—Women authors.   4. Indians
of North America—Fiction.   5. Indians of North America—
Legends.   6. Women—Literary collections.   I. Allen,
Paula Gunn.
PS508.I5S64 1989   810'.8'09287   88-47655
ISBN 0-8070-8100-0

I am a listener, said the American Indian. The White
Man does not ask Me what I think. The White Man thinks
he's always right.

No chei nu ca bache coo Whace.

Let every American Indian make it clear. We are not
interested in being made over as White Men or White
Women. Nor of the White Race. We are what we are.
Being Indians and members of the American Nations. And
as Citizens we are seeking Justice within the law of our
American Nation.

We are passing through a difficult cycle. . . .

I am a seeker of Truth.

And [I] search out all things regardless where. I am not a
Victim of tradition, nor am I a Victim intoxicated by the
remote idea that a *God* of the White Man has any more
Rights than any other so-called Man-made Creations unseen
and, to Me, unknown.

I suppose I am a *heathen*. I will Let it go at that.

— WaWa Calachaw Bonita Nuñez,
Spirit Woman

CONTENTS

Introduction / *Paula Gunn Allen* / 1

PART ONE: THE WARRIORS

A Woman's Fight / *Pretty Shield* / 27
A Warrior's Daughter / *Zitkala-Ša* / 30
Oshkikwe's Baby / *Delia Oshogay* / 37
American Horse / *Louise Erdrich* / 41
The Warrior Maiden / *Oneida Traditional* / 53
The Woman Who Fell from the Sky / *Iroquois (Mohawk) Traditional* / 56
As It Was in the Beginning / *E. Pauline Johnson* / 59
The Clearing in the Valley / *Soge Track* / 67
Blue Bird's Offering / *Ella Cara Deloria* / 83
The Warriors / *Anna Lee Walters* / 94
The Beginning and the End of the World / *Okanogan Traditional* / 106

PART TWO: THE CASUALTIES

Coyote Kills Owl-woman / *Okanogan Traditional* / 112
The Story of Green-blanket Feet / *Humishima* / 117
The Disposal of Mary Joe's Children / *Mary TallMountain* / 126
Grace / *Vickie L. Sears* / 145
Making Do / *Linda Hogan* / 162

PART THREE: THE RESISTANCE

The Power of Horses / *Elizabeth Cook-Lynn* / 174
Evil Kachina Steals Yellow Woman / *Cochiti Pueblo Traditional* / 182
Sun Steals Yellow Woman / *Cochiti Pueblo Traditional* / 186
Whirlwind Man Steals Yellow Woman / *Laguna Pueblo Traditional* / 187
Yellow Woman / *Leslie Marmon Silko* / 189

Contents

Deep Purple / *Paula Gunn Allen* / 198
An American in New York / *LeAnne Howe* / 212
Stories Don't Have Endings / *Misha Gallagher* / 221

Notes / 227
About the Authors / 229
For Further Reading / 233
Glossary / 235
Acknowledgments / 241

Paula Gunn Allen

INTRODUCTION

▽ ▽ ▽ ▽
▽

Throughout America, from north to south, the dominant culture
acknowledges Indians as objects of study, but denies them as
subjects of history. The Indians have folklore, not culture; they
practice superstitions, not religions; they speak dialects, not
languages; they make crafts, not arts.
— Eduardo Galeano

IN THE OLD WAYS practiced by many tribes, a person who is so inclined
and capable on occasion sits and tells stories. The stories are woven of
elements that illuminate the ritual tradition of the storyteller's people,
make pertinent points to some listener who is about to make a mistake or
who has some difficulty to resolve, and hold the listeners' attention so that
they can experience a sense of belonging to a sturdy and strong tradition.

The strength and sturdiness of that tradition reflect the strength and
sturdiness of a people, and that so many women from as many tribes as
are represented in this collection tell their stories with such power and
clarity attests, as much as political moves and community building do, to
the reemergence of American Indians as a significant voice in the American
community. But to hear our stories as we tell them, a non-Indian reader
needs to know where they come from, how we compose them, and something of their meaning for us.

I have entitled this volume *Spider Woman's Granddaughters* because it
contains all through it the light of intelligence and experience that, in the
Cherokee account, Grandmother Spider brought to the people. This light,
like that of long ago, is the light of thought about the past and present,
about the lives Native people live as hostages in our own land, and about
the overreaching power and living presence of the Land over which, finally,
no one can tyrannize. Like our sisters who resist in other ways, we Indian
women who write have articulated and rendered the experience of being

1

in a state of war for five hundred years. While non-Indians are largely unconscious of this struggle, we cannot afford that luxury. When the President of the United States can publicly denounce us, call our ancient and valued lifeways "primitive," and state that whites "shouldn't have let Indians maintain their primitive ways," the exact nature of our predicament becomes very clear. Although it is 1989 and not 1888 our situation vis-à-vis the civilization around us has changed little. We are here to testify that our traditions are valuable to us, and that we continue to resist obliteration either of our cultures or our personhood.

Context is important to understanding our stories, and for Indian people that context is both ritual and historical, contemporary and ancient. We are contemporary because we survive in the face of a brutal holocaust that seeks to wipe us out, and our context is as much historical as it is tribal.

Like tribal history since contact with Europe, tribal aesthetics are closely tied to what our stories mean. The stories in the oral tradition follow certain aesthetic processes that differ from the processes employed in the modern Western tradition. The stories in this collection employ the aesthetic processes from both the oral and Western traditions, choosing elements from each in ways that enrich both.

A number of literary conventions affect the composition of a collection such as this. One such convention segregates long stories from short, traditional stories from contemporary. Adherence to this convention leads Western readers to believe that there are major differences among the types that preclude mixing them, because doing so results in confusion and degradation of the purity of genre. To readers and critics not enculturated in Western assumptions, the confusion lies in the irrationality of taking those assumptions to be universal truths, not in the irrationality of mixing genres as they are defined in the West.

The dogmatism of the Western literary position has consequences that go well beyond the world of literature, which include the Western abhorrence of mixing races, classes, or genders (which is why homosexuality and lesbianism are so distressing to many Western minds). Similarly, the mixing of levels of diction, like the mixing of spiritual beliefs and attitudes, is disdained if not prohibited. This rigid need for impermeable classificatory boundaries is reflected in turn in the existence of numerous institutional, psychological, and social barriers designed to prevent mixtures from occurring. Western literary and social traditionalists are deeply purist, and today, millennia after Aristotle described the features that characterized Greek literature, his descendents proclaim and enforce purism's rules in thousands of ways large and small.

However pertinent his generic classifications may have been with regard to the Greek literature of his time, when applied to the entire range of American Indian literature in all of its varieties they become irrelevant. Attempts to make tribal literatures — whether traditional or modern — conform to Aristotelian dictates results in a serious dislocation of both Western literary theory and tribal literatures.

Intellectual apartheid of this nature helps create and maintain political apartheid; it tends to manifest itself in the practical affairs of all societies that subscribe to it. Contrary to popular and much scholarly opinion in Western intellectual circles, aesthetics are not extraneous to politics. And because political conquest necessarily involves intellectual conquest, educational institutions in this country have prevented people from studying the great works of minority cultures in light of critical structures that could illuminate and clarify those materials in their own contexts. The literatures and arts of non-Western peoples have thus remained obscure to people educated in Western intellectual modes. Moreover, non-Western literature and art appear quaint, primitive, confused, and unworthy of serious critical attention largely because they are presented that way.

Aesthetic colonization affects everyone. However, it particularly hampers writers from non-Western backgrounds in their work, both creatively and practically (for example, in getting published and critically recognized). Further and more tellingly, the obstacles emanate from home as much as from academia: I recall long ago John Rouillard, the then Santee Sioux director of Native American Studies in San Diego, asking the germane and humorous question, Do Indians write novels? during a Modern Language Association seminar on American Indian literature. We literary people in the session laughed, recognizing the quixotic nature of his query and our situation. Is it Indian to write novels — and by extension, to write poetry, plays, essays, short stories, and criticism? Every Indian in the room who engaged in any of these activities had to ask whether they were really Indian. Maybe not, if we were writers. We had to ask ourselves if we were traitors to our Indianness. Maybe we were so assimilated, so un-Indian, that we were doing white folks' work and didn't realize it!

I have come to recognize that a question like the one above is occasioned by thinking in terms of Western literary conventions, and can be adequately addressed when one examines the source of the defined categories and recognizes their relationship to the Anglo-European conquest of the Americas. Given that consideration, to which this introduction is devoted, one can reply, Yes, Indians do novels. And nowadays some of us write them. Writing them in the phonetic alphabet is the new part, that and the name. The rest of it, however, is as old as the hills, from which we take our sense of who we are. Novels are long stories that weave a number of elements into a coherent whole and, in their combinings, make significance of human and (for Native Americans, at least) nonhuman life.

Traditional Native novels are identified as "cycles" by folklorists when they are referring to a number of stories that cluster around a more or less central theme and often feature particular characters and events. The "Yellow Woman" stories of the Keres Pueblos, for example, can be called a cycle, and if all were put into an orderly sequence and transitions between were written in conformance with Western narrative conventions, a Western-style novel would result. Yellow Woman often appears as the daughter of Broken Prayer Stick, a war captain, and her sisters Blue Corn Woman, Red Corn Woman, and White Corn Woman often appear in the stories (or their existence is implied, at least in the minds of familiar audiences). Her stories are most often concerned with abduction, the birth of magical twins, isolation or exile from the community, and transformation that results in improvement of the fortunes of the community. That Yellow Woman is one of the Irriaku (sacred corn mothers) held in custody by the proper clan is also understood by the audience, as is the use of the color yellow to designate womanhood. Stories, like novels, exist within the minds of the audience as much as they exist in the mind of the storyteller. Context defines significance as much as fictional elements such as characterization, plot, setting, stance, style, and language do.

Native writers write out of tribal traditions, and into them. They, like oral storytellers, work within a literary tradition that is at base connected to ritual and beyond that to tribal metaphysics or mysticism. What has been experienced over the ages mystically and communally — with individual experiences fitting within that overarching pattern — forms the basis for tribal aesthetics and therefore of tribal literatures.

Native novels, whether traditional or "modern," operate in accordance with aesthetic assumptions and employ narrative structures that differ from Western ones. The white Anglo-Saxon secular-Protestant ethos holds that isolate, self-reliant, and self-motivated individuals formulate and render experience personal, profiting thereby. The ideal hero, a single individual, wreaks his will upon one or more hapless groups (who, one way or another, are generally perceived as in opposition to individualistic goals). He does so by means of engaging in conflict, bringing it to crisis, and resolving that crisis in such a way that individualistic values are affirmed. This classic fictional structure informs most of American culture, not only in its refined and popular aesthetic forms, but in most of its institutions as well.[1]

Western critical standards, as they apply to the short story, have also been shaped by the "three unities" — unity of time, place, and action — that Aristotle described. Unity and singularity are allied concepts, and it is the difference in perception of the significance of a people's collective experience that distinguishes American Indian short stories from non-Indian American ones.

In the Western canon, the classic short story has one hero and one theme. It is ideally situated in one geographic location and the action occurs in a brief time-frame. Stories that feature more than one main character, several settings, and several themes must be long. These longer stories, which usually occur over a greater span of time and certainly take much longer to read, are called novels. Even they, however, must reflect Aristotelian norms or readers become helplessly bewildered. This bewilderment leads them to identify narrative forms that do not conform to Western norms as folktales, story cycles, or "primitive" art.

But the Indian ethos is neither individualistic nor conflict-centered, and the unifying structures that make the oral tradition coherent are less a matter of character, time, and setting than the coherence of common understanding derived from the ritual tradition that members of a tribal unit share. The horrors that visit an Indian who attempts isolate individuality have been movingly depicted in the works of E. Pauline Johnson (*Moccasin Maker*), Mourning Dove (*Cogewea, the Half-Blood*), N. Scott Momaday (*House Made of Dawn*), D'Arcy McNickle (*The Surrounded*), Leslie Marmon Silko (*Ceremony*), James Welch (*Winter in the Blood* and *The Death of Jim Loney*), and Janet Campbell Hale (especially her *The Jailing of Cecilia Capture*). This concentration on the negative effect of individuality forms a major theme in the oral literatures of all tribes. In past as in present narratives, even socially encouraged experiences of isolation end with the isolate's reconnection with the community. The isolation is usually entered into for communitary purposes or is in accordance with communitary custom, such as isolation in times of mourning, childbirth, menstruation, and their masculine counterparts, meditation, vision-questing, or the year of wandering.

In the interests of developing a critical literary approach that will include more than Western works, I submit that it is not the presence of an individualistic hero that defines fiction as such. Rather, it is the presence in narratives of regularly occurring elements that are structured in definable, regularly occurring ways, employed to culturally defined ends and effects, that determines a work's literary identity.

The rules that define Native literatures — and they are many — are to be found in canonical Native works such as the Navajo chantways or the sacred texts of the Iroquois, Cherokee, Keres, or Maidu. Each tribe has its canonical works, and it is on the tradition of her own Indian nation that the writer draws. The stories included in this collection conform to those rules in that they employ the elements, structures, and contexts that inform the traditional stories of a given writer's people. There are some divergences from tribal narrative modes (more pronounced in some of the stories than in others) because present-day Native cultures and consciousness include Western cultural elements and structures. Assuming they do not seriously dislocate the tradition in which they are embedded, this inclusion makes them vital rather than impure or "decadent." If they are really good, they are as vital as the oral tradition which also informs and reflects contemporary Indian life. The Native literary tradition is dynamic; it changes as our circumstances change. It pertains to the daily life of the people, as that life reflects, refracts the light of the spiritual traditions within which we have our collective life and significance.

Among Native people, stories have been told from time immemorial into the present and a number of these stories have been published. The published stories are of two main kinds: those that are simply recordings of an orally told story, and those that are told-on-the-page. The latter, of course, are those that are recognized by Western readers as "short stories." But to a Native ear and eye, the told-on-the-page stories are sensible because they belong to the literary tradition the writer lives and thinks in. Whether that story is inscribed directly on minds by way of ears and eyes or is indirectly inscribed on them through the mediating agency of untreated wood and stone or chemically treated rolled-out sheets of wood is less a matter of qualification for inclusion in the world of literature than one of medium of choice. A work does not become literature because it is published. If that were true, my cigarette pack would be literature. The nature of a literary work is to be public, but whether that public consists of listeners, readers of rock-writing (petroglyphs), or readers of phonetic script is not the issue.

A work is defined as literature when it is primarily aesthetic in structure and significance, because it conveys a particular confluence of meanings in ways that are particular to literary discourse. The imagination, the community of experience, the major emotions, the aesthetics of personal experience that give it communal significance, that render the personal in ways that make it part of the universal, that move the personal from the isolation of the private to the communion of the communitary — these are the distinguishing characteristics of literary work, and when and how truly ("sublimely," as Horace termed it) a given narrative accomplishes these tasks determines its literary — that is, its communal — worth.

For all of us, Indian or not, stories are a major way we make communal, transcendent meaning out of human experience. What differs is structure and the respective communities' sense of the aesthetic. What also may differ are the experiences themselves. Indian experience is different in a variety of ways from non-Indian experience in the Americas (though tribal experience everywhere in the world may well share many features with that of Native Americans). Significance, what moves a person to the core, what instructs a person, and what enables a person to transcend the constricting limits of everyday concerns, is largely a culturally defined matter. Consider the use of the experience of enslavement in works by black writers. This is not a subject that plays much of a role in Indian narrative works, not because Indians weren't enslaved but because their traditions don't include the theme in the same form in which it appears in black American traditions. For us, the whole issue of enslavement is part of the issue of conquest and colonization. In that context, it becomes a theme that shows up frequently in Native writers' stories about jail, boarding school, war, and abduction. In all of these stories the underlying theme is about forced separation, signifying the loss of self and loss of personal meaning. Separation as loss (rather than as maturation or liberation) is a theme found all over Native America in both pre-contact[2] and modern forms, and is particularly central to Native women's stories in both their told-to-people and told-to-the-page modes.

The aesthetic imperative requires that new experiences be woven into existing traditions in order for personal experience to be transmuted into communal experience; that is, so we can understand how today's events harmonize with communal consciousness. We use aesthetics to make our lives whole, to explain ourselves to each other, to see where we fit into the scheme of things. But "the scheme of things" doesn't mean the world according to Aristotle; rather, it means "our common (tribal) reality" as articulated throughout the ages in our traditions. This is as true for ancient Greeks as for modern Chocktaws, as true for Harvard-educated literati as for Macon-reared blacks.

There are at least four fundamental facts of life for Native people that are particularly pertinent to this volume. First, for Native Americans, humans exist in community with all living things (all of whom are known to be intelligent, aware, and self-aware), and honoring propriety in those relationships forms one of our basic aesthetic positions. Second, in the eyes of America, we (like other wildlife) are extinct or soon will be. Native women must contend with yet a third fact, one more difficult to notice or tell about: if in the public and private mind of America Indians as a group are invisible in America, then Indian women are nonexistent. Finally, we are ever aware that we are occupied peoples who have no military power on earth ready to liberate us (as the Allies liberated France, say, or Greece or Lebanon earlier in this century). Against that backdrop, ever aware of our situation, we tell the tales of love, death, separation, and continuance. These four truths are always present in our consciousness and none takes precedence over the others. They are all givens, like the mountains or the sky, part of what is.

Because these facts are basic to our lives, they are basic to our stories. And because we are storytellers, we shape these traditional and historical facts within aesthetic matrices to form significances that carry us beyond (while including) the political, the historical, the sociological, or the psychological.

Right relationship, or right kinship, is fundamental to Native aesthetics. Right relationship is dictated by custom within a given tribal or cultural grouping, but everywhere it is characterized by considerations of proportion, harmony, balance, and communality. As Ella Cara Deloria wrote in *Speaking of Indians:*

> The ultimate aim of Dakota life, stripped of accessories, was quite simple: One must obey kinship rules; one must be a good relative. No Dakota who has participated in that life will dispute that. In the last analysis every other consideration was secondary — property, personal ambition, glory, good times, life itself. Without that aim and the constant struggle to attain it, the people would no longer be Dakotas in truth. They would no longer even be human. To be a good Dakota, then, was to be humanized, civilized. And to be civilized was to keep the rules imposed by kinship for achieving civility, good manners, and a sense of responsibility toward every individual dealt with. Thus only was it possible to live communally with success; that is to say, with a minimum of friction and a maximum of good will.[3]

While Deloria is speaking of her people in particular (she was Yankton "Sioux" or Dakota),[4] her remark applies to other Native communities. Essentially, the point she makes is that "the intricate system of relatedness, obligation and respect that governed the world of all Dakotas" necessarily governed their expressive forms as well. That Deloria chose to tell a long story (in other words, write a novel) founded on and concerned with the basic value of tribal consciousness, points to its primary in tribal aesthetics. Tribal art of all kinds embodies the principle of kinship, rendering the beautiful in terms of connectedness of elements in harmonious, balanced, respectful proportion of each and any to all-in-All.

What this signifies is a fundamental difference between the Western and the tribal sense of the beautiful. As mentioned earlier, singularity of consciousness is a central characteristic of modern Western fiction. Certainly this value informs the work of modern American, British, and French writers, male and female alike. One thinks of the Brontës, Austen, Woolf, Oates, Gilman, Mansfield, Twain, Hemingway, Hawthorne, and even Faulkner. But in the Indian way, singularity is antithetical to community. For Indians, relationships are based on commonalities of consciousness, reflected in thought and behavior; blood is only a reflection of that central definitive bond. In such a system, individualism (as distinct from autonomy or self-responsibility) becomes a negatively valued trait. Nor does the tribal community of relatives end with human kin: the supernaturals, spirit people, animal people of all varieties, the thunders, snows, rains, rivers, lakes, hills, mountains, fire, water, rock, and plants are perceived to be members of one's community. Which ones are one's close kin, one's distant kin, one's most revered, eldest kin are matters dictated by a given community's custom and one's position within that community of consciousness. Ultimately, Indian aesthetics are spiritual at base; that is, harmony, relationship, balance, and dignity are its informing principles because they are the principles that inform our spiritual lives.

In reading these stories, some grasp of Indian history since contact with Anglo-Europeans is useful. A comprehensive history is out of the question, but a sense of the cultural values that informed Anglo-European culture at the time of contact and throughout the conquest and colonization periods will aid the reader in understanding some of the differences between Native and non-Native understandings of both aesthetics and history.

At the time of Spain and Portugal's initial explorations of and assaults on the peoples of the Caribbean and Mexico, Europe was in the throes of religious and nationalistic wars that had lasted centuries. These internecine religious-political wars included the Inquisition, the various Protestant revolts, the persecution of the Jews, the destruction of gynocratic polities in Europe, Britain, and Ireland, industrial wars, and the subjugation of homosexuals of both genders. Various factions in these struggles also sought to eradicate tribal practices on the Continent and in the British Isles and further the rise of the individualistic ethos. The growing bourgeoisie, largely Protestant in loyalty, was flexing its political muscle and trying to overthrow the Holy Roman Empire, along with the aristocracies that were part and parcel of it, and to reorient it to accordance with its mercantile aspirations, which were individualistic in thrust and philosophy.[5] The formation of the United States in the last part of the eighteenth and the early nineteenth century marked a culmination in the power of the Protestant/mercantile individualistic ethos.

Thomas Jefferson, who brought off the Louisiana Purchase early in the nineteenth century by buying the homelands of several hundred tribes — not from the tribes themselves but from France — for the sum of nineteen million samollas, originated the idea of removing Native peoples from their lands. He was a purist who thought that Indians were degraded by proximity to whites and that the remedy was to remove the Indians. The Jefferson plan was carefully drafted into law as the Removal Act, under the stewardship of the Southern white supremacist and then secretary of war John C. Calhoun, and was implemented by Andrew Jackson. This president is generally held in high esteem by white historians as the great Democrat and populist because he didn't like Englishmen or aristocrats. Sad to say, he didn't like Indians either, though he had been raised by them, and though he had been allied with them during his great victory at New Orleans, which won him the presidency. Under the provisions of the Removal Act, thousands of people from many tribes of the Southeast and the prairie states were forced into exile in "Indian Territory," lands located in the southeast sector of Jefferson's canny purchase. These lands were set aside for Indians, and were to be theirs as long as the grass grows, the wind blows, and the waters run. It seems that grass, wind, and water dried up quickly.

Thirty or so years later, the Railroad Enabling Act, the Homestead Act, and the Indian Allotment Act were all passed shortly after the Civil War opened Western lands for settlement by eastern Americans (including numerous recently freed black people). This legislation spelled the death of the Indian Territory. Under the guise of punishing the Cherokee for siding with the Confederacy in the Civil War, the victorious Yankee legislators took the lion's share of Indian lands (interestingly, the Cherokee lost the least acreage) out of tribal hands, and under the provisions of the Allotment Act they doled out the remainder to Indian families and individuals in the same portions allowed under the separate but similar Homestead Act.

Indian people were forced to accept the provisions of this act because, as Senator Dawes, who sponsored the act, put it, "they lacked one thing to make them fully civilized," namely, greed. In the senator's view, greed, fueled by individualistic competition, would end tribal cooperation and bring tribal people into cultural and economic parity with other Americans. He noted that Indian people had a good literacy rate (the Cherokee could boast 98 percent literacy at the time), adequate food and shelter, medical care for all, and a thriving economic base, but he was disturbed because they continued to live communally. He wanted each man to head a nuclear household and gouge his neighbor to wrest a living for his family and himself alone — in short, to become civilized. As William Brandon observes, "Of the approximately 150 million acres owned by the Indians in 1880, most of it guaranteed by treaties made less than thirty or forty years before, over ninety million acres — an area roughly the size of Italy with a Switzerland or two thrown in — were extracted from the Indians' pocket."[6]

In 1907 Indian Territory became the state of Oklahoma. Today, one can drive along the tollway between Oklahoma City and Tulsa and read dozens of state-erected signs that point out tribal holdings with the dates during which each was allowed to retain its tribal identity. It is a beautiful drive, lined with tastefully designed billboards. On it one moves swiftly and comfortably through Oklahoma hill country, where beautiful groves of oak dot the roadside and lovely streams and rivers meander here and there. It is ugly only for those who know that each sign marks the site of starvation and slaughter. There is still a huge population of Indian people in Oklahoma. Census figures put it as the highest Indian population in the country, outstripping even New Mexico and Arizona (Texas drove out all its Native people during its brief life as the Lone Star Republic). The thruway costs a few dollars to travel; local history lessons exact a much higher price.

By 1870 California, having fallen into Anglo hands in 1848 by virtue of military defeat of the Catholic nation of Mexico and inundated with thousands of gold-hungry rugged individualists shortly thereafter, was all but denuded of Native people. Newspapers of the era filled their pages with hundreds of tales of murder, harassment, rape, and devastation. Generally, their tone is both fun-filled and self-congratulatory.

Under the provisions of Removal, Native people in Oregon, Montana, and Arizona were shipped to Oklahoma and even Georgia. As late as 1924 Geronimo, the feared and fearless Apache who swore vengeance on those who murdered his wife and children and obliterated his village, was imprisoned in Georgia, along with the remaining members of his band of Apaches, and later was removed to Fort Sill, Oklahoma, where he died. He nevertheless forced the United States to spend a million dollars per Apache captured or killed.

In addition to the Boomer movement and the Allotment and Homestead Acts, the Civil War, which itself engendered a great leap forward in military and industrial development and technology, contributed a great deal to Western conquest. It yielded well-trained, seasoned veterans and a military establishment that could train passable recruits with relative ease. These armies, followed closely by colonials (usually referred to as "pioneers" in history books) advanced upon the Plains, western Oregon, Washington, and southern New Mexico Territory, and the Indian Wars that followed were fought with greatly increased ferocity. There was no longer any hesitation on the part of the Anglo-Americans. They went for the throat, and in a space of twenty-five years had indulged in one of the bloodier displays of savagery the world has known before or since. There is no real way to know how many five-fingered beings died then. Certainly the figure is in the millions, and along with the five-fingered beings were destroyed the vast herds of buffalo (60 million in extent according to the United States bureau that keeps track of such things) and the grasslands that sustained them. The Great Mystery alone knows how many other beings perished in the holocaust.

The Civil War also furthered the goals of Anglo-American hegemony. Under wartime provisions, the provisional governor of the New Mexico Territory (whose tenure in office depended on New Mexico Territory remaining officially "at war" even though the small Southern resistance was easily quelled) was able to successfully wage war on the Navajo people. Under his command the famed Indian fighter Colonel Kit Carson took to the saddle with the New Mexico militia, massacring hundreds, killing livestock, trampling and salting cornfields, and burning settlements until thousands of starving Dine "came in" to Fort Defiance and were marched several hundred miles northeast to the infamous Bosque Redondo near Fort Sumner and held prisoner for four years. (It is heartwrenching to realize that the Navajo Nation's American Boy Scout troop is called the Kit Carson Troop.)

The wars to make North America safe for Anglo-Protestant mercantile interests and the individualism that was its weapon continued well into the twentieth century, and if one includes Mexico and Central America they continue without abatement today. Nor are the wars limited to armed aggression. There are more insidious and lasting means of waging war, and "education" is a primary tool of conquest. Seen in conjunction with economic and other forms of social pressure and propaganda disguised as arts and entertainment, it makes for a sinister and dispiriting picture.

To use educational warfare effectively you have to have your enemy in captivity. Thus the Indian school system was developed to aid the military and "legal" establishment in processing the resigned, defeated young Natives who fell into its hands. Schools that were little more than concentration camps for young people were erected all over the West, Midwest, and even in the East, where the star colonial establishment, Carlisle Indian School, was located. My great-grandmother got her education there. She learned how to be a literate, modest, excruciatingly exacting maid for well-to-do white farmers' and ranchers' wives. She didn't follow exactly the course laid out for her, and became the farmer-rancher's wife instead. The bitter fruits of her efforts are still being eaten by her grandchildren, great-grandchildren, and great-great grandchildren. I often wonder if we will recover from the poisonous effects of Indian-saving.

But Indian schools and mission schools are only special cases of the American school system in general. In these programs, from Head Start through graduate school, the young of this land are taught to view the world only through Protestant-derived, purist, Anglo-American eyes. The materials, values, cultural expression forms, models, and techniques, sciences, facts, and thinking processes taught are all cut from the Anglo-American model. Children who resist this intense, compulsory indoctrination are punished in a variety of ways: flunked out, forced out (or graduated illiterate in a society that requires literacy as the price of dinner), shamed, coerced, beaten, put in tiny cells in late-spring and early fall heat or winter cold, denied, discounted, and thrown away, as though human beings were yesterday's leavings.

The results of these methods, all of which were used in nineteenth- and twentieth-century Indian schools, can be seen on every reservation and every urban enclave where thousands of Native people suffer the ravages of despair brought on by too much shame, too much grief, and too much inexpressible and helpless fury.

As Native American political influence waned and Anglo-American influence increased, the Native world was buried in the deluge of immigrants from northern and eastern Europe and the ensuing flood of westward-moving settlers. Not only were vast populations imported from Europe and Africa (and smaller numbers from China) to provide cheap labor and occupation forces, at the same time our numbers were horrifyingly diminished. With loss of population on the Native side and enormous increase on the Western side, our land holdings, rights to self-governance, water, hunting, fishing, and religious rights were abrogated, and our most precious mainstay, the community of being with all our relatives, was severely curtailed. Not only were Native peoples held prisoners in forts, camps, and on reservations, not only were they forbidden to practice their religions or prevented from doing so by having their mobility restricted (most groups practice many religious ceremonies in places outside of the village or camp, sometimes great distances away), but the life forms and the land itself were altered beyond recognition, and in the course of white settlement from 1850 to 1950 all but destroyed.

By the end of World War I Native civilizations in the United States had all but ceased resistance to Anglo-Protestant rule. But their precipitous decline from self-ruling nations with powerful influence on European affairs to ignominious vassals of the victorious parties was not sufficient. Under the guise of protecting the Indian from extinction at the hands of numerous interests who thought extermination the best solution to "the Indian problem," Anglo-American liberals — among them scholars, Theosophists, ministers, writers, artists, philanthropists, photographers, and military men — pushed for cultural rather than physical genocide. Curiously, their position differed little from that taken by the Spanish branch of the Catholic Church three centuries earlier.[7]

Although the measures favored by white liberals did nothing to stem the pernicious effects of Anglo-European dominance, the situation improved when Native people themselves became involved. By the 1920s, through the intense work of activists like Zitkala-Ša (Gertrude Bonnin), WaWa Calachaw Bonita Nuñez, Dr. Carlos Montezuma, E. Pauline Johnson (in Canada and England), Geronimo, and Chief Joseph, the conscience of a few powerful Americans was awakened.

The General Federation of Women's Clubs, at the prodding of Zitkala-Ša, began to look for ways to alleviate the Native people's situation. The foment, even though it was confined to liberal elite coteries, attracted the attention of the gifted and well-connected journalist Helen Hunt Jackson. In her book *A Century of Dishonor*, she brought the plight of the Native people to the attention of those wealthy enough to do something about it. Governmental investigations, the Merriam Survey, and eventually the Indian Reorganization Act brought those tribes still in existence away from the brink of ultimate extinction.

In this century the population of Native people has grown from an estimated low of 270,000 in the early twentieth century to over a million today, and while Native life expectancy is still around forty-nine years, and while alcoholism, fetal alcohol syndrome, nonconsensual sterilization of both men and women, an appallingly high child and teen suicide rate, dismal employment opportunities on and off reservation, and intense community and intrapersonal conflicts continue to rob Native people of much of our strength and hardiness, still we have great hope.

The well-attended powwows in urban areas of any size, festivities enjoyed by Indian women and men in beautifully wrought costumes, adults and children dancing to powerful music from five or seven or even ten traditional drums, testify to the renewal of the Indian spirit moving across our lands once more. The signs of renewal are also evident in the number of young and estranged returning to be instructed in the old ways, the veterans who begin their recovery by learning and teaching the Good Red Road (a basically Lakota-designed alcoholism and drug-abuse recovery program), the students who somehow, against almost insurmountable obstacles (being whitewashed and retaining your cultural identity is incredibly difficult), stay in school and earn graduate degrees in every field. These and so many more trends point to Indian renewal.

The increasing publication of Indian-authored works also encourages our hope. When a people has no control over public perceptions of it, when its sense of self is denied at every turn in the books, films, and television and radio shows it is forced to imbibe, it cannot help but falter. But when its image is shaped by its own people, the hope of survival can be turned into a much greater hope: it can become a hope for life, for vitality, for affirmation.

It should be clear from this historical outline why Indian people didn't publish their work for the most part until this century. For one thing, literacy as understood in modern America is not particularly useful to tribal peoples who were once able to survive and prosper without it. For another, instruction in literacy was accomplished through humiliation, beatings, and isolation in huts, dark closets, and tiny prisons. When students are force-taught, half-starved, dipped in sheep-dip, shorn, redressed, renamed, forbidden to see their families for years on end, given half-rotted and barely digestible alien food, shamed and humiliated publicly, forbidden to speak their native language, and indoctrinated to believe that their loved ones are naked, murderous, shameful savages, hardly on a par with beasts (who used to be friends and allies), their reluctance to take up pen and write is hardly surprising.

Nor were Native people educated to become literati. Individualism works best for members of the mercantile class, not for their servants or laborers. Indian schools turned out soldiers or maids. Children were dressed in uniforms, forced to march and parade to the sound of martial tunes, and were made to do vast piles of laundry, prepare boarders' meals, and scrub floors. The militaristic rule that characterized Indian schools was not accidental. Indoctrinating people into American ways necessarily meant militarizing them into a mindless and destructive compliance with white authority. Literature was used as part of the indoctrination process, but we hardly presumed that we could emulate it.

In the face of this introduction to literacy, the miracle was that any Indian ever engaged in writing. But some daring persons did, mostly half-breeds, and mostly men. As the horrors of the nineteenth century faded, more and more took up the pen — or the typewriter — and began to tell their stories to the page. Journalists like John Rolling Ridge and social critics like Will Rogers and Vine Deloria, Jr., achieved considerable stature as critics of American life. Others confined themselves to writing down traditional stories, reporting customs, or writing legal briefs.

By the early 1980s the published, told-on-the-page works by women had reached respectable numbers; there was by then so much material, some of it recent, some of it recently reissued, that any attempt to treat each and every work in the scholarly manner it deserved had grown beyond the capabilities of any single scholar.

In the main, the as-told-to narratives collected by missionaries, Indian agents, folklorists, and ethnographers were gathered from men until well into the twentieth century. White students of Native cultures viewed Native women as the drudges of men, and Native men as hardly distinguishable from "lower" animals. As a result, only the rare singular individual — a chieftain or medicine man, or woman — bore listening to. Material collected from or about women (at least that which received any wide circulation) was generally confined to matters of menarche, childbearing, or food gathering. The majority of ethnographies contain chapters devoted to such "women's pursuits." Occasionally other stories crop up — tales about lesbians, woman warriors, woman chiefs — but they are viewed as anomalies or outright untruths foisted on some unsuspecting, inexperienced lore-gatherer.

There are a number of reasons why women's stories were never told, not all of them a consequence of white male chauvinism. Native men didn't feel qualified to tell about women's lives or activities, particularly to other men. Bolstered by the authority of long-standing custom, they believed that women had their own mouths, could tell their own stories, and should be able to do so. However, the women, for the most part, were not willing to disclose women's matters to men, however white they might be. It was not until famed anthropologist Franz Boas trained white women to do field work that we began to see women's stories in print.

One male anthropologist, Frank Linderman, did resolve this problem himself by seeking out a well-known medicine woman, Pretty Shield, and prevailing upon her to talk. Some of what she told him appears in this collection, but she was reticent. He was white, and male. The one was bad enough, but the combination strained her courtesy and sense of social responsibility to the limit.

Another white man named Lucullus McWhorter, faced with the difficulty of collecting material from women, hired a young Okanogan woman named Humishima — that is, Mourning Dove (her English name was Cristal Galler) — to gather folk tales from local people. Her *Coyote Tales*, published under his guidance, became a classic in Northwestern folklore, though she had to deal with the suspicious reluctance of the people she tried — often unsuccessfully — to interview. Humishima agreed to McWhorter's plans for gathering material with the proviso that he help her publish her novel, as yet unwritten. With only a third- or fourth-grade white education, she still longed to write and publish. Her novel, *Cogewea, the Half-Blood*, was the result of her agreement, though it took her sixteen years after completion of the manuscript during which she had to endure McWhorter's long interpolations into her text. She even had to pay several hundred dollars out of her migrant harvester wages to get it published. Happily, she was a persistent sort: her novel was one of the earliest in print written by an Indian, and the first by a Native woman.

Cogewea incorporates Okanogan history, spiritual practice, oral story, and contemporary life, weaving these disparate strains into a rousing western-style tale. Readers unfamiliar with popular westerns of the era might be put off by the style, tone, diction, and plot, but *Cogewea* is a classic of its type. It is an Indian story through and through, a half-breed story in every respect, combining cowboy and Indian in an innocence that underscores the deep comprehension of the situation in which Indian women found themselves in the early twentieth century. It is an Indian novel; that is, it is a long story, composed of a number of short stories. It is also part of the Chipmunk cycle (Cogewea means "chipmunk"), which is in turn part of the Old Woman cycle. In this regard it is not so much a novel as a continuation, in told-to-the-page/recorded form of an honored tradition. In fact, she may have been the first Indian writer to manage so felicitous a feat — one that would be repeated many times over throughout this century by other Indian writers, though they had never heard of her work.

But then they didn't have to. Intertextuality, for Indians, is use of tradition. If you write out of your consciousness, which must of necessity include your experience, you must write as Humishima wrote. You do so differently, of course: Leslie Marmon Silko embeds her story "Yellow Woman" in Yellow Woman traditions; E. Pauline Johnson embeds hers in Iroquois traditions (she was Mohawk, which is one of the Six Fires of the Iroquois Confederacy); Mary TallMountain embeds hers in Koyukan traditions. But the process is similar.

In choosing the stories for this volume, I used an Indian process as much as possible. That is, I did not try to include every story from every tribe in every region in the country. If I had, the volume would have run to a minimum of 30,000 pages. I have included stories I have read and cared about, stories from a variety of traditions to reflect the variety of Indian women's voices and experiences. The stories I have chosen are women's war stories or woman-warrior stories. They are about women who have entered battle, and have suffered defeat and captivity. They are about women who have resisted even though all hope, all chance of survival, of dignity, of happiness and liberty to live in their chosen way seemed lost. They are about women who do not give up hope, even when they are dying, their children are stolen, they are subject to emotional and physical battery; who continue to resist when all the forces of a wealthy, powerful, arrogant, ignorant, and uncaring nation are mustered to coerce their capitulation.

War stories seem to me to capture all the traditional themes of Indian women's narratives: the themes of love and separation, loss, and, most of all, of continuance. Certainly war has been the major motif of Indian life over the past five centuries, so it is perfectly fitting that we write out of our experience as women at war, women who endure during wartime, women who spend each day aware that we live in a war zone.

When it came to selections and writers, I thought immediately of the following: Elizabeth Cook-Lynn, whose traditional-contemporary stories possess a compelling beauty (her earliest ones, published in *Then Badger Said This*, which I read in 1977, still haunt me); Mary TallMountain, whose fiction I have shepherdessed and admired for over a decade and who has published widely; Anna Lee Walters, whose work I first encountered over a decade ago and whose recent collection *The Sun Is Not Merciful* is as profoundly moving a volume as I've read; Linda Hogan, another must because she is a tenacious and gifted writer who crafts a story as finely as she does a poem, and publishes them regularly (I have been moved by few works as completely as I was by "Making Do"); National Book Critics Circle Award winning novelist Louise Erdrich, whose novels conform closely to the story cycle tradition I have described; and Leslie Marmon Silko, whose several short stories have become a mainstay of women's studies literature classes in the past decade.

Among younger writers (young in terms of publication rather than age), I wanted to include Vickie L. Sears, whose stories about childhood abuse as it relates to Indian abuse (Indians being considered children by our paternal government, the "Great White Father" of movie fame) make profound statements about our situation during the whole of the twentieth century, and Misha Gallagher, whose poetry moves me deeply and who is a Native Californian.

Of the elder writers, our elder sisters, I knew of Humishima (Mourning Dove), WaWa Bonita Calachaw Nuñez, E. Pauline Johnson (but only as a poet), and Zitkala-Ša. I thought I would have to forego the latter two women, but as luck would have it, each had fictional work recently published or republished and Grandmother Spider guided my attention to each. While she was at it, she sent me a bonus in Ella Cara Deloria's recently published *Waterlily*, then threw in a "younger," LeAnne Howe, whose recently published collection *A Stand Up Reader* returns woman-as-writer to her ancient position as storyteller, but in a very contemporary way, for good measure.

The work of these writers forms the basis of my collection. Their told-to-the-page stories cover the greater part of the twentieth century. But their work alone doesn't quite suffice. The integral relationship between the contemporary oral tradition (told-to-people stories) and the told-to-the-page one requires inclusion of told-to-people stories, so that readers unfamiliar with tribal oral traditions and with the traditions' relationship to modern stories can get a sense of how the two modes of Indian narrative literature respectfully intertwine. In "Yellow Woman," for example, Silko refers to other Yellow Woman stories, making clear that her story is just another in the Yellow Woman cycle. I have included several Yellow Woman stories to read with hers so you can savor the relationship, but I should also say that what I've provided isn't the half of it.

The connection between modern and traditional stories is not always clear. Silko's use of the Yellow Woman stories, for example, leans more toward isolation of the protagonist from her people than toward connectedness — though even here her connection to herself is of necessity through the stories by way of her family. What specific tribal novel (i.e., story cycle) Hogan's "Making Do" or Sears's "Grace" arise from I don't know. Given the vastness of the oral traditions of the hundreds of tribal groups, many of whom have been relocated onto shared reserves, locating the cycle source is not an easy task. Moreover, the writers themselves do not necessarily recognize their own sources. Writers of any tradition often don't. We tend to think that what is in our minds got there in direct, memorable ways, or that we "made it up." In the Western tradition, "creativity" is thought to be a personal talent, arising without respect to the cultural matrix the creator lives in, a concept derived from the concept of private ownership. Ideas are seen as property, and the one who owns them is thought to be the legal beneficiary of whatever payments might accrue to the use of the ideas. This assumption also leads to the peculiar belief that myth and fiction are synonymous with lying, which does not seem so far-fetched when writers claim to have "made up" or "invented" their work.

The collective unconscious, while culture-specific in most particulars, is the ever-renewing source of all of our stories. Yet finding the traditional antecedents of any given narrative is about as simple as marking all the subtleties that distinguish Indian English as distinct from standard American English, and to complicate things farther, each narrative has countless tribal variations. The Indian collective unconscious, however, encompasses much more than goddesses, gods, and geometric symbols. More important than its characters are narrative strands, historical trauma, and other sorts of information that lend significance and pattern to individual and communal life.

In compiling and arranging this collection, one of my major concerns has been that these stories not be read as "women's literature" as that term has come to be applied in contemporary feminist writing. Rather, it is of great importance that they be read as tribal women's literature, an old and honored literary tradition in its own right. I want the reader to understand that tribal women — who have many differences from and with Indian men, to be sure — have even greater differences from non-Indian women, particularly white women. We are all — Chocktaw, Cherokee, Chickasaw, Mohawk, Laguna, Anishinabeg, Maidu, Crow Creek Sioux, Koyukan, Dakota, Chumash, Crow, Winnebago — part of a community of consciousness that differs in marked degree from the larger community surrounding us. Much of what we share is depicted, or at least hinted at, in these pages. And what we do not share with our white sisters is also portrayed. We are not so much "women," as American Indian women; our stories, like our lives, necessarily reflect that fundamental identity. And as American Indian women, we are women at war.

Thus this collection of women's war stories. War, in a traditional context, is as much a matter of metaphysics as of politics. Tribal understandings of the beautiful — the harmonious, connected, proper, and communitary — are derived from reciprocal relationships between the human and nonhuman persons with whom we share the planet. War stories are about the turmoil that ensues when one meets the enemy. They are about combat, about survival, about death, mutilation, indignity, and community destruction. Above all, they are about transformation, which is another term for ritual. Sometimes transformation occurs as a consequence of victory, but as often it occurs as a consequence of defeat. These stories of women at war are about the metaphysics of defeat. They are about being conquered, about losing the right and authority to control personal and community life. No holocaust in this millennium has been more destructive, and no survivors more helplessly victimized long after the shooting ended. As the Cree musician Buffy Saint Marie has said, the United States rebuilt Germany, but what has it done to the Native nations? We are indeed Raven's captives in this historical period.

But we are aware that, metaphysically speaking, there are greater, subtler victories than those of politics or economics. There are transformations occasioned by the endurance of communality, of aesthetics, of vision, and of truth. These stories belong as much to the literature of transcendence as to the annals of conquest. For in them, old and new, we see the same perceptions, the same interpretations, the same motifs and values. They are testaments to cultural persistence, to a vision and a spiritual reality that will not die.

So the stories go, from the long-ago through the traditional to the contemporary. The traditional remains always, but the situation of Indian women in this century requires varied styles, contents, themes, and structures. The women who tell stories to the page have demonstrated their adequacy to the task of portraying integrated Indian perception and identity through all the changes this century has brought to Indian country. These stories demonstrate the Indian slogan, "We shall endure," powerfully and tellingly. Although we've been disappeared from American consciousness, we never go away.

The women whose work appears here are grandmothers and granddaughters, single and married, widowed and divorced, lesbian and heterosexual, traditional and contemporary. Their stories are about love and death, poverty and pain, power politics and the power of the sacred. They belong to the time-honored tradition of storytelling in which the teller reminds us of our responsibilities, our gifts, and our right place in the interplay of energies that are at once sacred and frightening, ordinary and transcendent. The stories are informed with humor and rich in insight. They sing the songs of the tribes as we make our way from near extinction at the beginning of this century to increased health and vitality as we near its end.

The stories don't end here. They go on. Because, as Gallagher notes, "stories don't have endings." Not stories that come out of and go back to the mother tradition, ever part of her, ever telling our lives in the ancient and contemporary context that makes us five-fingered beings. As they say at Laguna when they've told a truth, "That long is my aunt's backbone."

THE WARRIORS

Americans have been raised on tales of brave wárriors who are sometimes portrayed as noble victims of white depredation, but more often as blood-thirsty savages howling down in vengeance upon helpless white settlers. In these tales and movies, the basic nature of the warpath has been ob-scured. Warriors are portrayed as primitive terrorists, and war is interpreted to mean "modern" warfare. The confusion is partly engendered by the language: in English, the term "war" means soldiers blasting away at military targets for the purpose of attacking or defending territory, ideals, or resources. In the tribal way, war means a ritual path, a kind of tao or spiritual discipline that can test honor, selflessness, and devotion, and put the warrior in closer, more powerful harmony with the supernaturals and the earth.

Generally, women did not go on the warpath, though as some of these stories attest, they could and did. One reason they did not do so was because their bleeding time every month served some of the same spiritual purposes, and childbirth served the others. (This discussion of "women" does not include dykes who, in social terms at least, were seen as male rather than female.)

There are a number of spiritual codes that govern a warrior's life, count-ing coup on the enemy, capturing an enemy, or stealing horses from an enemy being only means of demonstrating one's spiritual acumen. The main point was just that: development of spiritual acumen or competence.

The qualities of warriorhood characterize the women in the stories in this section, and a warrior's intrinsic relationship to the supernatural plays a clear part in each of the narratives. Comprehending the significances of these stories necessarily entails comprehending death as one way of coming to terms with the spiritual underpinnings of earth life; there are others, of course, chief among them childbirth. The old warriors used to say, "It is a good day to die." They had death songs ready for chanting when their time came. How different from Vietnam, where men had their minds destroyed along with their bodies because they were never taught how to live in a sacred manner. People who are raised in ways that secure their unattachment to earth, kin, and spirit cannot walk the ritual path of war. They can only destroy and be destroyed, horribly.

What is significant about the heroines of these stories, as about all warriors (as distinguished from soldiers), is their attachment: to self, to relatives, to earth and sky. Even the protagonist of E. Pauline Johnson's story, who because of her white father and his conflicts seems hell-bent on severing her attachments, is forced in the end to claim her connection to her tradition and her blood when she sees how unattachment and selfishness are conspiring in her destruction. Rather than resigning herself to the position of holy victim, she reverts to wildness and chooses to become a warrior instead.

Pretty Shield

A WOMAN'S FIGHT

V V V V

V

"A Woman's Fight" is a first-hand narrative, told to Frank B. Linderman by Pretty Shield, a Crow wise-woman. Linderman had contacted Pretty Shield, a woman of some renown among her people, because he saw a lack of information about significant Indian women in ethnographic publications. For reasons outlined in the Introduction, Pretty Shield was not too comfortable discussing women's lives and roles with a white man. However, perhaps because she was sorely in need of money to help support the grandchildren she cared for, or perhaps because she knew something he didn't, she agreed.

Her stories, many gained from his prodding, some given because she wanted to instruct him in proper ways and seemed to find his ignorance alarming and perhaps dangerous, provide a clear picture of womanhood among her people during her lifetime. She did not see whites until she was "six-winters old." She told him her stories in sign language, aided by the promptings of a translator, a Crow woman friend. She told this particular story because she was setting the record (among the Crow) straight, and because she was also letting the white man know that Crow women were strong and self-defining, regardless of popular male opinions about them. She suggests that real Crow life for women was not the women's lives men depicted to whites. Her point is well taken. Even recent ethnographers of the Crow see Crow society as belittling the status of women. Pretty Shield makes it clear: the one who tells the stories rules the world.

ONCE, WHEN I WAS EIGHT YEARS OLD, we moved our village from The-mountain-lion's-lodge [Pompey's Pillar] to the place where the white man's town of Huntley now stands. There were not many of us in this band. Sixteen men were with us when the women began to set up their lodges, and one man named Covered-with-grass was sent out as a wolf. I could see him on the hill when my mother was setting up her lodge-poles. I was dragging the poles of my play-lodge to a nice place that I had selected when I saw Covered-with-grass, the wolf on the hill, signal, "The enemy is coming."

Instantly two men leaped upon the backs of horses, their war-horses, that were always kept tied near lodges, and rode out on the plains to drive the other horses into camp.

There was great excitement, much running about by the women, who left their lodges just as they happened to be when the signal came. Some of the lodges had but a few poles up. Others, whose owners were quicker, had their lodge-skins tied, hanging loosely from the skin-poles.

Men, watching the hills, stationed themselves, one between every two lodges. Mothers, piling packs and parfleches into breast-works, called their children; and horses whinnied. Then I saw the horses that had been out on the plains coming fast, their hoofs making a great noise and much dust. I must get out of the way.

Dragging my poles, a load beneath each arm, I ran between two lodges whose lodge-skins were flapping in the wind, my own little lodge yet on my back. In came the horses, more than a hundred, sweeping into the camp between two lodges that were far apart, too far apart, I thought. And this thought gave me an idea. Why not close that wide gap between those two lodges? Why not set up my little lodge between the two big ones, and shut this wide place up?

While yet the horses were running around within the circle of the camp I dragged my poles to the spot, and quickly pitched my lodge there. I heard my mother calling me. I had to work very fast to shut up that wide place, believing that my little lodge would keep our horses from getting out, and the Lacota from getting in; but I did not finish pegging down my lodge-skin, not quite. Corn-woman found me. "Ho! Ho!" she cried out, "here is a brave little woman! She has shut the wide gap with her lodge. Ho! Ho!"

But just the same she picked me up in her arms and carried me to my mother, as though I were a baby. Corn-woman told this story every year until she died.

Now I shall have to tell you about the fighting, a little, because it was a woman's fight. A woman won it. The men never tell about it. They do not like to hear about it, but I am going to tell you what happened. I was there to see. And my eyes were good, too. [. . .]

Yes [. . .] a woman won that fight, and the men never tell about it. There was shooting by the time my play-lodge was pitched. A Lacota bullet struck one of its poles, and whined. Arrows were coming among the lodges, and bullets, when Corn-woman carried me to my mother, who made me lie down behind a pack. I saw what went on there.

Several horses were wounded and were screaming with their pain. One of them fell down near my mother's lodge that was not yet half pitched. Lying there behind that pack I did not cover my eyes. I was looking all the time, and listening to everything. I saw Strikes-two, a woman sixty years old, riding around the camp on a gray horse. She carried only her root-digger, and she was singing her medicine-song, as though Lacota bullets and arrows were not flying around her. I heard her say, "Now all of you sing, 'They are whipped. They are running away,' and keep singing these words until I come back."

When the men and even the women began to sing as Strikes-two told them, she rode out straight at the Lacota, waving her root-digger and singing that song. I *saw* her, I *heard* her, and my heart swelled, because she was a woman.

The Lacota, afraid of her medicine, turned and ran away. The fight was won, and by a woman.

Zitkala-Ša

A WARRIOR'S DAUGHTER

▼ ▼ ▼ ▼
▼

Zitkala-Ša's story, "A Warrior's Daughter," depicts a powerful woman whose beauty, desirability, and femininity cannot lessen her warrior devotion, loyalty, and honor.[1] Tusee may look like a beauty queen, but she is a fearless, respectful, prayerful warrior nonetheless. I suspect Zitkala-Ša is having her little vengeful joke on the white women she spent so much time with, trying to get them to work for Indians' rights. The delicacy of the ladies of privilege she knew must have been in stark contrast to the ideals of womanhood she had been raised with, and for which her life, and that of her mother, must have been models.

IN THE AFTERNOON SHADOW of a large tepee, with red-painted smoke lapels, sat a warrior father with crossed shins. His head was so poised that his eye swept easily the vast level land to the eastern horizon line.

He was the chieftain's bravest warrior. He had won by heroic deeds the privilege of staking his wigwam within the great circle of tepees.

He was also one of the most generous gift givers to the toothless old people. For this he was entitled to the red-painted smoke lapels on his cone-shaped dwelling. He was proud of his honors. He never wearied of rehearsing nightly his own brave deeds. Though by wigwam fires he prated much of his high rank and widespread fame, his great joy was a wee black-eyed daughter of eight sturdy winters. Thus as he sat upon the soft grass, with his wife at his side, bent over her bead work, he was singing a dance song, and beat lightly the rhythm with his slender hands.

His shrewd eyes softened with pleasure as he watched the easy movements of the small body dancing on the green before him.

Tusee is taking her first dancing lesson. Her tightly-braided hair curves over both brown ears like a pair of crooked little horns which glisten in the summer sun.

With her snugly moccasined feet close together, and a wee hand at her belt to stay the long string of beads which hang from her bare neck, she bends her knees gently to the rhythm of her father's voice.

Now she ventures upon the earnest movement, slightly upward and sidewise, in a circle. At length the song drops into a closing cadence, and the little woman, clad in beaded deerskin, sits down beside the elder one. Like her mother, she sits upon her feet. In a brief moment the warrior repeats the last refrain. Again Tusee springs to her feet and dances to the swing of the few final measures.

Just as the dance was finished, an elderly man, with short, thick hair loose about his square shoulders, rode into their presence from the rear, and leaped lightly from his pony's back. Dropping the rawhide rein to the ground, he tossed himself lazily on the grass. "Hunhe, you have returned soon," said the warrior, while extending a hand to his little daughter.

Quickly the child ran to her father's side and cuddled close to him, while he tenderly placed a strong arm about her. Both father and child, eyeing the figure on the grass, waited to hear the man's report.

"It is true," began the man, with a stranger's accent. "This is the night of the dance."

"Hunha!" muttered the warrior with some surprise.

Propping himself upon his elbows, the man raised his face. His features were of the Southern type. From an enemy's camp he was taken captive long years ago by Tusee's father. But the unusual qualities of the slave had won the Sioux warrior's heart, and for the last three winters the man had had his freedom. He was made real man again. His hair was allowed to grow. However, he himself had chosen to stay in the warrior's family.

"Hunha!" again ejaculated the warrior father. Then turning to his little daughter, he asked, "Tusee, do you hear that?"

"Yes, father, and I am going to dance tonight!"

With these words she bounded out of his arm and frolicked about in glee. Hereupon the proud mother's voice rang out in a chiding laugh.

"My child, in honor of your first dance your father must give a generous gift. His ponies are wild, and roam beyond the great hill. Pray, what has he fit to offer?" she questioned, the pair of puzzled eyes fixed upon her.

"A pony from the herd, mother, a fleet-footed pony from the herd!" Tusee shouted with sudden inspiration.

Pointing a small forefinger toward the man lying on the grass, she cried, "Uncle, you will go after the pony tomorrow!" And pleased with her solution of the problem, she skipped wildly about. Her childish faith in her elders was not conditioned by a knowledge of human limitations, but thought all things possible to grown-ups.

"Hähob!" exclaimed the mother, with a rising inflection, implying by the expletive that her child's buoyant spirit be not weighted with a denial.

Quickly to the hard request the man replied, "How! I go if Tusee tells me so!"

This delighted the little one, whose black eyes brimmed over with light. Standing in front of the strong man, she clapped her small, brown hands with joy.

"That makes me glad! My heart is good! Go, uncle, and bring a handsome pony!" she cried. In an instant she would have frisked away, but an impulse held her tilting where she stood. In the man's own tongue, for he had taught her many words and phrases, she exploded, "Thank you, good uncle, thank you!" then tore away from sheer excess of glee.

The proud warrior father, smiling and narrowing his eyes, muttered approval, "Howo! Hechetu!"

Like her mother, Tusee has finely pencilled eyebrows and slightly extended nostrils; but in her sturdiness of form she resembles her father.

A loyal daughter, she sits within her tepee making beaded deerskins for her father, while he longs to stave off her every suitor as all unworthy of his old heart's pride. But Tusee is not alone in her dwelling. Near the entrance-way a young brave is half reclining on a mat. In silence he watches the petals of a wild rose growing on the soft buckskin. Quickly the young woman slips the beads on the silvery sinew thread, and works them into the pretty flower design. Finally, in a low, deep voice, the young man begins:

"The sun is far past the zenith. It is now only a man's height above the western edge of land. I hurried hither to tell you tomorrow I join the war party."

He pauses for reply, but the maid's head drops lower over her deerskin, and her lips are more firmly drawn together. He continues:

"Last night in the moonlight I met your warrior father. He seemed to know I had just stepped forth from your tepee. I fear he did not like it, for though I greeted him, he was silent. I halted in his pathway. With what boldness I dared, while my heart was beating hard and fast, I asked him for his only daughter.

"Drawing himself erect to his tallest height, and gathering his loose robe more closely about his proud figure, he flashed a pair of piercing eyes upon me.

" 'Young man,' said he, with a cold, slow voice that chilled me to the marrow of my bones, 'hear me. Naught but an enemy's scalp-lock, plucked fresh with your own hand, will buy Tusee for your wife.' Then he turned on his heel and stalked away."

Tusee thrusts her work aside. With earnest eyes she scans her lover's face.

"My father's heart is really kind. He would know if you are brave and true," murmured the daughter, who wished no ill-will between her two loved ones.

Then rising to go, the youth holds out a right hand. "Grasp my hand once firmly before I go, Hoye. Pray tell me, will you wait and watch for my return?"

Tusee only nods assent, for mere words are vain.

At early dawn the round camp-ground awakes into song. Men and women sing of bravery and of triumph. They inspire the swelling breasts of the painted warriors mounted on prancing ponies bedecked with the green branches of trees.

Riding slowly around the great ring of cone-shaped tepees, here and there, a loud-singing warrior swears to avenge a former wrong, and thrusts a bare brown arm against the purple east, calling the Great Spirit to hear his vow. All having made the circuit, the singing war party gallops away southward.

Astride their ponies laden with food and deerskins, brave elderly women follow after their warriors. Among the foremost rides a young woman in elaborately beaded buckskin dress. Proudly mounted, she curbs with the single rawhide loop a wild-eyed pony.

It is Tusee on her father's warhorse. Thus the war party of Indian men and their faithful women vanish beyond the southern skyline.

A day's journey brings them very near the enemy's borderland. Nightfall finds a pair of twin tepees nestled in a deep ravine. Within one lounge the painted warriors, smoking their pipes and telling weird stories by the firelight, while in the other watchful women crouch uneasily about their center fire.

By the first gray light in the east the tepees are banished. They are gone. The warriors are in the enemy's camp, breaking dreams with their tom-ahawks. The women are hid away in secret places in the long thicketed ravine.

The day is far spent, the red sun is low over the west.

At length straggling warriors return, one by one, to the deep hollow. In the twilight they number their men. Three are missing. Of these absent ones two are dead; but the third one, a young man, is a captive to the foe.

"He-he!" lament the warriors, taking food in haste.

In silence each woman, with long strides, hurries to and fro, tying large bundles on her pony's back. Under cover of night the war party must hasten homeward. Motionless, with bowed head, sits a woman in her hiding-place. She grieves for her lover.

In bitterness of spirit she hears the warriors' murmuring words. With set teeth she plans to cheat the hated enemy of their captive. In the meanwhile low signals are given, and the war party, unaware of Tusee's absence, steal quietly away. The soft thud of pony-hoofs grows fainter and fainter. The gradual hush of the empty ravine whirrs noisily in the ear of the young woman. Alert for any sound of footfalls nigh, she holds her breath to listen. Her right hand rests on a long knife in her belt. Ah, yes, she knows where her pony is hid, but not yet has she need of him. Satisfied that no danger is nigh, she prowls forth from her place of hiding. With a panther's tread and pace she climbs the high ridge beyond the low ravine. From thence she spies the enemy's camp-fires.

Rooted to the barren bluff the slender woman's figure stands on the pinnacle of night, outlined against a starry sky. The cool night breeze wafts to her burning ear snatches of song and drum. With desperate hate she bites her teeth.

Tusee beckons the stars to witness. With impassioned voice and uplifted face she pleads:

"Great Spirit, speed me to my lover's rescue! Give me swift cunning for a weapon this night! All-powerful Spirit, grant me my warrior-father's heart, strong to slay a foe and mighty to save a friend!"

In the midst of the enemy's camp-ground, underneath a temporary dance-house, are men and women in gala-day dress. It is late in the night, but the merry warriors bend and bow their nude, painted bodies before a bright center fire. To the lusty men's voices and the rhythmic throbbing drum, they leap and rebound with feathered headgears waving.

Women with red-painted cheeks and long, braided hair sit in a large half-circle against the willow railing. They, too, join in the singing, and rise to dance with their victorious warriors.

Amid this circular dance arena stands a prisoner bound to a post, haggard with shame and sorrow. He hangs his disheveled head.

He stares with unseeing eyes upon the bare earth at his feet. With jeers and smirking faces the dancers mock the Dakota captive. Rowdy braves and small boys hoot and yell in derision.

Silent among the noisy mob, a tall woman, leaning both elbows on the round willow railing, peers into the lighted arena. The dancing center fire shines bright into her handsome face, intensifying the night in her dark eyes. It breaks into myriad points upon her beaded dress. Unmindful of the surging throng jostling her at either side, she glares in upon the hateful, scoffing men. Suddenly she turns her head. Tittering maids whisper near her ear:

"There! There! See him now, sneering in the captive's face. 'Tis he who sprang upon the young man and dragged him by his long hair to yonder post. See! He is handsome! How gracefully he dances!"

The silent young woman looks toward the bound captive. She sees a warrior, scarce older than the captive, flourishing a tomahawk in the Dakota's face. A burning rage darts forth from her eyes and brands him for a victim of revenge. Her heart mutters within her breast, "Come, I wish to meet you, vile foe, who captured my lover and tortures him now with a living death."

Here the singers hush their voices, and the dancers scatter to their various resting-places along the willow ring. The victor gives a reluctant last twirl of his tomahawk, then, like the others, he leaves the center ground. With head and shoulders swaying from side to side, he carries a high-pointing chin toward the willow railing. Sitting down upon the ground with crossed legs, he fans himself with an outspread turkey wing.

Now and then he stops his haughty blinking to peep out of the corners of his eyes. He hears someone clearing her throat gently. It is unmistakably for his ear. The wing-fan swings irregularly to and fro. At length he turns a proud face over a bare shoulder and beholds a handsome woman smiling.

"Ah, she would speak to a hero!" thumps his heart wildly.

The singers raise their voices in unison. The music is irresistible. Again lunges the victor into the open arena. Again he leers into the captive's face. At every interval between the songs he returns to his resting-place. Here the young woman awaits him. As he approaches she smiles boldly into his eyes. He is pleased with her face and her smile.

Waving his wing-fan spasmodically in front of his face, he sits with his ears pricked up. He catches a low whisper. A hand taps him lightly on the shoulder. The handsome woman speaks to him in his own tongue. "Come out into the night. I wish to tell you who I am."

He must know what sweet words of praise the handsome woman has for him. With both hands he spreads the meshes of the loosely woven willows, and crawls out unnoticed into the dark.

Before him stands the young woman. Beckoning him with a slender hand, she steps backward, away from the light and the restless throng of onlookers. He follows with impatient strides. She quickens her pace. He lengthens his strides. Then suddenly the woman turns from him and darts away with amazing speed. Clinching his fists and biting his lower lip, the young man runs after the fleeing woman. In his maddened pursuit he forgets the dance arena.

Beside a cluster of low bushes the woman halts. The young man, panting for breath and plunging headlong forward, whispers loud, "Pray tell me, are you a woman or an evil spirit to lure me away?"

Turning on heels firmly planted in the earth, the woman gives a wild spring forward, like a panther for its prey. In a husky voice she hissed between her teeth, "I am a Dakota woman!"

From her unerring long knife the enemy falls heavily at her feet. The Great Spirit heard Tusee's prayer on the hilltop. He gave her a warrior's strong heart to lessen the foe by one.

A bent old woman's figure, with a bundle like a grandchild slung on her back, walks round and round the dance-house. The wearied onlookers are leaving in twos and threes. The tired dancers creep out of the willow railing, and some go out at the entrance way, till the singers, too, rise from the drum and are trudging drowsily homeward. Within the arena the center fire lies broken in red embers. The night no longer lingers about the willow railing, but, hovering into the dance-house, covers here and there a snoring man whom sleep has overpowered where he sat.

The captive in his tight-binding rawhide ropes hangs in hopeless despair. Close about him the gloom of night is slowly crouching. Yet the last red, crackling embers cast a faint light upon his long black hair, and, shining through the thick mats, caress his wan face with undying hope.

Still about the dance-house the old woman prowls. Now the embers are gray with ashes.

The old bent woman appears at the entrance way. With a cautious, groping foot she enters. Whispering between her teeth a lullaby for her sleeping child in her blanket, she searches for something forgotten.

Noisily snored the dreaming men in the darkest parts. As the lisping old woman draws nigh, the captive again opens his eyes.

A forefinger she presses to her lip. The young man arouses himself from his stupor. His senses belie him. Before his wide-open eyes the old bent figure straightens into its youthful stature. Tusee herself is beside him. With a stroke upward and downward she severs the cruel cords with her sharp blade. Dropping her blanket from her shoulders, so that it hangs from her girdled waist like a skirt, she shakes the large bundle into a light shawl for her lover. Quickly she spreads it over his bare back.

"Come!" she whispers, and turns to go; but the young man, numb and helpless, staggers nigh to falling.

The sight of his weakness makes her strong. A mighty power thrills her body. Stooping beneath his outstretched arms grasping at the air for support, Tusee lifts him upon her broad shoulders. With half-running, triumphant steps she carries him away into the open night.

Delia Oshogay

OSHKIKWE'S BABY

V V V V
V

"Oshkikwe's Baby" is a traditional Chippewa (Anishinabeg) story, narrated by Delia Oshogay and interpreted by Maggie Lamorie. It was collected by Ernestine Friedl at Court Oreilles, Wisconsin in 1942. The two sisters, Matchikwewis and Oshkikwe, figure regularly in women's stories collected in the Court Oreilles area. Said to be daughters of Wenebojo, the trickster figure of the Chippewa, they are at least one-quarter supernatural themselves, as Wenebojo was conceived by his mother from a supernatural father, as is Oshkikwe's son in this story. Their warpath is a supernatural odyssey, and knowledge and skill of the supernatural warrior is necessary to the successful outcome. That is to say, both women are wise women, which may be one reason why the Old Woman steals the baby. Certainly there are occult resonances in the story, but traditional life inevitably is concerned with the occult as well as the spiritual — an association that is more obvious to nontribal people. To traditional folk the distinction is not so sharp, nor the boundaries so clear.

MATCHIKWEWIS AND OSHKIKWE were out picking cranberries and staying by themselves. One day Oshkikwe found a tiny pipe with a little face on it. The eyes were looking at her and would wink at her. She showed it to her older sister and said, "Look at this little pipe! I guess we're not really alone in the world. There must be somebody else in the world."

Matchikwewis said that they had once lived in a village and that their father had been the head man. When he died, she took Oshkikwe away, because she didn't want her to be abused by the people.

Matchikwewis knew that her sister was going to give birth to a child because of the pipe. One time, when they woke up, they saw a *tikinagan* (cradleboard) with wraps and everything set for a baby, including a little bow and arrow. Oshkikwe took sick and found a little boy and a little pup.

Matchikwewis took good care of her sister, and everything was going fine. One day Matchikwewis told her sister that she'd had a dream which told her not to leave the baby out of her sight for ten days but always stay with him, for otherwise an old witch would come for him. Once Oshkikwe just went outside to get a stick of wood, and when she came back she could see the swing moving. The pup used to guard the little cradleboard. While she went out, she heard the pup barking. When she got back, both the baby and the pup were gone. All that remained was a piece of the hindquarters of the witch which the dog must have bitten off and a little piece of the *tikinagan* which the pup must have got too.

As soon as she saw this, she said that she'd get ready to look for the child and the pup. She told her sister she'd be gone for ten days. The sister told her to work on her breasts, so they wouldn't run dry. She had been nursing the baby on one breast and the pup on the other. The sister also said that the further the witch went with the child, the bigger he'd get, and soon he'd become a man.

The mother started walking, and she crossed a deer trail. She kept on going and came to another trail: a man's tracks, deer tracks, and a dog's tracks. This was her son's tracks, because the witch had so much power that it didn't take the child long to grow up. Finally, Oshkikwe came to a wigwam. Outside of it, she saw a man who must have been her son already grown up.

The man went into the wigwam to tell his "mother" what he had seen. He told her that he had seen a young woman. But the witch said, "Don't you dare look at that woman, because she's just a dirty old witch. As soon as you look at her, you'll become ugly."

The young man said, "Well, I don't like to see her trying to build a wigwam of old birchbark and things. Why don't you give her some nice birchbark, so it won't rain on her?"

The witch didn't like to do it, but she had to. Whenever this old witch knew that there was a new-born boy, she'd kidnap him, and as soon as they got into her territory, the boy would grow up and go hunting and work for her, so she got all the profit out of it.

This man of Oshkikwe's got home early one afternoon, because he had to make arrows before it got dark. Just as he went by Oshkikwe's wigwam, she had her breasts open. The pup was hanging around Oshkikwe, because he remembered her.

While the young man was whittling his arrows, the first thing he knew Oshkikwe was sitting on a woodpile, showing her breasts to her son. He knew that there was something he couldn't remember, but he couldn't remember what it was. He suspected something, though. In his dream he made a wish that his "mother" would sleep soundly, so that he could go over and visit this young woman whom his "mother" called an old witch. So his "mother" slept soundly that night. He went to see the young woman, accompanied by the pup. When the pup got there, he went to nurse at the woman's left breast. Oshkikwe said to him, "You are my son, and here is the milk you lived on before this old witch got hold of you."

He couldn't remember, but she told him, and she brought a piece of his cradleboard made of cedar and shells, and also a piece of the old witch's hindquarters, and showed them to her son. He asked his mother how she managed to live and whether the old witch gave her anything to eat. Oshkikwe said, "When she gives me something, she brings only the livers and dirties them on the way." Then the man told his mother he'd go back with her, but not for a while. The minute he'd go back to her, he'd turn right into a baby. At the same time, though, he had to find out the real facts about who his mother was.

That night he pretended to be sick and started to moan. His "mother" asked him what was the matter, and he said he was dying and that the only thing that would save him would be the sight of his old cradleboard. The old lady went out and got a very old cradleboard, but he said that wasn't his. Then she got his real one, with the pretty shells, and he saw that part of it was missing, and he knew then that Oshkikwe was right, since she had the missing part. Then he started to moan again. His "mother" asked him what the matter was. He said he had to taste the milk he used to nurse on. She pulled out her own breast and squeezed out some old yellow stuff and gave it to him to taste. He thought it was funny that he'd ever grown up with such awful stuff for food. He had to find out one more thing. He said, "The only way I can live is if you pull up your skirts high and dance around a little." So she danced for him and lifted up her buckskin dress. He called out, "Higher, ma!" Then he knew that Oshkikwe was right. The old witch went to sleep after that.

The man went back to his mother and told her that he'd go hunting the next morning. He planned to kill a deer and hang it high up on a tree, and then come back and tell the old witch to go and bring it back because his feet were all blistered.

The next morning he came back and told the witch that he'd killed two deer, one near and one far. He told the witch to send Oshkikwe to go and get the more distant deer, and she should get the other one. They both set out, but instead of going on, Oshkikwe came right back.

The old witch had two children. The man banged them both on the head with a club and killed them. Then he stuck two sugar cookies in their mouths and made it look as though they were still alive.

Then he and his mother picked up one stake of the wigwam and went down into that hole a long ways. The man and the puppy got smaller and smaller. By the time the old witch got home, her boy was gone, and here were her two children with sugar cookies in their mouths. She yelled at the kids, because they were eating something she was saving for their brother; but when she got closer to them, she saw that they were dead.

Then she spoke aloud to her son: "Huh! What do you think? This world is too small for you to get away from me!" She found the hole they had gone down and followed them. By this time the man and the puppy had become very small. He told his mother to put him in the cradleboard which she'd brought along. The last thing he managed to tell his mother was that she should make a big mark with his arrow, and there the earth would split. She took the arrow and marked the ground just as the witch came along. Then the witch fell into the split, and that was the end of her. When Oshkikwe got home, she found her sister all dressed up and her hair oiled. She said that if Oshkikwe hadn't arrived that night, she would have gone after her the next day.

Louise Erdrich
AMERICAN HORSE

V V V V
V

In Louise Erdrich's story "American Horse," Albertine, like her disowned
cousin Officer Harmony, is a Michif (otherwise known as Metis). Michifs
are Indians of Cree, Sioux, and Chippewa (Anishinabeg) ancestry who
intermarried long ago with Scotsmen in the western Great Lakes region.
Eventually French blood was mixed in, and their language, culture, and
kinship system combined their predecessors' tribal ways with Catholic practices. In the process, they developed over two or three hundred years into a
distinctive group of people who presently reside in southern Canada and
the northern midwestern United States. In the nineteenth century, under
the leadership of Louis Reil, they gave the British a run for their money.

Also during the nineteenth century some Lakota dissidents fled persecution in the United States by going to Canada, where they attempted
unsuccessfully to throw in with the rebellious Michif — among them members of Sitting Bull's band and perhaps relatives of American Horse. After
a short time the refugees returned to the United States and Sitting Bull
gave in: he went so far as to urge his band's children to attend white schools.
In the end a number of Michif fled from Canada to the western United
States, where they settled in Montana. My mother's father was one of the
survivors of the abortive Michif revolution.

When read in conjunction with "Oshkikwe's Baby," the underlying Anishinabeg women's motif in "American Horse" becomes apparent, as does
the history of the Michif trapped by geopolitical exigencies in the United
States. The theft of a miraculous child, son of a deceased father (and father's
people), by a wicked witch and the trickery involved are pertinent here. The
resolution in which Albertine-Oshkikwe reclaims her child is not included
in the story — perhaps because it has yet to occur in historical time. The
final scene, with Buddy taking and eating the chocolate bar, is reminiscent
of Northwestern stories about how Raven (another evil force who abducts
Indian women and children and holds them captive for the purposes of

enslavement) ensures the enthrallment of his victims: he tricks them into eating shit (literally). Because they have done so, they cannot escape his clutches. Only when they succeed in reversing the trick can they gain their freedom.[1]

THE WOMAN SLEEPING on the cot in the woodshed was Albertine American Horse. The name was left over from her mother's short marriage. The boy was the son of the man she had loved and let go. Buddy was on the cot too, sitting on the edge because he'd been awake three hours watching out for his mother and besides, she took up the whole cot. Her feet hung over the edge, limp and brown as two trout. Her long arms reached out and slapped at things she saw in her dreams.

Buddy had been knocked awake out of hiding in a washing machine while herds of policemen with dogs searched through a large building with many tiny rooms. When the arm came down, Buddy screamed because it had a blue cuff and sharp silver buttons. "Tss," his mother mumbled, half awake, "wasn't nothing." But Buddy sat up after her breathing went deep again, and he watched.

There was something coming and he knew it.

It was coming from very far off but he had a picture of it in his mind. It was a large thing made of metal with many barbed hooks, points, and drag chains on it, something like a giant potato peeler that rolled out of the sky, scraping clouds down with it and jabbing or crushing everything that lay in its path on the ground.

Buddy watched his mother. If he woke her up, she would know what to do about the thing, but he thought he'd wait until he saw it for sure before he shook her. She was pretty, sleeping, and he liked knowing he could look at her as long and close up as he wanted. He took a strand of her hair and held it in his hands as if it was the rein to a delicate beast. She was strong enough and could pull him along like the horse their name was.

Buddy had his mother's and his grandmother's name because his father had been a big mistake.

"They're all mistakes, even your father. But *you* are the best thing that ever happened to me."

That was what she said when he asked.

Even Kadie, the boyfriend crippled from being in a car wreck, was not as good a thing that had happened to his mother as Buddy was. "He was a medium-size mistake," she said. "He's hurt and I shouldn't even say that, but it's the truth." At the moment, Buddy knew that being the best thing in his mother's life, he was also the reason they were hiding from the cops.

He wanted to touch the satin roses sewed on her pink tee-shirt, but he knew he shouldn't do that even in her sleep. If she woke up and found him touching the roses, she would say, "Quit that, Buddy." Sometimes she told him to stop hugging her like a gorilla. She never said that in the mean voice she used when he oppressed her, but when she said that he loosened up anyway.

There were times he felt like hugging her so hard and in such a special way that she would say to him, "Let's get married." There were also times he closed his eyes and wished that she would die, only a few times, but still it haunted him that his wish might come true. He and Uncle Lawrence would be left alone. Buddy wasn't worried, though, about his mother getting married to somebody else. She had said to her friend, Madonna, "All men suck," when she thought Buddy wasn't listening. He had made an uncertain sound, and when they heard him they took him in their arms.

"Except for you, Buddy," his mother said. "All except for you and maybe Uncle Lawrence, although he's pushing it."

"The cops suck the worst though," Buddy whispered to his mother's sleeping face, "because they're after us." He felt tired again, slumped down, and put his legs beneath the blanket. He closed his eyes and got the feeling that the cot was lifting up beneath him, that it was arching its canvas back and then traveling, traveling very fast and in the wrong direction for when he looked up he saw the three of them were advancing to meet the great metal thing with hooks and barbs and all sorts of sharp equipment to catch their bodies and draw their blood. He heard its insides as it rushed toward them, purring softly like a powerful motor and then they were right in its shadow. He pulled the reins as hard as he could and the beast reared, lifting him. His mother clapped her hand across his mouth.

"Okay," she said. "Lay low. They're outside and they're gonna hunt."

She touched his shoulder and Buddy leaned over with her to look through a crack in the boards.

They were out there all right, Albertine saw them. Two officers and that social worker woman. Vicki Koob. There had been no whistle, no dream, no voice to warn her that they were coming. There was only the crunching sound of cinders in the yard, the engine purring, the dust sifting off their car in a fine light brownish cloud and settling around them.

The three people came to a halt in their husk of metal — the car emblazoned with the North Dakota State Highway Patrol emblem which is the glowing profile of the Sioux policeman, Red Tomahawk, the one who killed Sitting Bull. Albertine gave Buddy the blanket and told him that he might have to wrap it around him and hide underneath the cot.

"We're gonna wait and see what they do." She took him in her lap and hunched her arms around him. "Don't you worry," she whispered against his ear. "Lawrence knows how to fool them."

Buddy didn't want to look at the car and the people. He felt his mother's heart beating beneath his ear so fast it seemed to push the satin roses in and out. He put his face to them carefully and breathed the deep, soft powdery woman smell of her. That smell was also in her little face cream bottles, in her brushes, and around the washbowl after she used it. The satin felt so unbearably smooth against his cheek that he had to press closer. She didn't push him away, like he expected, but hugged him still tighter until he felt as close as he had ever been to back inside her again where she said he came from. Within the smells of her things, her soft skin and the satin of her roses, he closed his eyes then, and took his breaths softly and quickly with her heart.

They were out there, but they didn't dare get out of the car yet because of Lawrence's big, ragged dogs. Three of these dogs had loped up the dirt driveway with the car. They were rangy, alert, and bounced up and down on their cushioned paws like wolves. They didn't waste their energy barking, but positioned themselves quietly, one at either car door and the third in front of the bellied-out screen door to Uncle Lawrence's house. It was six in the morning but the wind was up already, blowing dust, ruffling their short moth-eaten coats. The big brown one on Vicki Koob's side had unusual black and white markings, stripes almost, like a hyena and he grinned at her, tongue out and teeth showing.

"Shoo!" Miss Koob opened her door with a quick jerk.

The brown dog sidestepped the door and jumped before her, tiptoeing. Its dirty white muzzle curled and its eyes crossed suddenly as if it was zeroing its cross-hair sights in on the exact place it would bite her. She ducked back and slammed the door.

"It's mean," she told Officer Brackett. He was printing out some type of form. The other officer, Harmony, a slow man, had not yet reacted to the car's halt. He had been sitting quietly in the back seat, but now he rolled down his window and with no change in expression unsnapped his holster and drew his pistol out and pointed it at the dog on his side. The dog smacked down on its belly, wiggled under the car and was out and around the back of the house before Harmony drew his gun back. The other dogs vanished with him. From wherever they had disappeared to they began to yap and howl, and the door to the low shoebox-style house fell open.

"Heya, what's going on?"

Uncle Lawrence put his head out the door and opened wide the one eye he had in working order. The eye bulged impossibly wider in outrage when he saw the police car. But the eyes of the two officers and Miss Vicki Koob were wide open too because they had never seen Uncle Lawrence in his sleeping get up or, indeed, witnessed anything like it. For his ribs, which were cracked from a bad fall and still mending, Uncle Lawrence wore a thick white corset laced up the front with a striped sneakers lace. His glass eye and his set of dentures were still out for the night so his face puckered here and there, around its absences and scars, like a damaged but fierce little cake. Although he had a few gray streaks now, Uncle Lawrence's hair was still thick, and because he wore a special contraption of elastic straps around his head every night, two oiled waves always crested on either side of his middle part. All of this would have been sufficient to astonish, even without the most striking part of his outfit — the smoking jacket. It was made of black satin and hung open around his corset, dragging a tasseled belt. Gold thread dragons struggled up the lapels and blasted their furry red breath around his neck. As Lawrence walked down the steps, he put his arms up in surrender and the gold tassels in the inner seams of his sleeves dropped into view.

"My heavens, what a sight." Vicki Koob was impressed.

"A character," apologized Officer Harmony.

As a tribal police officer who could be counted on to help out the State Patrol, Harmony thought he always had to explain about Indians or get twice as tough to show he did not favor them. He was slow-moving and shy but two jumps ahead of other people all the same, and now, as he watched Uncle Lawrence's splendid approach, he gazed speculatively at the torn and bulging pocket of the smoking jacket. Harmony had been inside Uncle Lawrence's house before and knew that above his draped orange-crate shelf of war medals a blue-black German luger was hung carefully in a net of flat-headed nails and fishing line. Thinking of this deadly exhibition, he got out of the car and shambled toward Lawrence with a dreamy little smile of welcome on his face. But when he searched Lawrence, he found that the bulging pocket held only the lonesome-looking dentures from Lawrence's empty jaw. They were still dripping denture polish.

"I had been cleaning them when you arrived," Uncle Lawrence explained with acid dignity.

He took the toothbrush from his other pocket and aimed it like a rifle.

"Quit that, you old idiot." Harmony tossed the toothbrush away. "For once you ain't done nothing. We came for your nephew."

Lawrence looked at Harmony with a faint air of puzzlement.

"Ma Frere, listen," threatened Harmony amiably, "those two white people in the car came to get him for the welfare. They got papers on your nephew that give them the right to take him."

"Papers?" Uncle Lawrence puffed out his deeply pitted cheeks. "Let me see them papers."

The two of them walked over to Vicki's side of the car and she pulled a copy of the court order from her purse. Lawrence put his teeth back in and adjusted them with busy workings of his jaw.

"Just a minute," he reached into his breast pocket as he bent close to Miss Vicki Koob. "I can't read these without I have in my eye."

He took the eye from his breast pocket delicately, and as he popped it into his face the social worker's mouth fell open in a consternated O.

"What is this," she cried in a little voice.

Uncle Lawrence looked at her mildly. The white glass of the eye was cold as lard. The black iris was strangely charged and menacing.

"He's nuts," Brackett huffed along the side of Vicki's neck. "Never mind him."

Vicki's hair had sweated down her nape in tiny corkscrews and some of the hairs were so long and dangly now that they disappeared into the zippered back of her dress. Brackett noticed this as he spoke into her ear. His face grew red and the backs of his hands prickled. He slid under the steering wheel and got out of the car. He walked around the hood to stand with Leo Harmony.

"We could take you in too," said Brackett roughly. Lawrence eyed the officers in what was taken as defiance. "If you don't cooperate, we'll get out the handcuffs," they warned.

One of Lawrence's arms was stiff and would not move until he'd rubbed it with witch hazel in the morning. His other arm worked fine though, and he stuck it out in front of Brackett.

"Get them handcuffs," he urged them. "Put me in a welfare home."

Brackett snapped one side of the handcuffs on Lawrence's good arm and the other to the handle of the police car.

"That's to hold you," he said. "We're wasting our time. Harmony, you search that little shed over by the tall grass and Miss Koob and myself will search the house."

"My rights is violated!" Lawrence shrieked suddenly. They ignored him. He tugged at the handcuff and thought of the good heavy file he kept in his tool box and the German luger oiled and ready but never loaded, because of Buddy, over his shelf. He should have used it on these bad ones, even Harmony in his big-time white man job. He wouldn't last long in that job anyway before somebody gave him what for.

"It's a damn scheme," said Uncle Lawrence, rattling his chains against the car. He looked over at the shed and thought maybe Albertine and Buddy had sneaked away before the car pulled into the yard. But he sagged, seeing Albertine move like a shadow within the boards. "Oh, it's all a damn scheme," he muttered again.

"I want to find that boy and salvage him," Vicki Koob explained to Officer Brackett as they walked into the house. "Look at his family life — the old man crazy as a bedbug, the mother intoxicated somewhere."

Brackett nodded, energetic, eager. He was a short hopeful redhead who failed consistently to win the hearts of women. Vicki Koob intrigued him. Now, as he watched, she pulled a tiny pen out of an ornamental clip on her blouse. It was attached to a retractable line that would suck the pen back, like a child eating one strand of spaghetti. Something about the pen on its line excited Brackett to the point of discomfort. His hand shook as he opened the screendoor and stepped in, beckoning Miss Koob to follow.

They could see the house was empty at first glance. It was only one rectangular room with whitewashed walls and a little gas stove in the middle. They had already come through the cooking lean-to with the other stove and washstand and rusty old refrigerator. That refrigerator had nothing in it but some wrinkled potatoes and a package of turkey necks. Vicki Koob noted that in her perfect-bound notebook. The beds along the walls of the big room were covered with quilts that Albertine's mother, Sophie, had made from bits of old wool coats and pants that the Sisters sold in bundles at the mission. There was no one hiding beneath the beds. No one was under the little aluminum dinette table covered with a green oilcloth, or the soft brown wood chairs tucked up to it. One wall of the big room was filled with neatly stacked crates of things — old tools and springs and small half-dismantled appliances. Five or six television sets were stacked against the wall. Their control panels spewed colored wires and at least one was cracked all the way across. Only the topmost set, with coathanger antenna angled sensitively to catch the bounding signals around Little Shell, looked like it could possibly work.

Not one thing escaped Vicki Koob's trained and cataloguing gaze. She made note of the cupboard that held only commodity flour and coffee.

The unsanitary tin oil drum beneath the kitchen window, full of empty surplus pork cans and beer bottles, caught her eye as did Uncle Lawrence's physical and mental deteriorations. She quickly described these "benchmarks of alcoholic dependency within the extended family of Woodrow (Buddy) American Horse" as she walked around the room with the little notebook open, pushed against her belly to steady it. Although Vicki had been there before, Albertine's presence had always made it difficult for her to take notes.

"Twice the maximum allowable space between door and threshold," she wrote now. "Probably no insulation. 2–3 inch cracks in walls inadequately sealed with whitewashed mud." She made a mental note but could see no point in describing Lawrence's stuffed reclining chair that only reclined, the shadeless lamp with its plastic orchid in the bubble glass base, or the three-dimensional picture of Jesus that Lawrence had once demonstrated to her. When plugged in, lights rolled behind the water the Lord stood on so that he seemed to be strolling although he never actually went forward, of course, but only pushed the glowing waves behind him forever like a poor tame rat in a treadmill.

Brackett cleared his throat with a nervous rasp and touched Vicki's shoulder.

"What are you writing?"

She moved away and continued to scribble as if thoroughly absorbed in her work. "Officer Brackett displays an undue amount of interest in my person," she wrote. "Perhaps?"

He snatched playfully at the book, but she hugged it to her chest and moved off smiling. More curls had fallen, wetted to the base of her neck. Looking out the window, she sighed long and loud.

"All night on brush rollers for this. What a joke."

Brackett shoved his hands in his pockets. His mouth opened slightly, then shut with a small throttled cluck.

When Albertine saw Harmony ambling across the yard with his big brown thumbs in his belt, his placid smile, and his tiny black eyes moving back and forth, she put Buddy under the cot. Harmony stopped at the shed and stood quietly. He spread his arms wide to show her he hadn't drawn his big police gun.

"Ma Cousin," he said in the Michif dialect that people used if they were relatives or sometimes if they needed gas or a couple of dollars, "why don't you come out here and stop this foolishness?"

"I ain't your cousin," Albertine said. Anger boiled up in her suddenly. "I ain't related to no pigs."

She bit her lip and watched him through the cracks, circling, a big tan punching dummy with his boots full of sand so he never stayed down once he fell. He was empty inside, all stale air. But he knew how to get to her so much better than a white cop could. And now he was circling because he wasn't sure she didn't have a weapon, maybe a knife or the German luger that was the only thing that her father, Albert American Horse, had left his wife and daughter besides his name. Harmony knew that Albertine was a tall strong woman who took two big men to subdue when she didn't want to go in the drunk tank. She had hard hips, broad shoulders, and stood tall like her Sioux father, the American Horse who was killed threshing in Belle Prairie.

"I feel bad to have to do this," Harmony said to Albertine. "But for godsakes, let's nobody get hurt. Come on out with the boy why don't you. I know you got him in there."

Albertine did not give herself away this time. She let him wonder. Slowly and quietly she pulled her belt through its loops and wrapped it around and around her hand until only the big oval buckle with turquoise chunks shaped into a butterfly stuck out over her knuckles. Harmony was talking but she wasn't listening to what he said. She was listening to the pitch of his voice, the tone of it that would tighten or tremble at a certain moment when he decided to rush the shed. He kept talking slowly and reasonably, flexing the dialect from time to time, even mentioning her father.

"He was a damn good man. I don't care what they say, Albertine, I knew him."

Albertine looked at the stone butterfly that spread its wings across her fist. The wings looked light and cool, not heavy. It almost looked like it was ready to fly. Harmony wanted to get to Albertine through her father but she would not think about American Horse. She concentrated on the sky-blue stone.

Yet the shape of the stone, the color, betrayed her.

She saw her father suddenly, bending at the grille of their old grey car. She was small then. The memory came from so long ago it seemed like a dream — narrowly focused, snapshot clear. He was bending by the grille in the sun. It was hot summer. Wings of sweat, dark blue, spread across the back of his work shirt. He always wore soft blue shirts, the color of shade cloudier than this stone. His stiff hair had grown out of its short haircut and flopped over his forehead. When he stood up and turned away from the car, Albertine saw that he had a butterfly.

"It's dead," he told her. "Broke its wings and died on the grille."

She must have been five, maybe six, wearing one of the boy's tee-shirts Mama bleached in hilex-water. American Horse took the butterfly, a black and yellow one, and rubbed it on Albertine's collarbone and chest and arms until the color and the powder of it were blended into her skin.

"For grace," he said.

And Albertine had felt a strange lightening in her arms, in her chest, when he did this and said, "For grace." The way he said it, grace meant everything the butterfly was. The sharp delicate wings. The way it floated over grass. The way its wings seemed to breathe fanning in the sun. The wisdom of the way it blended into flowers or changed into a leaf. In herself she felt the same kind of possibilities and closed her eyes almost in shock or pain, she felt so light and powerful at that moment.

Then her father had caught her and thrown her high into the air. She could not remember landing in his arms or landing at all. She only remembered the sun filling her eyes and the world tipping crazily behind her, out of sight.

"He was a damn good man," Harmony said again.

Albertine heard his starched uniform gathering before his boots hit the ground. Once, twice, three times. It took him four solid jumps to get right where she wanted him. She kicked the plank door open when he reached for the handle and the corner caught him on the jaw. He faltered, and Albertine hit him flat on the chin with the butterfly. She hit him so hard the shock of it went up her arm like a string pulled taut. Her fist opened, numb, and she let the belt unloop before she closed her hand on the tip end of it and sent the stone butterfly swooping out in a wide circle around her as if it was on the end of a leash. Harmony reeled backward as she walked toward him swinging the belt. She expected him to fall but he just stumbled. And then he took the gun from his hip.

Albertine let the belt go limp. She and Harmony stood within feet of each other, breathing. Each heard the human sound of air going in and out of the other person's lungs. Each read the face of the other as if deciphering letters carved into softly eroding veins of stone. Albertine saw the pattern of tiny arteries that age, drink, and hard living had blown to the surface of the man's face. She saw the spoked wheels of his iris and the arteries like tangled threads that sewed him up. She saw the living net of springs and tissue that held him together, and trapped him. She saw the random, intimate plan of his person.

She took a quick shallow breath and her face went strange and tight. She saw the black veins in the wings of the butterfly, roads burnt into a map, and then she was located somewhere in the net of veins and sinew that was the tragic complexity of the world so she did not see Officer Brackett and Vicki Koob rushing toward her, but felt them instead like flies caught in the same web, rocking it.

"Albertine!" Vicki Koob had stopped in the grass. Her voce was shrill and tight. "It's better this way, Albertine. We're going to help you."

Albertine straightened, threw her shoulders back. Her father's hand was on her chest and shoulders lightening her wonderfully. Then on wings of her father's hands, on dead butterfly wings, Albertine lifted into the air and flew toward the others. The light powerful feeling swept her up the way she had floated higher, seeing the grass below. It was her father throwing her up into the air and out of danger. Her arms opened for bullets but no bullets came. Harmony did not shoot. Instead, he raised his fist and brought it down hard on her head.

Albertine did not fall immediately, but stood in his arms a moment. Perhaps she gazed still farther back behind the covering of his face. Perhaps she was completely stunned and did not think as she sagged and fell. Her face rolled forward and hair covered her features, so it was impossible for Harmony to see with just what particular expression she gazed into the headsplitting wheel of light, or blackness, that overcame her.

Harmony turned the vehicle onto the gravel road that led back to town. He had convinced the other two that Albertine was more trouble than she was worth, and so they left her behind, and Lawrence too. He stood swearing in his cinder driveway as the car rolled out of sight. Buddy sat between the social worker and Officer Brackett. Vicki tried to hold Buddy fast and keep her arm down at the same time, for the words she'd screamed at Albertine had broken the seal of antiperspirant beneath her arms. She was sweating now as though she'd stored an ocean up inside of her. Sweat rolled down her back in a shallow river and pooled at her waist and between her breasts. A thin sheen of water came out on her forearms, her face. Vicki gave an irritated moan but Brackett seemed not to take notice, or take offense at least. Air-conditioned breezes were sweeping over the seat anyway, and very soon they would be comfortable. She smiled at Brackett over Buddy's head. The man grinned back. Buddy stirred. Vicki remembered the emergency chocolate bar she kept in her purse, fished it out, and offered it to Buddy. He did not react, so she closed his fingers over the package and peeled the paper off one end.

The car accelerated. Buddy felt the road and wheels pummeling each other and the rush of the heavy motor purring in high gear. Buddy knew that what he'd seen in his mind that morning, the thing coming out of the sky with barbs and chains, had hooked him. Somehow he was caught and held in the sour tin smell of the pale woman's armpit. Somehow he was pinned between their pounds of breathless flesh. He looked at the chocolate in his hand. He was squeezing the bar so hard that a thin brown trickle had melted down his arm. Automatically, he put the bar in his mouth.

As he bit down he saw his mother very clearly, just as she had been when she carried him from the shed. She was stretched flat on the ground, on her stomach, and her arms were curled around her head as if in sleep. One leg was drawn up and it looked for all the world like she was running full tilt into the ground, as though she had been trying to pass into the earth, to bury herself, but at the last moment something had stopped her.

There was no blood on Albertine, but Buddy tasted blood now at the sight of her, for he bit down hard and cut his own lip. He ate the chocolate, every bit of it, tasting his mother's blood. And when he had the chocolate down inside him and all licked off his hands, he opened his mouth to say thank you to the woman, as his mother had taught him. But instead of a thank you coming out he was astonished to hear a great rattling scream, and then another, rip out of him like pieces of his own body and whirl onto the sharp things all around him.

Oneida Traditional
THE WARRIOR MAIDEN

V   V   V   V
V

"The Warrior Maiden" is a traditional story. Unfortunately, I don't know whether the story comes from the Iroquois Oneida or Wisconsin Oneida, but as the two are related its placement near E. Pauline Johnson's story seems germane. The themes of the two are intertwined, for both treat the power of warrior women. The woman in this story is responsible for saving a number of people, almost in a true Western heroic tradition. The similarity between this story and those dear to the hearts of Americans probably didn't escape the attention of the original collectors.

LONG AGO, in the days before the white man came to this continent, the Oneida people were beset by their old enemies, the Mingoes. The invaders attacked the Oneida villages, stormed their palisades, set fire to their longhouses, laid waste to the land, destroyed the cornfields, killed men and boys, and abducted the women and girls. There was no resisting the Mingoes, because their numbers were like grains of sand, like pebbles on a lake shore.

The villages of the Oneida lay deserted, their fields untended, the ruins of their homes blackened. The men had taken the women, the old people, the young boys and girls into the deep forests, hiding them in secret places among rocks, in caves, and on desolate mountains. The Mingoes searched for victims, but could not find them. The Great Spirit himself helped the people to hide and shielded their places of refuge from the eyes of their enemies.

Thus the Oneida people were safe in their inaccessible retreats, but they were also starving. Whatever food they had been able to save was soon eaten up. They could either stay in their hideouts and starve, or leave them in search of food and be discovered by their enemies. The warrior chiefs and sachems met in council but could find no other way out.

53

Then a young girl stepped forward in the council and said that the good spirits had sent her a dream showing her how to save the Oneida. Her name was Aliquipiso and she was not afraid to give her life for her people.

Aliquipiso told the council: "We are hiding on top of a high, sheer cliff. Above us the mountain is covered with boulders and heavy sharp rocks. You warriors wait and watch here. I will go to the Mingoes and lead them to the spot at the foot of the cliff where they all can be crushed and destroyed."

The chiefs, sachems, and warriors listened to the girl with wonder. The oldest of the sachems honored her, putting around her neck strands of white and purple wampum. "The Great Spirit has blessed you, Aliquipiso, with courage and wisdom," he said. "We, your people, will always remember you."

During the night the girl went down from the heights into the forest below by way of a secret path. In the morning, Mingoe scouts found her wandering through the woods as if lost. They took her to the burned and abandoned village where she had once lived, for this was now their camp. They brought her before their warrior chief. "Show us the way to the place where your people are hiding," he commanded. "If you do this, we shall adopt you into our tribe. Then you will belong to the victors. If you refuse, you will be tortured at the stake."

"I will not show you the way," answered Aliquipiso. The Mingoes tied her to a blackened tree stump and tortured her with fire, as was their custom. Even the wild Mingoes were astonished at the courage with which the girl endured it. At last Aliquipiso pretended to weaken under the pain. "Don't hurt me any more," she cried, "I'll show you the way!"

As night came again, the Mingoes bound Aliquipiso's hands behind her back and pushed her ahead of them. "Don't try to betray us," they warned. "At any sign of it, we'll kill you." Flanked by two warriors with weapons poised, Aliquipiso led the way. Soundlessly the mass of Mingoe warriors crept behind her through thickets and rough places, over winding paths and deer trails, until at last they arrived beneath the towering cliff of sheer granite. "Come closer, Mingoe warriors," she said in a low voice, "gather around me. The Oneidas above are sleeping, thinking themselves safe. I'll show you the secret passage that leads upwards." The Mingoes crowded together in a dense mass with the girl in the center. Then Aliquipiso uttered a piercing cry: "Oneidas! The enemies are here! Destroy them!"

The Mingoes scarcely had time to strike her down before huge boulders and rocks rained upon them. There was no escape; it seemed as if the angry mountain itself were falling on them, crushing them, burying them. So many Mingoe warriors died there that the other bands of Mingoe invaders stopped pillaging the Oneida country and retired to their own hunting grounds. They never again made war on Aliquipiso's people.

The story of the girl's courage and self-sacrifice was told and retold wherever Oneidas sat around their campfires, and will be handed down from grandparent to grandchild as long as there are Oneidas on this earth.

The Great Mystery changed Aliquipiso's hair into woodbine, which the Oneidas call "running hairs" and which is a good medicine. From her body sprang honeysuckle, which to this day is known among her people as the "blood of brave women."

Iroquois (Mohawk) Traditional

THE WOMAN WHO FELL
FROM THE SKY

V V V V

V

"The Woman Who Fell from the Sky" is a traditional Iroquois narrative that I have adapted. I include it here because E. Pauline Johnson, also Iroquois, retains certain of its narrative features and character traits in her story. This account tells of a Sacred Woman who overcomes her enemy (whom she married at her father's behest) and through an act of great courage, power, and self-assertion turns his perfidy into a new planet, Earth, with its sun and moon. The story shows the importance of the rules of obedience, respect, focus, and discipline through which one gains meta-physical power sufficient to create planetary systems. It also forms part of the creation story of the Iroquois.

ONCE UPON A TIME, long ago so far, a young woman was told by her dead father to go and marry a stranger. Being a strange woman, she did as he said, not taking her mother's counsel in the matter as she should have done. She journeyed to the place where the dead father had directed her to go, and there found the man she was to marry.

Now this man was a renowned magician, a sorcerer. He heard her proposal that they marry skeptically. He said to himself, "This woman is but a girl. It would be more fitting for her to ask to be my servant rather than my wife." But he only listened silently to her, then he said, "It is well. If you can meet my tests, we will see if I will make you my wife."

He took her into his lodge and said, "Now you must grind corn." She took the corn and boiled it slightly, using wood he brought her for the fire. When the kernels were softened, she began to grind them on the grinding stone. And though there were mounds and mounds of stuff to be ground, still she was done with the task in a very short time. Seeing this, the sorcerer was amazed, but he kept silent. Instead he ordered her to remove all her clothing. When she was naked, he told her to cook the corn in the huge pot that hung over the fire. This she did, though the hot corn popped and spattered scalding, clinging mush all over her. But she did not flinch, enduring the burns with calm.

When the mush was done, the woman told the sorcerer it was ready. "Good," he said. "Now you will feed my servants." He noted that her body was covered with cornmush. Opening the door, he called in several huge beasts who ran to the woman and began to lick the mush from her body with their razor sharp tongues, leaving deep gashes where their tongues sliced her flesh. Still she did not recoil but endured the torment, not letting her face lose its look of calm composure.

Seeing this, the sorcerer let the beasts back out, then said she and he would be married, and so they were. After four nights that they spent sleeping opposite each other with the soles of their feet touching, he sent her back to her village with gifts of meat for the people. He commanded her to divide the meat evenly among all the people, and further to see to it that every lodge had its roof removed that night, as he was going to send a white corn rain among them. She did as she was told, and after the village had received its gifts, the meat and the white corn rain, she returned to her husband's lodge.

Outside his lodge there grew a tree that was always filled with blossoms so bright they gave light to his whole land. The woman loved the tree, loved to sit under it and converse with the spirits and her dead father, whom she held dear in her heart. She so loved the light tree that once, when everyone was sleeping, she lay down under it and opened her legs and her body to it. A blossom fell on her vagina then, touching her with sweetness and a certain joy. And soon after she knew she was pregnant.

About that time her husband became weak and ill. His medicine people could not heal him, but told him that his sickness was caused by his wife. He was certain they were right, for he had never met anyone so powerful as she. He feared that her power was greater than his own, for hadn't she been able to withstand his most difficult tests? "What should I do?" he asked his advisors. They did not advise him to divorce her, because that kind of separation was unknown to them. They did not advise him to kill her, because death was unknown among them. The only death that had occurred was of the woman's father, and they did not understand what had happened to him.

After deliberating on the matter for four days, the advisors told the sorcerer that he should uproot the tree of light. Then, lying beside it, he should call his wife to come and sit with him. He should by some ruse get her to fall over the edge of the hole the uprooted tree would leave, and she would fall into the void. When she had fallen, they said, he was to replace the tree and then he would recover his health and his power.

That afternoon he went outside his lodge and pulled up the tree. He peered over the edge of the hole it left, and he could see another world below. He called his wife to come and see it. When she came, he said, "Lean over the edge. You can see another world below." She knelt beside the hole and leaning over the edge, looked down. She saw darkness, and a long way below, she saw blue, a shining blue that seemed filled with promise and delight. She looked at her husband and smiled, eyes dancing with pleasure. "It looks like a beautiful place there," she said. "Who would have thought that the tree of light would be growing over such a place!"

"Yes," her husband agreed. "It surely seems beautiful there." He regarded her for a moment carefully, then said, "I wonder what it is like there. Maybe somebody could go down there and find out."

Astonished, the woman looked at her husband. "But how would someone do that?"

"Jump." The husband said.

"Jump?" she asked, looking down through the opening, trying to calculate the distance. "But it is very far."

"Someone of your courage could do it," he said. "You could jump. Become the wind or a petal from this tree." He indicated the tree lying fallen next to them. "A petal could fall, gently, on the wind it would be carried. You could be a petal in the wind. You could be a butterfly, a downgliding bright bird."

She gazed for a long time at the shining blue below her. "I could jump like that. I could float downward. I could fall into the shining blue world below us."

"Yes," he said. "You could."

For another long moment she knelt gazing downward, then taking a deep breath she stood, and flexing her knees and raising her arms high over her head she leaned into the opening and dove through.

For some time the sorcerer watched her body as it fell downward through the dark, toward the blue. "She jumped," he finally said to the council as they made their way slowly toward him. "She's gone."

And they raised the tree and placed it back firmly in its place, covering the opening to the other world with its roots.

E. Pauline Johnson
AS IT WAS IN THE BEGINNING

V V V V
V

E. Pauline Johnson wrote around the turn of the century. Her stories appeared mainly in The Mother Magazine, *which was published in Elgin, Illinois, as early as 1907, and her poems, the earliest of which were written in the 1870s, were published as early as the 1880s. Johnson was the daughter of a dedicated Indian rights activist George Henry Martin Johnson (her mother was English), much of her poetry and fiction reflect her involvement in that struggle.* The Moccasin Maker,[1] *her collection of short stories and nonfiction articles (from which the following story was taken), was published in 1913, the year she died.*

While virtually unknown in the United States, Johnson was hailed as Canada's "poet laureate" during much of her professional life. She toured in England, Canada, and the United States, reading from her works. She seems to have been a victim of love's arrows, as she might have phrased it; disastrous love affairs weakened her and made both touring and writing very difficult for her.

THEY ACCOUNT FOR IT by the fact that I am a Redskin, but I am something else, too — I am a woman.

I remember the first time I saw him. He came up the trail with some Hudson's Bay trappers, and they stopped at the door of my father's tepee. He seemed even then, fourteen years ago, an old man; his hair seemed just as thin and white, his hands just as trembling and fleshless as they were a month since, when I saw him for what I pray his God is the last time.

My father sat in the tepee, polishing buffalo horns and smoking; my mother, wrapped in her blanket, crouched over her quill-work, on the buffalo-skin at his side; I was lounging at the doorway, idling, watching, as I always watched, the thin, distant line of sky and prairie; wondering, as I always wondered, what lay beyond it. Then he came, this gentle old man with his white hair and thin, pale face. He wore a long black coat, which I now know was the sign of his office, and he carried a black leather-covered book, which, in all the years I have known him, I have never seen him without.

The trappers explained to my father who he was, the Great Teacher, the heart's Medicine Man, the "Blackcoat" we had heard of, who brought peace where there was war, and the magic of whose black book brought greater things than all the Happy Hunting Grounds of our ancestors.

He told us many things that day, for he could speak the Cree tongue, and my father listened, and listened, and when at last they left us, my father said for him to come and sit within the tepee again.

He came, all the time he came, and my father welcomed him, but my mother always sat in silence at work with the quills; my mother never liked the Great "Blackcoat."

His stories fascinated me. I used to listen intently to the tale of the strange new place he called "heaven," of the gold crown, of the white dress, of the great music; and then he would tell of that other strange place — hell. My father and I hated it; we feared it, we dreamt of it, we trembled at it. Oh, if the "Blackcoat" would only cease to talk of it! Now I know he saw its effect upon us, and he used it as a whip to lash us into his new religion, but even then my mother must have known, for each time he left the tepee she would watch him going slowly away across the prairie; then when he was disappearing into the far horizon she would laugh scornfully, and say:

"If the white man made this Blackcoat's hell, let him go to it. It is for the man who found it first. No hell for Indians, just Happy Hunting Grounds. Blackcoat can't scare me."

And then, after weeks had passed, one day as he stood at the tepee door he laid his white, old hand on my head and said to my father: "Give me this little girl, chief. Let me take her to the mission school; let me keep her, and teach her of the great God and His eternal heaven. She will grow to be a noble woman, and return perhaps to bring her people to the Christ."

My mother's eyes snapped. "No," she said. It was the first word she ever spoke to the "Blackcoat." My father sat and smoked. At the end of a half-hour he said:

"I am an old man, Blackcoat. I shall not leave the God of my fathers. I like not your strange God's ways — all of them. I like not His two new places for me when I am dead. Take the child, Blackcoat, and save her from hell."

The first grief of my life was when we reached the mission. They took my buckskin dress off, saying I was now a little Christian girl and must dress like all the white people at the mission. Oh, how I hated that stiff new calico dress and those leather shoes! But, little as I was, I said nothing, only thought of the time when I should be grown, and do as my mother did, and wear the buckskins and the blanket.

My next serious grief was when I began to speak the English, that they forbade me to use any Cree words whatever. The rule of the school was that any child heard using its native tongue must get a slight punishment. I never understood it, I cannot understand it now, why the use of my dear Cree tongue could be a matter for correction or an action deserving punishment.

She was strict, the matron of the school, but only justly so, for she had a heart and a face like her brother's, the "Blackcoat." I had long since ceased to call him that. The trappers at the post called him "St. Paul," because, they told me, of his self-sacrificing life, his kindly deeds, his rarely beautiful old face; so I, too, called him "St. Paul," though oftener "Father Paul," though he never liked the latter title, for he was a Protestant. But as I was his pet, his darling of the whole school, he let me speak of him as I would, knowing it was but my heart speaking in love. His sister was a widow, and mother to a laughing yellow-haired little boy of about my own age, who was my constant playmate and who taught me much of English in his own childish way. I used to be fond of this child, just as I was fond of his mother and of his uncle, my "Father Paul," but as my girlhood passed away, as womanhood came upon me, I got strangely wearied of them all; I longed, oh, God, how I longed for the old wild life! It came with my womanhood, with my years.

What mattered it to me now that they had taught me all their ways? — their tricks of dress, their reading, their writing, their books. What mattered it that "Father Paul" loved me, that the traders at the post called me pretty, that I was a pet of all, from the factor to the poorest trapper in the service? I wanted my own people, my own old life, my blood called out for it, but they always said I must not return to my father's tepee. I heard them talk amongst themselves of keeping me away from pagan influences; they told each other that if I returned to the prairies, the tepees, I would degenerate, slip back to paganism, as other girls had done; marry, perhaps, with a pagan — and all their years of labor and teaching would be lost.

I said nothing, but I waited. And then one night the feeling overcame me. I was in the Hudson's Bay store when an Indian came in from the north with a large pack of buckskin. As they unrolled it a dash of its insinuating odor filled the store. I went over and leaned above the skins a second, then buried my face in them, swallowing, drinking the fragrance of them, that went to my head like wine. Oh, the wild wonder of that wood-smoked tan, the subtlety of it, the untamed smell of it! I drank it into my lungs, my innermost being was saturated with it, till my mind reeled and my heart seemed twisted with a physical agony. My childhood recollections rushed upon me, devoured me. I left the store in a strange, calm frenzy, and going rapidly to the mission house I confronted my Father Paul and demanded to be allowed to go "home," if only for a day. He received the request with the same refusal and the same gentle sigh that I had so often been greeted with, but *this* time the desire, the smoke-tan, the heart-ache, never lessened.

Night after night I would steal away by myself and go to the border of the village to watch the sun set in the foothills, to gaze at the far line of sky and prairie, to long and long for my father's lodge. And Laurence — always Laurence — my fair-haired, laughing, child playmate, would come calling and calling for me: "Esther, where are you? We miss you; come in, Esther, come in with me." And if I did not turn at once to him and follow, he would come and place his strong hands on my shoulders and laugh into my eyes and say, "Truant, truant, Esther; can't *we* make you happy?"

My old child playmate had vanished years ago. He was a tall, slender young man now, handsome as a young chief, but with laughing blue eyes, and always those yellow curls about his temples. He was my solace in my half-exile, my comrade, my brother, until one night it was, "Esther, Esther, can't *I* make you happy?"

I did not answer him; only looked out across the plains and thought of the tepees. He came close, close. He locked his arms about me, and with my face pressed up to his throat he stood silent. I felt the blood from my heart sweep to my very finger-tips. I loved him. Oh God, how I loved him! In a wild, blind instant it all came, just because he held me so and was whispering brokenly, "Don't leave me, don't leave me, Esther; *my* Esther, my child-love, my playmate, my girl-comrade, my little Cree sweetheart, will you go away to your people, or stay, stay for me, for my arms, as I have you now?"

No more, no more the tepees; no more the wild stretch of prairie, the intoxicating fragrance of the smoke-tanned buckskin; no more the bed of buffalo hide, the soft, silent moccasin; no more the dark faces of my people, the dulcet cadence of the sweet Cree tongue — only this man, this fair, proud, tender man who held me in his arms, in his heart. My soul prayed to his great white God, in that moment, that He let me have only this.

It was twilight when we re entered the mission gate. We were both excited, feverish. Father Paul was reading evening prayers in the large room beyond the hallway; his soft, saint-like voice stole beyond the doors, like a benediction upon us. I went noiselessly upstairs to my own room and sat there undisturbed for hours.

The clock downstairs struck one, startling me from my dreams of happiness, and at the same moment a flash of light attracted me. My room was in an angle of the building, and my window looked almost directly down into those of Father Paul's study, into which at that instant he was entering, carrying a lamp. "Why, Laurence," I heard him exclaim, "what are you doing here? I thought, my boy, you were in bed hours ago."

"No, uncle, not in bed, but in dreamland," replied Laurence, arising from the window, where evidently he, too, had spent the night hours as I had done.

Father Paul fumbled about for a moment, found his large black book, which for once he seemed to have got separated from, and was turning to leave, when the curious circumstance of Laurence being there at so unusual an hour seemed to strike him anew. "Better go to sleep, my son," he said simply, then added curiously, "Has anything occurred to keep you up?"

Then Laurence spoke: "No, uncle, only — only, I'm happy, that's all. "
Father Paul stood irresolute. Then: "It is — ?"
"Esther," said Laurence quietly, but he was at the old man's side, his hand was on the bent old shoulder, his eyes proud and appealing.

Father Paul set the lamp on the table, but, as usual, one hand held that black book, the great text of his life. His face was paler than I had ever seen it — graver.

"Tell me of it," he requested.

I leaned far out of my window and watched them both. I listened with my very heart, for Laurence was telling him of me, of his love, of the new-found joy of that night.

"You have said nothing of marriage to her?" asked Father Paul.
"Well — no; but she surely understands that — "
"Did you speak of *marriage*?" repeated Father Paul, with a harsh ring in his voice that was new to me.
"No, uncle, but — "
"Very well, then; very well."
There was a brief silence. Laurence stood staring at the old man as though he were a stranger; he watched him push a large chair up to the table, slowly seat himself; then mechanically following his movements,

he dropped onto a lounge. The old man's head bent low, but his eyes were bright and strangely fascinating. He began:

"Laurence, my boy, your future is the dearest thing to me of all earthly interests. Why, you *can't* marry this girl — no, no, sit, sit until I have finished," he added, with raised voice, as Laurence sprang up, remonstrating. "I have long since decided that you marry well; for instance, the Hudson's Bay factor's daughter."

Laurence broke into a fresh, rollicking laugh. "What, uncle," he said, "little Ida McIntosh? Marry that little yellow-haired fluff ball, that kitten, that pretty little dolly?"

"Stop," said Father Paul. Then, with a low, soft persuasiveness, "She is *white*, Laurence."

My lover started. "Why, uncle, what do you mean?" he faltered.

"Only this, my son: poor Esther comes of uncertain blood; would it do for you — the missionary's nephew, and adopted son, you might say — to marry the daughter of a pagan Indian? Her mother is hopelessly uncivilized; her father has a dash of French somewhere — half-breed, you know, my boy, half-breed." Then, with still lower tone and half-shut, crafty eyes, he added: "The blood is a bad, bad mixture, *you* know that; you know, too, that I am very fond of the girl, poor dear Esther. I have tried to separate her from evil pagan influences; she is the daughter of the Church; I want her to have no other parent; but you never can tell what lurks in *a caged animal that has once been wild*. My whole heart is with the Indian people, my son; my whole heart, my whole life, has been devoted to bringing them to Christ, *but it is a different thing to marry with one of them.*"

His small old eyes were riveted on Laurence like a hawk's on a rat. My heart lay like ice in my bosom.

Laurence, speechless and white, stared at him breathlessly.

"Go away somewhere," the old man was urging, "to Winnipeg, Toronto, Montreal; forget her, then come back to Ida McIntosh. A union of the Church and the Hudson's Bay will mean great things, and may ultimately result in my life's ambition, the civilization of this entire tribe, that we have worked so long to bring to God."

I listened, sitting like one frozen. Could those words have been uttered by my venerable teacher, by him whom I revered as I would one of the saints in his own black book? Ah, there was no mistaking it. My white father, my life-long friend who pretended to love me, to care for my happiness, was urging the man I worshipped to forget me, to marry with the factor's daughter — because of what? Of my red skin; my good, old, honest pagan mother; my confiding French-Indian father. In a second all the care, the hollow love he had given me since my childhood, were as things that never existed. I hated that old mission priest as I hated his white man's hell. I hated his long, white hair; I hated his thin, white hands; I hated his body, his soul, his voice, his black book — oh, how I hated the very atmosphere of him!

Laurence sat motionless, his face buried in his hands, but the old man continued: "No, no; not the child of that pagan mother; you can't trust her, my son. What would you do with a wife who might any day break from you to return to her prairies and her buckskins? *You can't trust her.*" His eyes grew smaller, more glittering, more fascinating then, and leaning with an odd, secret sort of movement towards Laurence, he almost whispered, "Think of her silent ways, her noiseless step; the girl glides about like an apparition; her quick fingers, her wild longings — I don't know why, but with all my fondness for her, she reminds me sometimes of a strange — *snake.*"

Laurence shuddered, lifted his face, and said hoarsely: "You're right, uncle; perhaps I'd better not; I'll go away, I'll forget her, and then — well, then — yes, you are right, it *is* a different thing to marry one of them." The old man arose. His feeble fingers still clasped his black book; his soft white hair clung about his forehead like that of an Apostle; his eyes lost their peering, crafty expression; his bent shoulders resumed the dignity of a minister of the living God; he was the picture of what the traders called him — "St. Paul."

"Good-night, son," he said.

"Good-night, uncle, and thank you for bringing me to myself."

They were the last words I ever heard uttered by either that old arch-fiend or his weak, miserable kinsman. Father Paul turned and left the room. I watched his withered hand — the hand I had so often felt resting on my head in holy benedictions — clasp the door-knob, turn it slowly, then, with bowed head and his pale face rapt in thought, he left the room — left it with the mad venom of my hate pursuing him like the very Evil One he taught me of.

What were his years of kindness and care now? What did I care for his God, his heaven, his hell? He had robbed me of my native faith, of my parents, of my people, of this last, this life of love that would have made a great, good woman of me. God! How I hated him!

I crept to the closet in my dark little room. I felt for a bundle I had not looked at for years — yes, it was there, the buckskin dress I had worn as a little child when they brought me to the mission. I tucked it under my arm and descended the stairs noiselessly. I would look into the study and speak good-bye to Laurence; then I would —

I pushed open the door. He was lying on the couch where a short time previously he had sat, white and speechless, listening to Father Paul. I moved towards him softly. God in heaven, he was already asleep. As I bent over him the fullness of his perfect beauty impressed me for the first time; his slender form, his curving mouth that almost laughed even in sleep, his fair, tossed hair, his smooth, strong-pulsing throat. God! How I loved him!

Then there arose the picture of the factor's daughter. I hated her. I hated her baby face, her yellow hair, her whitish skin. "She shall not marry him," my soul said. "I will kill him first — kill his beautiful body, his lying, false heart." Something in my heart seemed to speak; it said over and over again, "Kill him, kill him; she will never have him then. Kill him. It will break Father Paul's heart and blight his life. He has killed the best of you, of your womanhood; kill *his* best, his pride, his hope — his sister's son, his nephew Laurence." But how? How?

What had that terrible old man said I was like? A *strange snake*. A snake? The idea wound itself about me like the very coils of a serpent. What was this in the beaded bag of my buckskin dress? this little thing rolled in tan that my mother had given me at parting with the words, "Don't touch much, but sometime maybe you want it!" Oh! I knew well enough what it was — a small flint arrow-head dipped in the venom of some *strange snake*.

I knelt beside him and laid my hot lips on his hand. I worshipped him, oh, how, how I worshipped him! Then again the vision of *her* baby face, *her* yellow hair — I scratched his wrist twice with the arrow-tip. A single drop of red blood oozed up; he stirred. I turned the lamp down and slipped out of the room — out of the house.

I dream nightly of the horrors of the white man's hell. Why did they teach me of it, only to fling me into it?

Last night as I crouched beside my mother on the buffalo-hide, Dan Henderson, the trapper, came in to smoke with my father. He said old Father Paul was bowed with grief, that with my disappearance I was suspected, but that there was no proof. Was it not merely a snake bite?

They account for it by the fact that I am a Redskin.

They seem to have forgotten I am a woman.

Soge Track

THE CLEARING IN THE VALLEY

▼ ▼ ▼ ▼

▼

Soge Track's story "The Clearing in the Valley" is about a young girl's induction into a Pueblo tradition, that of war captain, or "watcher." While I do not think that girls or women really serve as hochin, and thus take the story to be fiction in that regard, the events she recounts are real enough, even in the late 1960s when the story is set. Her "paranormal" experience with the recently deceased previous hochin is usual enough (even if it takes place in a somewhat unusual context).

Many gynecentric societies did not engage in the warpath. The Pueblo peoples of the southwest are a prime example of this. When Pueblo people did participate in warfare, long purification ceremonies were required before the combatant was allowed to reenter village life. In those conflict-phobic cultures, the sacred path analogous to the warrior path was the position and duty of the hochin or "war captain." This person was a watcher who read the calendar, keeping track of the ceremonial time by which the people regulated their lives, announced upcoming events and daily news to the people at sundown, and saw to it that ditch-cleaning and house renewal proceeded in the proper ways at the proper time. In olden times the hocheni led certain officiants on missions to locate lost or stolen sacred objects (such as the Yellow Woman Corn Mother referred to in "Evil Kachina Steals Yellow Woman"), a ritual affair that entailed a number of pre- and post-warfare ceremonies and prayerful visits to sacred spots outside the village perimeters. "The Clearing in the Valley" belongs to this tradition.

EAST FROM THE PUEBLO a dirt road, very narrow, leads up into the mountains. If you take this road, say for two miles, you will come to a clearing in a valley. The boys of the Pueblo have done an excellent job of clearing what was once just a thicket. Now it is a fine place for family outings. It is used, not only for family outings, but for a religious ceremony sacred to our Indian religion.

It is said that this place is also haunted. In broad daylight many people have had stones thrown at them from out of nowhere. Once, during a round dance — the one we call a "49" — one man who was in the middle of the dance, drumming, was pulled out of the circle by a woman wrapped in a black shawl.

No one thought this very strange and neither did the man who was being led into the thickets by this woman. But then, the man reached for the woman to ask her where they were going. He turned her so she was facing him and let out a horrified cry. No one was wrapped under the shawl. The empty shawl fell to the ground.

So this was supposed to be a really weird place. People showed their fright by not wanting to pass there after sunset. Even in the daytime they avoided going through there alone.

I suppose I've heard a hundred stories about it, but the weirdest thing of all is that I never get scared when I think of this place. Instead, I get a peaceful feeling. I think this started when . . . yes, now I remember. How clearly I can see myself! That was a fine year — the year I was nine.

It is no longer summer at the Pueblo. My favorite tree which stands in back of North Pueblo, the side where I live, is naked. It has been stripped of its clothes, yet it is not embarrassed. A few dull, straw-colored leaves still hold onto dry gray twigs that stick out like crooked fingers, trying their best to claw down the heavens. I know not what kind of tree it is, but it has been there for as long as I can remember. It is so huge, taller than the Pueblo, because when I go after water from the creek I can see my tree, extending its branches to the sky.

The two five-story Pueblos stand dark brown against a slowly clearing blue-gray sky. It is in the dawn as the sun, Our Father, is not yet over our mountain. From where I lie I can hear faint noises of the Pueblo people getting up, and Pueblo creek rippling peacefully through the center of the plaza. This is the beginning of a new day for us. Oh, but so early it starts! It's so dark yet! But that is our way — be up before the sun so that we may pray as soon as he appears.

I decide to get up. I quickly slip into my one blue-flower printed dress and up the ladder I go. You see, we live on the second story and our way of entering our abode is by way of a trapdoor through the roof. When I reach the top I look around, up, and below me. Oh, such beauty!

Many times I have seen this, but I still get such a feeling that I stand and turn round and round, trying to get my eyes full of this beauty. With my arms stretched out, I yawn.

I stand for a while with my head bent down, my long tangled hair over my face. Suddenly every bit of my body feels warm. With my eyes closed I turn my face toward the east and look. I can see that the heavens have opened a path for our sun. Still looking with eyes half-closed, I pull back my hair from my face, stretch my arms to the sun and take his light into my body.

I say, "My Father, it is the start of another day. For this day, I ask for good thoughts."

In Grandmother's soft voice, I hear, "My Granddaughter, you must hurry if you want your breakfast. I have much to do."

I go up the ladder and, going down the next ladder, almost fall because of my hair tangled over my face. I wish I were allowed to cut my hair but, if it were so, I would be the laughingstock of the village.

Down to the creek I run and quickly wash my face. Lying down, I take a quick drink of water. The odor of hot, blue cornmeal bread waiting makes me want to run, but a woman is getting water. She has a rust-colored pottery jug which she is dipping into the water. As she does this, the purple plaid shawl which she wears touches the water.

When she looks up I give her the usual salutation, "Ta," which all young people give to elders. Now I want to run back, but she must not see me running because I have to act with respect. Trying to walk fast, I start back.

When I get back I start to go down the ladder of our abode, I see Old Man sitting on the fifth story. He sits with his back to the wall, his legs bent under him. His dark, wrinkled face which looks like a dried apple, I cannot see because he is wearing his pink J. C. Penney blanket wrapped around his head. Beside him is his crooked, brown cane. At one time it was beige, a fresh-peeled stick, but that was when it was new.

I wave and say, "Good morning, my Father." I have to give him a special salutation for he is one of the wise elders.

He looks down at me and gives me a toothless grin and says, "Good morning, Granddaughter." With this he adds, "Why the rush?"

I, in reply, say, "I haven't eaten yet and I am much hungry."

He waves his hand for me to continue.

When I enter our abode, Grandmother says, "My Granddaughter, you have a very hard head. I told you to hurry. Instead, you take your time, talking to the rocks, weeds, and trees."

When she says this, I giggle and go to where she is in the corner, combing her coal-black hair which falls to one side of her somber face. She holds me on her lap and reaches for the small straw broom and starts to comb my long tangled hair.

Grandmother says, "If you would act like a lady and stop this running around, your hair wouldn't get so tangled. Your hair looks just like our old horse's mane."

I try not to let her see that I am almost in tears. If she does, she will only scold me more. I ask, "Where is my Grandfather?"

"Where is my Grandfather? Where? Where? This you ask all the time. He went after the horses so he can get us wood for this winter. If you will get ready you just might be able to go with him."

As she braids my hair, I reach for some piñon which is in a bowl to my right.

"Sit still," she says, "or you will have one braid different from the other."

I sit still and when she is finally finished she pushes me to my feet, telling me, "Get the buffalo grease."

I reach up to a crevice to the left of our small fireplace. When I find it I sit on her right side for her to put the buffalo grease on my face. Evenly she spreads it on the palm of her dark, stubby hand.

"Turn your face," she says. Taking a little grease with her short, soft fingers she starts to rub it on my forehead, then on my cheeks in a circular motion. This feels so soothing that I start to close my eyes. Teasing me, Grandmother says, "Wake up! Your Grandfather is here."

I pretend to be startled, but I am not so easily fooled. I know what a long walk it is to get the horses.

Grandmother now finishes putting grease on my face by massaging my chin and lips. The rest of the grease she rubs into her hands, then rubs my arms and legs. Now, with my face washed and my hair combed, Grandmother tells me to sit by the fireplace.

I sit down crosslegged and put my hands to the fire. I am so hungry that I start to eat the piñons that I could not get awhile ago.

Grandmother puts before me a bowl of blue cornmeal drink, some dry, pounded deer meat, and some blue cornmeal bread. Then she starts to fold up our bedding. While I eat, Grandmother does not talk to me and I tell her nothing. It would be disrespectful if we talked while eating.

On top of the fireplace is a small pottery bowl of salt which I reach up for. As I am about to bring it down, I hear the familiar cough of my Grandfather. I get so excited that I drop the bowl. With a thump it breaks and the salt, which was a hard mass, is now many grains of salt.

Grandfather comes down the ladder and, without saying a word, cleans up what I have done and makes a gesture for me to continue eating.

I pick up some of the salt that has fallen to the dirt floor and put it in my blue cornmeal drink, then I stir it up with my finger and take a big gulp. It is so good that it makes me even more hungry than I was to start with. I cut a piece of cornmeal bread off and, along with some dry meat, stick it into my mouth.

Grandfather puts a large pottery bowl on the hearth and joins me in eating. As I stick my long skinny fingers into the bowl in which I know are cooked Indian plums, I look at my Grandfather and smile.

He sits with his legs crossed and with a very straight back. He isn't a tall man or, for that matter, neither are the rest of the Pueblo people. He is, say, five feet four inches. As I look at him now I can see that he is getting a few white hairs in his long straight hair which he wears in braids. In each braid a green ribbon one inch wide is interbraided. His face is soft, smooth, and dark with a few laughing wrinkles under each deep-set, brown eye. Where his eyebrows are supposed to be there are none, only a greyish-blue marking. This comes from a sort of initiation that all men and boys must go through. Grandfather's nose is very straight — like a Greek god's. Once I asked him how he got such a straight nose and he told me that it was because his mother would massage it for him every night. His lips are full and rough. To me, he is the best-looking man at the Pueblo.

Until now I have been in a trance, looking at my Grandfather. I look at my food and am a little shocked because I have eaten almost everything. I get up, stretch, and say to my Grandfather, "I am ready. Are you?"

"Yes," he says, "but you are not. Help your Grandmother finish up so that we may be on our way fast and return before sunset."

Grandmother has almost everything done so I start to clean the floor where Grandfather and I have eaten.

Grandmother says, "Daughter, get the water bag hanging near you. Fill it up and give it to your Grandfather to take out to the wagon."

After I do this, I go to the corner opposite our entrance where there is a wooden box. I lift up the lid and get my own water bag. This is one of my favorite things for it was given to me by my Grandmother's father and it means much to me. It is made of a deer's hoof with a strip of buckskin attached to it so I can carry it around my neck. I sling it around my neck and scamper up the ladder, then down another ladder.

When I reach the ground, I take off at a run to the back of the Pueblo where the wagon is. Grandfather is putting an ax into the wagon. I run up to our old black horse, and pat his neck. So the other horse won't feel bad, I do the same thing to his neck. By this time, Grandmother is coming with the food and Grandfather is sitting in the wagon, waiting.

Grandmother puts the food in the wagon and gets in. At the same time, I run and jump on, letting my legs hang from the back of the wagon.

We are now on our way. We start to go east. As we go along we meet some people and, as we pass them, I wave. I lie back and, as the Pueblo is getting smaller because we are getting farther away, I wave to the Pueblo, and Grandfather starts to sing in a soft flowing voice.

I suddenly remember my slingshot and I sit up. At this, Grandmother looks back at me.

In a demanding voice, she says, "What's wrong with you?"

I put my head down and whimper, "Nothing." I know that if I tell her I forgot my slingshot and that is why I am acting this way, she will scold me. So I just sit still.

As Grandfather sings my favorite Indian song, I start to hum along with him, "Hey no we no hey wa . . ."

Grandmother says, "Would you come sit up front with us for a little while?"

I get up and crawl onto the bench. She puts her arms around me and closes my eyes with her fingers. Then she takes her arms from my shoulders and puts my hands out flat. Then she says, "Open your eyes."

I open my eyes and on my hands lays my slingshot.

"See, you were pouting for nothing."

Says Grandfather, "You know your Grandmother would never forget anything."

I crawl back to the back of the wagon and let my legs hang out again. I reach into the brown leather pouch that is hanging from the leather thong tied around my waist. I reach in for some dried Indian plums and piñon. I eat only a few piñon and, with my slingshot around my neck, I get an idea that I can use the plums as rocks. I shoot a few when I realize that if Grandfather saw me he would scold me for wasting food. I eat the meat of the plum first after that and the seed I use to shoot. "He, he, he," with gurgling sounds I laugh to myself.

"What's going on back there?" Grandmother asks in her deep laughing voice.

"I aimed for a post and hit it. I am good with my slingshot, yes?"

"I guess your Grandfather would know that better than I would. You spend more time with him."

I am taken aback by this — my Grandmother has never seen me use my slingshot. Excitedly, I say, "Grandmother, you do not know how good I am with the slingshot. I will show you. What do you want me to hit?"

"Whatever you want, my child."

Getting up on my knees, I look around for something to hit. We are coming around a bend and ahead of us is a young aspen, standing in a small clearing. "Look, Grandmother."

I take careful aim and pull back the small leather piece which holds the seed. I am really using all my strength to pull for I am shaking. The black innertube rubber is being stretched closer and closer to my face. I can see the tree so clearly! Now I am ready. I let go. My whole body is tense as I strain to hear the seed hit the tree.

"Yes, my Granddaughter, you are good. You hit the tree right where you aimed," Grandmother tries to comfort me. But it is no use. No matter how soft or tender her voice may be, she cannot comfort me.

"I didn't hit the tree, Grandmother." The muttered words come out in a whisper. My voice is hoarse. I'm going to cry. I so much wanted to impress my Grandmother, but I failed. She will never know that I really am good with my slingshot.

Grandfather hears my whimpering and says, "My Granddaughter missed a tree today, but there will be a day when she will not miss. It will not be just for you, but for the both of us. It won't be a tree. It will be much more important than that, dealing with life."

I stop my whimpering and the wagon is also coming to a stop. There is a small clearing where wagons have been, probably for the same purpose as our wagon.

"Whoa," and Grandfather is out of the wagon. He walks around for a while, arranging the small blanket that is wrapped around his waist.

Grandmother slowly gets down and takes a purple scarf from the wagon and ties it around her head. "Before you come down from the wagon, hand me the food box," she tells me.

"Are we going to eat now?"

"Right now? We just got through eating not long ago."

"Let's get some chips and a few pieces of wood. Then I will build a fire to make coffee."

Grandfather is unharnessing the horses. "Granddaughter, let the horses loose down by the creek." While swinging the double-edged ax, he heads for the thickets.

Grandmother calls out after him, "Do not be gone long. We will eat soon."

"Me too?"

"No, you help your Grandmother pick up small pieces of wood around here."

Grandmother has the fire going and she is picking up small pieces of wood, throwing them into the wagon. "Take that coffee can and run down and get me some water."

Jumping over logs and rocks, I run to get the water. Grandfather is near because I can hear the thump of his ax hitting wood with the echo sounding like a thunderclap. As I take the water back to our camp, I hear the mellow chirping of a bluejay. "Birdie, come play with me," I sing and it flies away.

Grandmother takes the water from me and sets the can on three rocks in the fire. "Help me pick up wood so we can finish and get home before dark."

I feel like jumping around, but since I have to help I might as well get it over with. Time passes and I am hungry and tired. Grandmother and I have gathered quite a lot of wood. I am sitting down, my slingshot in hand, taking in the quietness, the delectable smell of coffee. The smell of pine is like incense. I can hear the trickling of water over rocks, the murmur of leaves brushing against each other.

All of this is pushed aside by the racket my Grandfather is making while bringing back . . . well, dragging back, some pieces of wood. "Oh, that was tiring."

"Well, don't go back for more," Grandmother says. "We will eat now."

"No, I won't go back. I have the wood in stacks all ready to bring back. After I eat and rest I will bring it back. Then we can leave, before dark comes."

"My Granddaughter and I have gathered enough little wood. After we eat, we're going to look for some wild onions."

Grandfather takes the big green canvas from the wagon and spreads it on the ground for us to eat on. He then lies down on a corner of it. "Granddaughter, come step on my back."

I run to where he is, take off my moccasins and walk down his back, starting from the top.

Grandmother is putting the food on the canvas. Dry deer meat, tortillas, baked apples and coffee — these are our noon meal.

Grandfather, in a relaxed voice, says, "That is enough, my child. Let us eat."

We are all sitting on the canvas with the food in the middle of our small circle. I have a feeling of restlessness and can't sit still.

Grandmother, in her deep, laughing voice, says, "You are like a young colt, wanting only to run. Here, have some coffee."

Coffee tastes so good in the mountains, well, all food does. It has an ambrosial taste.

After we have eaten, Grandfather lies back down. Grandmother puts the food away, and I also decide to take a nap. I am thinking about the birds that are singing around me and then nothing . . .

I am awakened by a cool breeze hitting my face. I look up. The sun is behind a dark rain cloud and the trees around me are blowing in the wind.

Smoothing my hair, I sit up and call for Grandfather. When I get no answer, I call, "Grandmother, where are you?" Still no answer.

I jump up and run to the river. I have a lump in my throat and I feel hot tears running down my face, no sound, just tears. I run back to our little camp. I see the wagon with more wood in it than was there before I went to sleep. This means that Grandfather has brought some wood and gone back for more, and Grandmother is looking for onions. I wipe the tears from my eyes and giggle.

"Well, since they are both gone, I will take a walk. I too will look for something. What it is I do not know." Saying this aloud, I head for the river.

It is gloomy for the sun is still behind the rain cloud. It will probably rain. Oh well, I'm still going to walk in the water. Oh-h-h! the water is cold, but I still walk in the water. The cool wind blows my hair back from my face and blows my dress, goes through my dress and makes my body cold to touch, but inside I am warm. I walk and walk and walk until I come to a valley. I pass it a little ways, but just then the sun comes out from behind the cloud.

A road runs right through the center of the valley and, on the sides, trees, small bushes and grass are starting to turn tan, for it is in the harvest time when nature dresses in her prettiest colors. I step out of the water and walk up to a fallen tree that is lying under the shade of another tree. A part of the fallen tree is sticking out from under the shade, with the sun hitting it.

It's so warm and smooth for the bark has been stripped off. I lie on my stomach and the front of my body becomes warm. Now my back is cold, so I turn over. It is so nice here that I want to go to sleep again. Yawning and stretching, I close my eyes. Once again, I listen to the birds. This time I am listening for one particular bird. Whenever I go to the pasture just outside our village I can hear him chirping, "Hunting house flower, I have brought you a bucket." Lying on the tree trunk I also hear the splashing and gurgling sounds of water hitting rocks. I am thinking about these things, but slowly I am falling into the delectation of sleep.

Suddenly I hear the low drumming of thunder and feel small drops of rain hit me, going through my dress and making me get goose bumps. I jump off the trunk and sit under the tree. With my back against the tree trunk, I bend my knees, pulling my dress over them and tucking it around me. I just sit there in that position, clinging to my slingshot which is still around my neck.

I watch the rain come down, first in spurts, then soon there are so many spurts that it is pouring down and, once in a while, I hear the thunder rolling overhead. I put my head down on my knees and think: When will it ever stop? I am hungry. I want to get back to the camp. I don't want my Grandparents to leave me. Now Grandmother will have something to say to the effect that I am a tomboy or colt or goat or something!

I have been sitting with my head down for some time. I stand up. Getting up on the fallen tree trunk, I look about and take a deep breath. Everything is so fresh looking! Drops of rain on the leaves reflect the sun and give the valley a golden-glow effect. I take another breath and inhale the earthy odor of wet dirt and wet foliage. My hair is wet too. So is my dress and, now that the rain has completely stopped, I get my moccasins from under the snake leaves where I had hidden them so they wouldn't get wet. I sit on the tree trunk to let the sun dry me off.

I sit, eating my piñons and plums and shooting pebbles in the air with my slingshot. My slingshot makes me remember my attempt to hit the tree to show my Grandmother how great I am. I decide to practice on a low branch about thirty steps from me. Taking aim, I let the pebble go and hit the branch. Again and again I aim for the branch and never miss it. I am disgusted with myself for being able to hit the branch which is a lot harder to hit than the aspen tree I chose to hit for my Grandmother.

I look around for another target and see to the left of the branch a tree which looks like a good target because, where the trunk ends, two big branches are sticking up. I decide to try to shoot between these two branches where they are the closest. I take aim, let the pebble go, and — crack! — I hit one of the branches. At the bottom of the trunk I notice a pink growth of some kind. This time I take aim at the pink thing. I let the pebble go and I hit it, but it moves. What have I hit?

Cautiously, I walk towards it, picking up a stick on the way. When I get closer, it is an old man, cozily wrapped in his pink blanket.

I run up to him and ask in a surprised voice, "Old Man, how did you get way up here?"

"Well, child, since you want to know, I came with the wind. There, I answer your question, now you tell me what you are doing here."

I answer, very proud, "My Grandfather, Grandmother, and I have come after wood for the winter. They are not far from here. Would you like to come to our camp? We will give you something to eat, then we will give you a ride back to the village."

"Thank you, little one, but I won't be going back to the village and I don't think your Grandparents would appreciate seeing me now."

"But . . . wha — "

"Ask no more, child, but sit and listen to what I have to say and then say nothing of me to anyone. If you do, you will be thought of as an insane little girl who tells lies and you do not want that, do you?"

In a shaky voice, I answer, "No-o." His voice which is very low and sounds like a frog, and the things he has told me have made me a little scared.

"Don't be afraid. Listen. What it is that I am going to tell you, not very many people know about. Only a few chosen people know. You are one of them. You are only a little girl, so full of life, like a newborn colt."

Now he sounds like my Grandmother, I decide, but he is going on.

"A new colt tries to get up but falls down, then tries again and again until he makes it up and stays up. Then he runs and runs. That is the little girl in you. There is the wiseness of the coyote in you when you sit, as you are now, with the expression of interest in your face. You know what is going on, but maybe inside you do not know what I am saying. If you don't know, don't worry about it. One day soon, maybe after a while, it will hit you. When that day does come, then you will know what I am saying. Use it to gain wisdom and knowledge about life.

"You are here and so am I. So different in age, but that is all the difference for we are of the same people. My time has come to leave the ones I love and the place I love. I know all that I should know but, for you, life is just beginning.

"In our beginning we did not have to tell our young people things like this for we did not have to. Nothing was explained, it was already known. The young were brought up with this knowledge. Now we have neighbors in town with whom we rub shoulders. This is not wrong, it is only that we will not be good to each other forever because of our differences. Even now we are having our disagreements where we exchange crude words. This you must know. You must be prepared for it."

"Why, Old Man?"

Ignoring my words, he continues, "Our neighbors in town have things which we do not. Our young people like these things, our youth want change. It is not their fault if they were not told what I am telling you."

When he says this I fell very honored that he is telling me, so I sit with a very straight back so that I look stately.

"The young were not prepared for what the man in town had to offer. They were not told not to take and so they took, not knowing what it was they accepted."

Again I interrupt. "What did the man in town give them?"

"The man in town gave them things they did not understand. Now they do not know what to do with these things. They should be proud of their

Indianness, but they were not told this. The old took it for granted that the young realized this." The Old Man wags his head from side to side. His eyes are sad. "We will not drive him out. Our young people still want change."

All this is really strange to me and now I am scared of the man in town. I do not understand all this about "youth" and "the young" and "change" and "the old." What do I have to do with it? I have not done anything wrong. Yes, I have seen the man in town. He is different from us.

I remember one time when I went to town with Grandfather in the wagon. We went into a house with many things inside. There was no bedding or fireplace just . . . I don't know . . . so much stuff for one house.

Grandfather pointed to a white sack. The man gave it to him and Grandfather gave him something in his hand. The man took it and put it in a little box. Then he said something and then "fren."

Grandfather taught me that word. He said it meant a good person to you. Well, all this time I was holding onto Grandfather's blanket which was around his waist and, when we were leaving, the man held out something to me which he took out of a big jar for I had been watching him very closely.

Grandfather took it from his hand and gave it to me, saying, "Take it and eat it. It is good."

All the way back home, I ate my sweet stick, saving a little for Grandmother.

Now, Old Man's husky voice brings me back to the present.

"Old Man," I say, "I do not know why you are telling me these things. If you are trying to scare me because I shot at you with my slingshot a while ago when I saw you from where I was sitting, you are not scaring me." And I get up. "I am going back to our camp."

"Little one," Old Man says and his voice compels me to turn back to him, "I realize that you are still very young, but I must tell you what I know in the hope that you will not be like the rest, that you will help our people."

Without thinking, I sit down again to listen.

"You do not know from where we come or why we are here. I know this and I know my time has come to go, so why should I take this knowledge with me? I shall give you my knowledge to make the best use of it.

"My child, you see or you shall see many kinds of peoples — good, bad, and people with different color skin from yours. I tell you this, child, never judge people from what other people say, but think of them as you wish in your own eyes. Long ago, when your Grandfather's father's fathers were on this land, when they lived where we live now, all the peoples were good. They all loved one another. Life was good. Then one day something came over them, they were changing. Greed, hate, and other things overpowered them. They no longer cared for each other but each one for himself. His Indianness was slowly dying. He no longer prayed. The people too were dying, slowly but surely. They were starving for faith, hope, and love.

"There was an old man at the Pueblo. He always carried a cane with him. He had no family as everyone else did because he thought of all peoples as his family. Well, when all this was happening to his people, he became very concerned. He called them together and told them to pray and they answered in voices of hate and anger. 'What can we pray to? We are dying. We have nothing.'

"He told them, 'My people, you do have something. It is right in front of your eyes, but your greed and hate have made you blind.' With tears in his eyes he told them, 'But, my people, I cannot turn against you even if you throw your beauty away, for I love you too much.' He said, 'I will need the strongest of the young men who are left.'

"The weakest of the people forced some young men to do what the old man asked of them. He told them to step up to him, one by one. The first one came and he told him, 'Go north of here, over our mountain. Come to a pile of rocks, to where the snakes live. Go unto the rocks with a good heart. Pray, ask for forgiveness, that the snakes will have mercy on you. After you have done this, go farther up and get the snake leaf with the red life line and, on your way back down, stop again at the rocks and ask for the food that is there. Eat only enough to give you strength to make it back with the leaf. Go now, my son.'

"The next young man came up and he told him, 'You, my son, are to go along the river and come to the beaver's home and help him build his home for one morning while he watches from the bank of the river. Then after a while, he will bring a stick and add it to his home. Take that stick and take his home apart and at the bottom in the middle you will find the blossoms of the plum bush. Take these and bring them back. On your way back, you will see an aspen tree with small purple flowers. In one of the branches of that tree will be a basket of food. Eat only a small amount of food and hurry back with the blossoms.'

"The next young man comes up to the old man. 'You will go to yonder hill, the one called Coyote Ears. When you get to the bottom there is a gully with many sharp rocks. Walk in the gully. Follow it up to the ear which is to the north. There is a cave. Inside you will find a male coyote and a female coyote with some cubs. Go in with a good heart and no harm will come to you. Sit down and talk to them. Tell them what has happened here. Ask for help. They will give you a basket of food. Thank them and take the basket. When you get to the bottom of the hill, empty the food on an ant hill and on the bottom of the basket will be seven grains of wheat. Bring the seven grains of wheat back with you. Go now.'

"The last young man steps up to the old man. 'You are the last to go and your job is to go south to where there is the mountain, the Home-of-the-Sun. There you will find seven pottery bowls with sand in the first one. Bring that one back with you. After you take the bowl wait for one morning and go back to the spot where the bowl was. You will see that it will have been replaced with a basket of food. Take sand and sprinkle some on top of the food. Then bring the rest of the sand back here. Go and be strong.'

"The rest of the people he told to go into the kiva and wait for the return of the young men.

"Mournfully, the people went into the kiva. For four days the people waited. Each day the old man would go to the fifth story of the Pueblo to watch for the young men. He would try to think of good things — to take his mind off the mournful weeping of the people. Then, on the fourth day, the old man saw the first young man, coming back from the north.

"The old man called to him.

"He came.

"The old man told him to sit.

"He sat.

" 'Did you go where I asked you to go?'

" 'Yes.'

" 'Did you get the leaf?'

" 'No, I looked but I could not find it.'

" 'My son, listen to our people's cries. For days I have sat here listening to them. We have all been waiting for your return and now that you are here you say you did not find the leaf. My son, you are lying. You did not look for the leaf. Hunger overtook you, you ate all the food, you are no longer weak, but strong. This strength will not last forever. For this, in black shall you roam this earth. The people, hearing your cries will repel you — you, my son, the crow.'

By this time I am really involved with the story that Old Man is telling and I want him to hurry, but he continues in his slow, dull, frog-like voice.

"The next young man came back from the beaver's home and he was strong, but he was also empty-handed. He had eaten the food and did not bring back what the old man told him to bring back. For this, the old man told him, he would forever be in the hot sun. The journey he took was the last time he was to see the greenness and feel the coolness of the mountains. He was sent to the desert to be a low crawling animal with nothing — the lizard of the desert.

"The next young man came back with the same story of finding nothing at Coyote Ears hill. The old man told him he would be a bird. No, not an ugly bird, but just a bird in search of cherries for this was to be the only food he would want. The people, not knowing why, would chase him away from their orchard, and the young boys would kill him and take him back to their mothers to roast.

"The last young man returned and went up to the old man who was sitting on the fifth story of the Pueblo with his head bent. He did not want to look at the young man.

" 'My father, here is the sand from the mountain where the sun lives,' the young man said.

"The old man looked up and tears of joy rushed to his eyes.

"The young man put the pottery bowl in front of the old man, then he collapsed. He was so weak that there could be no hope for him to recover.

"The old man said in a voice as loud as silence, 'The sparrow — in beauty shall you live, in beauty shall you sing for your people.'

"One by one, the people came out of the kiva. With faith, hope, and love restored, the few people who were left started life anew. Each day, they waited for the sparrow to sing and he, up to this day, has never failed to sing in beauty."

"My Granddaughter," Old Man finished, "it is time you went back to your camp and for me to be on my way. Now remember what I have told you."

I am thinking about the story . . . Then I remember, yes, I do have to get back to the camp. Jumping up, I run back. When I get close to the camp, I see Grandfather and Grandmother, sitting in the wagon ready to leave. I run up to them and climb the side of the wagon onto the top of the wood close behind them.

They are both irritated, and Grandfather says, "Now if we told you to run off, you would stay right here and do nothing, but since you knew we wanted to get back before nightfall, you took off and kept us waiting. And I suppose you think that is good?"

"No, Grandfather, but I have heard a great story."

"A story?" Grandmother's voice is disgusted. "Oh, what is the use!" Then she leans back and hugs me.

As we pass the spot where the Old Man and I were sitting, I look around for him, but he is nowhere in sight. I just smile and look straight ahead of me. I can see the Pueblo now and all that Old Man had told me runs through my head. Looking at my Grandfather and then at my Grandmother, I think to myself that someday I will help my people. We will love one another and there will be peace.

The next day after the time we went for wood, I was playing in the corral when Grandmother called me. I hurried up to her and we both went into the abode.

She had tears in her eyes and she said, "Granddaughter, you remember Old Man? Well, he is no longer here. Yesterday, when we were not here, he was coming down the ladder when he slipped and fell. He is dead. So his spirit won't be left with you, I am doing this."

She told me to stand right by the entrance and she took the straw broom and brushed it down from the top of my head to my toes.

I cannot cry or say anything.

Grandmother sends me on my way, and I go up to the fifth story and take watch for Old Man.

Ella Cara Deloria

BLUE BIRD'S OFFERING

▼ ▼ ▼ ▼

▼

Ella Cara Deloria's novel Waterlily, *from which the following excerpts are taken, was completed by 1944, though it did not find its way into print until 1988. Set in the period before contact with Europe,* Waterlily *is concerned with the effect war has on women's lives. Primarily a linguist and ethnographer, Deloria published her classic* Dakota Texts *in 1932.* Dakota Grammar *(written in collaboration with Franz Boas) and* Speaking of Indians *were published in the 1940s, as her novel would have been had not World War II and, presumably, other more pressing activities intervened. After the war she continued to work with Boas and then, after his death, with Ruth Benedict until Benedict's death in 1948. It may be that Benedict's death played an important role in delaying publication of* Waterlily, *for she had received a copy of the manuscript from Deloria in 1944 and had suggested lengthy editing and revision. Fortunately, the excellence and prolific nature of Deloria's linguistic and ethnographic work prevented her novel from disappearing entirely.*

BLUE BIRD HAD NEVER BEEN entirely happy either in her marriage or in her life in a camp circle that was not her own. It was not that the people were unkind; quite the contrary. But she could not feel satisfied there. She never ceased to yearn for her own people. It was almost four years now she and her grandmother had been staying there. Sometimes she wished they had risked everything and struck out alone in search of their own camp circle. Even if they had perished on the way, it would have been worth trying.

Her childhood among her own many loving kinsmen was a happy one, but that time was like a dream vanished. Try as she would, she could never recapture the feel of that carefree life, so cruelly ended in a day. Tonight for the first time, with her infant, Waterlily, asleep beside her, she was again completely happy. This was a different kind of happiness, satisfying, if subdued. But it was good. She lay idly reminiscing in the dark tipi of her cousin, who was out somewhere. With singular detachment she was able for the first time to recall in detail the events of that tragic day that had robbed her of her family. Tonight it seemed remote, like something that had happened to someone else long ago in a far-off place.

She had been fourteen years old at the time. Her father had decided to leave the camp circle for a few days of deer hunting because their supply of meat was dwindling fast and no buffalo had been sighted in a long time. He took his wife and his mother and his three children, Blue Bird and her brothers, ten and six years of age.

The family made their temporary camp near a wood and immediately went out to cut the poles and boughs needed to set up their working arrangements, drying racks for the meat, and an arbor of leaves. Soon the father was bringing in deer and other game at such a rate that the two women had to work steadily from dawn to dusk caring for the meat, for they were a frugal family and saved every bit that could be used.

But busy as they were, the old grandmother took time out one afternoon for a walk under the tall cottonwoods nearby. The next day she announced, as they sat eating, "There is a large cache of earth beans over yonder, where many little paths under the matted grass come together from all directions. The field mice, too, have been busy preparing for winter."

"Well, that is indeed good news," her son's wife said. "Now maybe we can take back earth beans as well as meat. I hope you can remember where the cache is."

"Oh, yes. And anyway I set up a stick to mark the spot," the old woman assured her, adding, "I could easily have thumped in the dirt roof right then with my club and brought the beans home. But of course I waited."

The younger boy, who dearly relished them, pouted, "Oh, Grandmother, you should have! Then I could be having some beans now."

Blue Bird cut in, "You can't do that, silly! Don't you know that you have to leave a return gift for the mice when you take away their food? They have to have something to live on, too."

That was no way for a girl to speak to a brother, and few adults would fail to correct such a slip. Blue Bird's mother said gently but firmly, "Daughter, one does not call one's brother 'silly.' " And then she turned to her mother-in-law, saying, "I have some dried corn in that rawhide box. Will it answer?"

The old woman was delighted. "Of course. It will be just the thing, Too good, I should say. For who are they, to have green corn dried for them? They should be too happy with it to think of bewitching me — I hope." She said this laughingly, but it was plain she half feared the common belief about the powers of resentful mice.

Blue Bird went with her grandmother to open the cache and they found an abundance of beans, unusually large and meaty. They would cook up rich and sweet, the old woman said. She found more caches and went to work at once, happily drawing out handfuls of the black, earth-caked store and piling it on her blanket, spread out to receive it. For each handful she religiously returned a handful of green corn that had been parboiled and then sundried, a treat for the mice indeed. When she was through, she and Blue Bird grasped the corners of the blanket and tossed the beans high to winnow out the dirt. The loose, fine dust was carried off on the breeze. The clumps settled to the bottom and could easily be removed later.

The old woman gathered the blanket to form a bag holding the beans and tied a thong around it tightly, bending over. When she straightened up, she groaned a bit over a kink in her back, as was her habit. Then, shielding her eyes with one hand, she studied the sun. "Come, child, we must be going now. It is getting on," she said. But she could not resist hurriedly picking up a few dried sticks. "We can always do with more firewood." She made a bundle of them with the pack strap she always wore for a belt. From a lifetime of practice she flung the bundle expertly onto her back. At last she and Blue Bird started home, carrying the beans suspended between them.

Out of the woods and into the clear they came, but when they looked toward their camp, it was not there. Everything was in ruins. How could it have happened so quickly, so quietly? It was unbelievable that in the short time since Blue Bird and her grandmother had left it, an enemy war party had raided their camp. Yet that was the case.

The destruction could hardly have been more thorough. The skin tent was slashed beyond mending, the poles were all broken or askew, and the drying racks filled with jerked meat were completely dismantled. The two boys lay dead, flat on their faces, not far from the tipi. They had been shot while running away, impaled by arrows in their backs. The parents had vanished without a trace. Whether they too had been killed or were taken captive the two survivors were never to know.

They hurriedly covered the bodies of the boys, but this was no time to mourn. Shocked as they were, they could not entertain both grief and fear at the same time. One emotion must wait, and fear took precedence. Lest the marauders return and find them, the grandmother decided they must hasten into hiding. She and Blue Bird did so, lying concealed under bushes and behind rocks by day and traveling by night. Under an overcast sky they lost their way and wandered blindly, with no idea of their destination.

The second day at dawn they happened upon a large camp circle, though it was not theirs. But the people were their kind and spoke their dialect, so they knew they had found refuge. On learning of their plight and their recent tragedy, the magistrates sent the crier out from the council tipi to announce their arrival and rally the people to their aid.

The response was quick. Someone gave the newcomers a tipi to live in, while public-spirited collectors carried around the circle a great bull hide into which contributions were placed. Women came running out of their tipis to add their gifts, such items as clothing and food. And thus all in a day Blue Bird and her grandmother were equipped to start life anew. From time to time the wives and mothers of hunters brought them meat, and at the next several feasts they were invited as special guests. In such ways did the people help them establish themselves in their new camp circle. And when at last, in the privacy of their newly acquired home, the two could give way to their grief and wail at leisure, their women neighbors came in to wail with them in sympathy, as was the custom. And the members of the camp circle adopted the newcomers as relatives.

It was true enough that here Blue Bird and her grandmother fell into the category of the humbler folk of the community. Without any male relatives to give them backing, they made no pretensions to importance in the social life of the camp circle. Nor were they expected to. Nevertheless, their lowly station in no way degraded them in the popular esteem. The Tetons did not have to put on airs in that way. If one's circumstances did not allow it, one did not need to give feasts or take part in the conspicuous give-away ceremonies. The grandmother and grandchild, accepting their situation, were content to remain quietly in the background. Since they could not return to the camp circle where they did have position, and with it certain social obligations, it was enough that they had fallen in with their own kind of people and that they had been taken in as relatives in social kinship.

As the seasons passed, the young men of the village could not fail to see that Blue Bird was maturing and that her growing beauty was remarkable. But this fact troubled her grandmother greatly, and she felt the need of someone with whom to share the responsibility for the girl until she should be safely married. Knowing well how some reckless young men played at courtship, she feared for Blue Bird. She must be warned at once that many a girl had come to ruin by taking their smooth wooing seriously, and the grandmother was the only one to tell her. "I shall have a talk with her tomorrow." But each day she put it off, dreading the ordeal. "I am too old for this; would that her mother were here," she said to herself. "Or perhaps I should simply give the girl away in marriage now, to some kind and able householder, to be a co-wife. Then she can be honorably married before any trouble can befall her. Yes, that would be best."

But just whom to give her to was a puzzle. And what wife would want her? Being co-wife was not necessarily bad, provided the man was kind. She had been a co-wife herself. But then, she was the wife's sister and therefore was well received. In fact, as she remembered now, it was that elder sister who had offered to take her into the family. Ah, but Blue Bird had no sister in this camp circle. A head wife might resent her. That too must be considered. Slowly and timidly the old woman turned the problem over in her mind many times. But she had not yet acted when Blue Bird said to her one day, "Grandmother, one of the young men at the courting place has been urging me to marry him. His name is Star Elk."

The old woman shook her head emphatically, "No! No! Not that one. It would be good for you to marry, grandchild. We are so alone and helpless without a man to provide for our home. But not that one. Only last night the women around the campfire were talking about him. 'He is no hunter,' they said. 'He takes no interest in anything. Always he has been headstrong and unfriendly, even as a boy,' they said. That is not the kind of man for you, grandchild."

"But I have told him I would marry him, Grandmother."

The silence that followed was ominous. When the old woman again found her voice, she said, "Ah, if only you had told me he was courting you so I could have warned you, grandchild. Since you have promised already, there is nothing I can do. Once she gives it, an honorable Dakota woman does not break her word to a man. Those who make false promises are ever after derided. To give your word is to give yourself." With that she stumbled out of the little tipi and began to wail in a quavering voice the following lament: "Ah, my son! Ah, my daughter-in-law! You have left me alone to struggle on. What can I do, frail and full of years as I am?" Far into the night she wailed.

Blue Bird's marriage was inevitable now. But even after resigning herself to it, the grandmother went about with a heavy heart. "If only I had had someone to help me arrange a suitable marriage for her," she muttered to herself from time to time. That the girl might run off with Star Elk was a dreaded possibility, even while there was a feeble hope that perhaps the young man had been misrepresented as altogether undesirable. Perhaps he was not that bad after all, and perhaps he would soon do the honorable thing — marry the girl openly, with tribal approval.

The most glamorous kind of marriage was by purchase. A woman who married in that way was much respected, for it meant that she had kept herself so unattainable that the man, who wanted her at all costs, thought nothing of giving horses for her, even at the risk of her rejecting him publicly. "I do not aspire to that for my poor orphaned grandchild," the grandmother said. "All I ask is a valid marriage, and then I should die happy." He might come to live with them or take her to his people openly. Whichever way, it should be planned and aboveboard, and then Blue Bird would be respected.

But Star Elk lived up to his reputation. He lured the girl away, the very thing her grandmother had feared. What a gamble that was! A Teton girl who accepted marriage on such shabby terms took the supreme risk with her honor. How did she know that the man was not just trifling with her? Too often an elopement ended disastrously for the girl, while the man always went free. Momentarily the old woman looked for the girl's return, after the man tired of her. She would of course receive her back; was she not her grandchild? But the disgrace would be lasting.

As it happened, though, Blue Bird was lucky. Star Elk did not dally on the way but took her straight home to his people. And for her grandmother that was the one mitigating fact. Soon the new relatives-in-law came for her and placed her tipi in among their family group that they might care for her. Thus, even though Blue Bird had married in the least honorable way, the material condition of her grandmother was bettered, and that was something.

Because Star Elk had taken Blue Bird home to his people, the marriage was accepted as tolerably valid, and in due time the foolish step was forgiven the girl. The usual sharp censure of the eloping woman was toned down considerably by the circumstances. Condoning it, women began saying, "Well, what could you expect since the girl is very young and pretty and lacks a mother to guide her? What could a tottering grandmother do, anyway? It is good that the girl did not get into real trouble and bear a fatherless child." Thus Blue Bird, by not being "discarded in the wilds" (abandoned far from the camp circle) or bearing a "fatherless child," came in time to be counted among the blameless women of the camp circle. By the slimmest of margins — but she was in.

Even so, things were far from ideal. Star Elk was lazy and petulant and given to jealous fits. It was his relatives who received her kindly and treated her well, partly for their own reputation as correct in-laws, and partly to compensate for his failures. This made up in a measure for the poor bargain

Blue Bird had made. But, kind as they were, it might have been better if they had been remiss in some details, or even outright hostile to her, if only her husband had been more satisfactory. The marriage had been unfortunate from the beginning.

The tipis of skin were opaque at night. Unless the fire was flaming, occupants must feel their way about. The cousin entered the tipi at a late hour and moved with caution toward her place. Perhaps Blue Bird was asleep. Nevertheless she spoke to her softly, "Cousin, are you resting well? We shall be by ourselves. I have sent the children and their father to sleep in his mother's tipi. Wake me at once if you need anything."

"I am quite all right, cousin, and I think I can sleep now. I was just thinking of the past; that is all."

The two women said nothing further. There was in the language no formality equivalent to "Good night." One quite well indicated one's goodwill and good wishes by tonal quality. After a little, Blue Bird reached out drowsily and touched her baby, smiling in the dark as she did so. "This is all I want," she murmured. "Let him do his worst!" And presently she slept. How could she guess to what lengths he would go to spite her for staying away?

Star Elk had grown more and more ill-tempered each day of his married life. The truth was that he was tormented with jealousy over his wife. He continually imagined that other men looked upon her with desire, and accused her of encouraging them furtively. She used to enjoy looking on at the celebrations and dances, but after a time he even forbade her to do that. And when she was with child, he once declared in a rage that it was not his. That was pure nonsense, as was nearly everything he said of or to his wife.

And now that the baby was born, he behaved still more outrageously. When he learned that Blue Bird was staying away for a while, he pouted and refused to see her and the baby. It was reported that all day and late into the night he lay out in the tall grass, among the horses that were picketed behind the cousin's tipi, and watched to see who went to call on Blue Bird. When this was rumored around, people laughed at him. "How shameful, to pout like a woman," the men said. "He has always been a queer fellow . . . without close friends . . . even as a boy he had none . . ." "His kind do not take to fasting or warfare — but if at least he were a tolerable hunter."

But neither the disapproval of the older men nor the ridicule of his contemporaries spurred Star Elk to be more dutiful as a husband. If anything, the effect was to make him more and more active in finding ways to hurt his wife. He reached the limit when he decided to "throw her away publicly."

During a great victory dance, attended by many visitors from neighboring camp circles, he waited until the crowd was biggest, and then, at an intermission, he forced his way in, snatched one of the highly decorated sticks used by the drummers, and stood motionless, holding it high. That was the way to gain an audience's full attention when one wanted to take part in the ceremonial give-away. Only persons of social standing were qualified to do this, because of their past record of hospitality, generosity, war achievements, or the like. But here was Star Elk, who had no such record. The crowd waited in silence. What was this fellow going to do?

Arrogantly he held the stick high for one dramatic moment and then cried out, "This is that woman! Whoever needs a woman to fetch his fuel and water can have her!" He flung the heavy drumstick into the crowd. Fearful of being struck, the people pushed back in waves. Nobody scrambled for the stick. He knew nobody would; all he wanted was to hurt and shame Blue Bird — and that he did.

It was a foolish and uncalled-for act but wholly characteristic. Instead of enhancing the man, as it might if he had cried, "This is a horse for the needy!" what he said only lowered his already low standing. Moreover, Star Elk had insulted a victory dance. "Throwing away a wife" was a custom, to be sure, but this was not the place. If it must be done at all, it should be at some social dance where the mood was properly light and reckless. Even then it was a custom shunned by men of standing, who considered it beneath them to air their emotions publicly. The way to leave an unfaithful wife was to send her away or to walk out of her life without so much as a backward glance. Only vain and weak men gave vent to their temper in public as Star Elk had done. It was also wrong because Blue Bird had not been unfaithful, and this was generally known. Star Elk not only succeeded in losing a good wife and making a fool of himself; he earned such public disfavor that he could not remain in the camp circle. He left immediately, his destination unknown.

Naturally, Blue Bird was hurt by that undeserved public insult. But she was not nearly so crushed as Star Elk had intended her to be. The fact was that at the time of the festivities in the center of the camp circle she sat in her cousin's tipi, sick at heart over something infinitely more vital to her even than her honor, for her baby was dying.

Do what she would, Blue Bird could see that the little Waterlily was growing steadily weaker. All that day she had lain motionless and refused to eat. Nor did any of the medicinal roots the cousin brought from neighbors help her. When a mother from the opposite side of the circle heard of the symptoms, she came hurrying across with a powdery substance obtained in the badlands and known as "earth-smoke," saying, "Try this next. It always cured my children — a pinch of it in a little water." But Waterlily could not swallow it.

All hope was dwindling fast. In a few hours the child would die unless something was done. Blue Bird must pray. Inexperienced in such holy matters, she nevertheless determined to make some kind of appeal for divine aid. But how to proceed?

Mechanically she thrust her hand into the flat rawhide bag which was her purse and which contained her personal effects and a small otterskin very evenly painted a brilliant red. She had hurriedly salvaged this one object from her father's belongings that fatal day and had prized it ever since. She was sure it must be potent with supernatural power, although her father had never said so. She only knew that he had venerated it above all else. Perhaps, possibly, it would save her baby.

Then she took some smoking mixture of tobacco and red willow bark and tied a bit of it into squares of deerskin, making ten tiny bundles no bigger than her thumb. She knew she must make some sacrificial offerings. Fumbling in her haste, she muttered to herself, "Is that right? Alas, what do I know about it? Those who know tell of the Something Holy — *Taku Wakan* — that has supreme power, but I never understood. It is so remote. What right have I?" All the while she worked in a desperate race with death.

Throughout the Great Plains and the wooded country near the Rockies, wherever the people moved, she had seen here a rock or there a tree with red paint on it, and sometimes a once beautiful blanket or other gift rotting there. She knew what that meant. Everyone knew. Those rocks and those trees had been set apart and consecrated; they were individual altars where people had prayed in times of stress. She was going to make her own altar now.

Taking up the baby and clutching in her free hand the bag with its special contents, Blue Bird left the tipi and walked away unnoticed. On and on she walked, until the noise of the festivities died away and the camp circle was no longer in sight. She stopped in utter stillness beside a great rock in the midst of an empty plain. She studied the rock and saw that though it was well embedded in the earth, the exposed part was nearly as tall as she. It sat apart from any other object as though already reserved for her. It sat on virgin ground. Surely no human had ever stood where she now stood.

She carefully laid the all but lifeless infant on her wrap spread on the ground and set immediately to work, covering one side of the rock with red ocher face paint. Then she carefully spread her father's hallowed otterskin on the top of the rock, like a covering for its head. Next she planted a stick upright in front of it. (The painted side had become the rock's face. She had personalized it.) To the top of the stick, which stood waist high, she tied the ten little tobacco bundles. They were on short strings of uneven lengths and dangled, now clustering and now separating, in the faint breeze that came and went. In descriptions of sacrificial altars where men fasted and prayed in some lonely spot, the essential property was unvarying: one hundred bundles of tobacco. But ten was all she could manage; it would have to do.

The hot summer sun beat down in all its fury. The earth danced in continuous ripples around the rim where it met the sky. Once the baby whimpered weakly. Everything was as ready as Blue Bird could make it. Now for the prayer, which was of utmost importance. "Prayer should be audibly released into the infinite" she had heard somewhere. She began speaking to the Great Spirit (*Wakan Tanka*) in the rock. Aloud but haltingly, fearful lest she not pray correctly, she said: "O, Grandfather, hear me! Since the very beginning you have been here. Before there were any men you were here. And it is certain that long after we are all gone you will remain. Hear me, Grandfather, and pity me. I want my baby to live."

Right or wrong, that was her prayer. Overwhelmed by her daring, she stood motionless, waiting — for what, she did not know. Presently someone said in her ear quite clearly, *"Hao!"* It was the Dakota word of approval and consent.

Quickly Blue Bird covered her face with both hands and bowed her head for whatever was to follow. A man must have stolen up from behind while she was praying, maybe an enemy, ready to kill her. So be it. Inert and without clear thought she waited a long time, but nothing happened. Very slowly she raised her head and uncovered her face to look about her — behind her and then farther off and finally to the whole round horizon. In that vast emptiness she stood alone.

"I have prayed aright and my prayer is heard! My baby, my baby will live!" A strange lightness, an unearthly joy, seized her, and a new boldness born of confidence swept away all her girlhood diffidence. Holding her hands to her mouth like a trumpet, she first called out, then shouted, and finally screamed her enraptured thanks: "Grandfather, you have made me thankful!" Screaming this over and over until her throat ached, she whirled about, throwing her voice in all directions in a frantic aim to reach the whole of space with her thanks.

But that sort of elation could not last. Soon enough she was back to reality and began to contemplate her unhappy lot. Through no fault of her own she had just been cruelly shamed in public. It was so merciless, so unfair. Feeling sorry for herself, she wailed aloud. In the customary way she addressed all her dead relatives in turn, her parents, brothers, aunts, and uncles, ending with the forlorn question no one can answer, "Where have you gone? Where have you gone?"

It was always good to let sorrow out and bad to hold it in. She felt much better when she had had her fill of unrestrained weeping. She dried her eyes, fitting the base of her palm into her eye sockets as all women did. She picked up her child, but its limp body no longer distressed her as she departed, leaving the rare otterskin to be the Great Spirit's forever. To no one less would she ever have relinquished what her father once venerated.

Everyone was at the dancing when she reentered her cousin's tipi. She was glad it was vacant, that she would not have to account for herself. What she had been through was not for common telling. Once more she offered the earth-smoke and Waterlily was able to swallow it this time. Gradually the infant seemed not to be in such pain as before. She fell asleep and after a while was recovered. Blue Bird was not surprised. She had prayed for that and had her answer already.

Elated about her child, she heard almost without emotion that visitors from another camp circle had recognized her old grandmother as one of the family who had never come back, and would take the news of her and her granddaughter back home. "Your grandson Black Eagle has long mourned for you," the grandmother was told. "As soon as we get home he will be coming for you." And so he did, and at last Blue Bird, her child, and her grandmother were back where they belonged, where their many relatives welcomed them with tears of grief for the dead and of joy for the living.

Anna Lee Walters

THE WARRIORS

∨ ∨ ∨ ∨

∨

This American Indian fiction classic tells about how one Indian family clung to tradition in the face of devastation. We all know who lives near the railroad tracks: the cast-offs, the unmodern, the traditionals, the ones who cannot belong to a society that has no time for things of the spirit, and whose attitude toward human and animal life is one of exploitation. But a warrior does not forget, even in the midst of devastation, where she comes from. She does not forget that beauty is what we have, what we share, what gives human beings dignity. In the midst of the ugliness of alcoholism and dislocation, the life of a warrior goes on.

There are strong parallels in this story between the mother and her brother: both retain their identity, however they suffer and grieve, and both maintain their way of life. Some students of mine, reading this story, have responded to the mother as though she were the villain. To do so is to miss an important theme: although her brother Ralph must be dealt with, still he is her brother, her daughters' uncle. His disease cannot be trivialized or ignored. In her strength, her courage to confront his disease, she also displays a warrior's dignity. Together she and her brother teach the young how to keep their sense of value intact in the face of a brutal and hostile world.

IN OUR YOUTH, we saw hobos come and go, sliding by our faded white house like wary cats who did not want us too close. Sister and I waved at the strange procession of passing men and women hobos. Just between ourselves, Sister and I talked of that hobo parade. We guessed at and imagined the places and towns we thought the hobos might have come from or had been. Mostly they were white or black people. But there were Indian hobos, too. It never occurred to Sister and me that this would be Uncle Ralph's end.

Sister and I were little, and Uncle Ralph came to visit us. He lifted us over his head and shook us around him like gourd rattles. He was Momma's younger brother, and he could have disciplined us if he so desired. That was part of our custom. But he never did. Instead, he taught us Pawnee words. "*Pari* is Pawnee and *pita* is man," he said. Between the words, he tapped out drumbeats with his fingers on the table top, ghost dance and round dance songs that he suddenly remembered and sang. His melodic voice lilted over us and hung around the corners of the house for days. His stories of life and death were fierce and gentle. Warriors dangled in delicate balance.

He told us his version of the story of Pahukatawa, a Skidi Pawnee warrior. He was killed by the Sioux, but the animals, feeling compassion for him, brought Pahukatawa to life again. "The Evening Star and the Morning Star bore children and some people say that these offspring are who we are," he often said. At times he pointed to those stars and greeted them by their Pawnee names. He liked to pray for Sister and me, for everyone and every tiny thing in the world, but we never heard him ask for anything for himself from *Atius*, the Father.

"For beauty is why we live," Uncle Ralph said when he talked of precious things only the Pawnees know. "We die for it, too." He called himself an ancient Pawnee warrior when he was quite young. He told us that warriors must brave all storms and odds and stand their ground. He knew intimate details of every battle the Pawnees ever fought since Pawnee time began, and Sister and I knew even then that Uncle Ralph had a great battlefield of his own.

As a child I thought that Uncle Ralph had been born into the wrong time. The Pawnees had been ravaged so often by then. The tribe of several thousand when it was at its peak over a century before were then a few hundred people who had been closely confined for more than a hundred years. The warrior life was gone. Uncle Ralph was trapped in a transparent bubble of a new time. The bubble bound him tight as it blew around us.

Uncle Ralph talked obsessively of warriors, painted proud warriors who shrieked poignant battle cries at the top of their lungs and died with honor. Sister and I were little then, lost from him in the world of children who saw everything with children's eyes. And though we saw with wide eyes the painted warriors that he fantasized and heard their fierce and haunting battle cries, we did not hear his. Now that we are old and Uncle Ralph has been gone for a long time, Sister and I know that when he died, he was tired and alone. But he was a warrior.

The hobos were always around in our youth. Sister and I were curious about them, and this curiosity claimed much of our time. They crept by the house at all hours of the day and night, dressed in rags and odd clothing. They wandered to us from the railroad tracks where they had leaped from slow-moving boxcars onto the flatland. They hid in high clumps of weeds and brush that ran along the fence near the tracks. The hobos usually traveled alone, but Sister and I saw them come together, like poor families, to share a can of beans or a tin of sardines that they ate with sticks or twigs. Uncle Ralph also watched them from a distance.

One early morning, Sister and I crossed the tracks on our way to school and collided with a tall, haggard white man. He wore a very old-fashioned pin-striped black jacket covered with lint and soot. There was fright in his eyes when they met ours. He scurried around us, quickening his pace. The pole over his shoulder where his possessions hung in a bundle at the end bounced as he nearly ran from us.

"Looks just like a scared jackrabbit," Sister said, watching him dart away.

That evening we told Momma about the scared man. She warned us about the dangers of hobos as our father threw us a stern look. Uncle Ralph was visiting but he didn't say anything. He stayed the night and Sister asked him, "Hey, Uncle Ralph, why do you suppose they's hobos?"

Uncle Ralph was a large man. He took Sister and put her on one knee. "You see, Sister," he said, "hobos are a different kind. They see things in a different way. Them hobos are kind of like us. We're not like other people in some ways and yet we are. It has to do with what you see and feel when you look at this old world."

His answer satisfied Sister for a while. He taught us some more Pawnee words that night.

Not long after Uncle Ralph's explanation, Sister and I surprised a black man with white whiskers and fuzzy hair. He was climbing through the barbed-wire fence that marked our property line. He wore faded blue overalls with pockets stuffed full of handkerchiefs. He wiped sweat from his face. When it dried, he looked up and saw us. I remembered what Uncle Ralph had said and wondered what the black man saw when he looked at us standing there.

"We might scare him," Sister said softly to me, remembering the white man who had scampered away.

Sister whispered, "Hi," to the black man. Her voice was barely audible.

"Boy, it's sure hot," he said. His voice was big and he smiled.

"Where are you going?" Sister asked.

"Me? Nowheres, I guess," he muttered.

"Then what you doing here?" Sister went on. She was bold for a seven-year-old kid. I was older but I was also quieter. "This here place is ours," she said.

He looked around and saw our house with its flowering mimosa trees and rich green mowed lawn stretching out before him. Other houses sat around ours.

"I reckon I'm lost," he said.

Sister pointed to the weeds and brush further up the road. "That's where you want to go. That's where they all go, the hobos."

I tried to quiet Sister but she didn't hush. "The hobos stay up there," she said. "You a hobo?"

He ignored her question and asked his own. "Say, what is you all? You not black, you not white. What is you all?"

Sister looked at me. She put one hand on her chest and the other hand on me. "We Indians!" Sister said.

He stared at us and smiled again. "Is that a fact?" he said.

"Know what kind of Indians we are?" Sister asked him.

He shook his fuzzy head. "Indians is Indians, I guess," he said.

Sister wrinkled her forehead and retorted, "Not us! We not like others. We see things different. We're Pawnees. We're warriors!"

I pushed my elbow into Sister's side. She quieted.

The man was looking down the road and he shuffled his feet. "I'd best go," he said.

Sister pointed to the brush and weeds one more time. "That way," she said.

He climbed back through the fence and brush as Sister yelled, "Bye now!" He waved a damp handkerchief.

Sister and I didn't tell Momma and Dad about the black man. But much later Sister told Uncle Ralph every word that had been exchanged with the black man. Uncle Ralph listened and smiled.

Months later when the warm weather had cooled and Uncle Ralph came to stay with us for a couple of weeks, Sister and I went to the hobo place. We had planned it for a long time. That afternoon when we pushed away the weeds, not a hobo was in sight.

The ground was packed down tight in the clearing among the high weeds. We walked around the encircling brush and found folded cardboards stacked together. Burned cans in assorted sizes were stashed under the cardboards, and there were remains of old fires. Rags were tied to the brush, snapping in the hard wind.

Sister said, "Maybe they're all in the boxcars now. It's starting to get cold."

She was right. The November wind had a bite to it and the cold stung our hands and froze our breaths as we spoke.

"You want to go over to them boxcars?" she asked. We looked at the Railroad Crossing sign where the boxcars stood.

I was prepared to answer when a voice roared from somewhere behind us.

"Now, you young ones, you git on home! Go on! Git!"

A man crawled out of the weeds and looked angrily at us. His eyes were red and his face was unshaven. He wore a red plaid shirt with striped gray and black pants too large for him. His face was swollen and bruised. An old woolen pink scarf hid some of the bruise marks around his neck, and his topcoat was splattered with mud.

Sister looked at him. She stood close to me and told him defiantly, "You can't tell us what to do! You don't know us!"

He didn't answer Sister but tried to stand. He couldn't. Sister ran to him and took his arm and pulled on it. "You need help?" she questioned.

He frowned at her but let us help him. He was tall. He seemed to be embarrassed by our help.

"You Indian, ain't you?" I dared to ask him.

He didn't answer me but looked at his feet as if they could talk so he wouldn't have to. His feet were in big brown overshoes.

"Who's your people?" Sister asked. He looked to be about Uncle Ralph's age when he finally lifted his face and met mine. He didn't respond for a minute. Then he sighed. "I ain't got no people," he told us as he tenderly stroked his swollen jaw.

"Sure you got people. Our folks says a man's always got people," I said softly. The wind blew our clothes and covered the words.

But he heard. He exploded like a firecracker. "Well, I don't! I ain't got no people! I ain't got nobody!"

"What you doing out here anyway?" Sister asked. "You hurt? You want to come over to our house?"

"Naw," he said. "Now you little ones, go on home. Don't be walking round out here. Didn't nobody tell you little girls ain't supposed to be going round by themselves? You might git hurt."

"We just wanted to talk to hobos," Sister said.

"Naw, you don't. Just go on home. Your folks is probably looking for you and worrying 'bout you."

I took Sister's arm and told her we were going home. Then we said bye to the man. But Sister couldn't resist a few last words, "You Indian, ain't you?"

He nodded his head like it was a painful thing to do. "Yeah, I'm Indian."

"You ought to go on home yourself," Sister said. "Your folks probably looking for you and worrying 'bout you."

His voice rose again as Sister and I walked away from him. "I told you kids, I don't have no people!" There was exasperation in his voice.

Sister would not be outdone. She turned and yelled, "Oh yeah? You Indian ain't you? Ain't you?" she screamed. "We your people!"

His topcoat and pink scarf flapped in the wind as we turned away from him.

We went home to Momma and Dad and Uncle Ralph then. Uncle Ralph met us at the front door. "Where you all been?" he asked looking toward the railroad tracks. Momma and Dad were talking in the kitchen.

"Just playing, Uncle," Sister and I said simultaneously.

Uncle Ralph grabbed both Sister and me by our hands and yanked us out the door. "*Awkuh!*" he said, using the Pawnee expression to show his dissatisfaction.

Outside, we sat on the cement porch. Uncle Ralph was quiet for a long time, and neither Sister nor I knew what to expect.

"I want to tell you all a story," he finally said. "Once, there were these two rats who ran around everywhere and got into everything all the time. Everything they were told not to do, well they went right out and did. They'd get into one mess and then another. It seems that they never could learn."

At that point Uncle Ralph cleared his throat. He looked at me and said, "Sister, do you understand this story? Is it too hard for you? You're older."

I nodded my head up and down and said, "I understand."

Then Uncle Ralph looked at Sister. He said to her, "Sister, do I need to go on with this story?"

Sister shook her head from side to side. "Naw, Uncle Ralph," she said.

"So you both know how this story ends?" he said gruffly. Sister and I bobbed our heads up and down again.

We followed at his heels the rest of the day. When he tightened the loose hide on top of his drum, we watched him and held it in place as he laced the wet hide down. He got his drumsticks down from the top shelf of the closet and began to pound the drum slowly.

"Where you going, Uncle Ralph?" I asked. Sister and I knew that when he took his drum out, he was always gone shortly after.

"I have to be a drummer at some doings tomorrow," he said.

"You a good singer, Uncle Ralph," Sister said. "You know all them old songs."

"The young people nowadays, it seems they don't care 'bout nothing that's old. They just want to go to the Moon." He was drumming low as he spoke.

"We care, Uncle Ralph," Sister said.

"Why?" Uncle Ralph asked in a hard, challenging tone that he seldom used on us.

Sister thought for a moment and then said, "I guess because you care so much, Uncle Ralph."

His eyes softened as he said, "I'll sing you an *Eruska* song, a song for the warriors."

The song he sang was a war dance song. At first Sister and I listened attentively, but then Sister began to dance the men's dance. She had never danced before and tried to imitate what she had seen. Her chubby body whirled and jumped the way she'd seen the men dance. Her head tilted from side to side the way the men moved theirs. I laughed aloud at her clumsy effort, and Uncle Ralph laughed heartily, too.

Uncle Ralph went in and out of our lives after that. We heard that he sang at one place and then another, and people came to Momma to find him. They said that he was only one of a few who knew the old ways and the songs.

When he came to visit us, he always brought something to eat. The Pawnee custom was that the man, the warrior, should bring food, preferably meat. Then, whatever food was brought to the host was prepared and served to the man, the warrior, along with the host's family. Many times Momma and I, or Sister and I, came home to an empty house to find a sack of food on the table. Momma or I cooked it for the next meal, and Uncle Ralph showed up to eat.

As Sister and I grew older, our fascination with the hobos decreased. Other things took our time, and Uncle Ralph did not appear as frequently as he did before.

Once while I was home alone, I picked up Momma's old photo album. Inside was a gray photo of Uncle Ralph in an army uniform. Behind him were tents on a flat terrain. Other photos showed other poses but only in one picture did he smile. All the photos were written over in black ink in Momma's handwriting. "Ralphie in Korea," the writing said.

Other photos in the album showed our Pawnee relatives. Dad was from another tribe. Momma's momma was in the album, a tiny gray-haired woman who no longer lived. And Momma's momma's dad was in the album; he wore old Pawnee leggings and the long feathers of a dark bird sat upon his head. I closed the album when Momma, Dad, and Sister came home.

Momma went into the kitchen to cook. She called me and Sister to help. As she put on a bibbed apron, she said, "We just came from town, and we saw someone from home there." She meant someone from her tribal community.

"This man told me that Ralphie's been drinking hard," she said sadly. "He used to do that quite a bit a long time ago, but we thought it had stopped. He seemed to be all right for a few years." We cooked and then ate in silence.

Washing the dishes, I asked Momma, "How come Uncle Ralph never did marry?"

Momma looked up at me but was not surprised by my question. She answered, "I don't know, Sister. It would have been better if he had. There was one woman who I thought he really loved. I think he still does. I think it had something to do with Mom. She wanted him to wait."

"Wait for what?" I asked.

"I don't know," Momma said, and sank into a chair.

After that we heard unsettling rumors of Uncle Ralph drinking here and there.

He finally came to the house once when only I happened to be home. He was haggard and tired. His appearance was much like that of the white man that Sister and I met on the railroad tracks years before.

I opened the door when he tapped on it. Uncle Ralph looked years older than his age. He brought food in his arms. "*Nowa*, Sister," he said in greeting. "Where's the other one?" He meant my sister.

"She's gone now, Uncle Ralph. School in Kansas," I answered. "Where you been, Uncle Ralph? We been worrying about you."

He ignored my question and said, "I bring food. The warrior brings home food. To his family, to his people." His face was lined and had not been cleaned for days. He smelled of cheap wine.

I asked again, "Where you been, Uncle Ralph?"

He forced himself to smile. "Pumpkin Flower," he said, using the Pawnee name, "I've been out with my warriors all this time."

He put one arm around me as we went to the kitchen table with the food. "That's what your Pawnee name is. Now don't forget it."

"Did somebody bring you here, Uncle Ralph, or are you on foot?" I asked him.

"I'm on foot," he answered. "Where's your Momma?"

I told him that she and Dad would be back soon. I started to prepare the food he brought.

Then I heard Uncle Ralph say, "Life is sure hard sometimes. Sometimes it seems I just can't go on."

"What's wrong, Uncle Ralph?" I asked.

Uncle Ralph let out a bitter little laugh. "What's wrong?" he repeated. "What's wrong? All my life, I've tried to live what I've been taught, but Pumpkin Flower, some things are all wrong!"

He took a folded pack of Camel cigarettes from his coat pocket. His hand shook as he pulled one from the pack and lit the end. "Too much drink," he said sadly. "That stuff is bad for us."

"What are you trying to do, Uncle Ralph?" I asked him.

"Live," he said.

He puffed on the shaking cigarette a while and said, "The old people said to live beautifully with prayers and song. Some died for beauty, too."

"How do we do that, Uncle Ralph, live for beauty?" I asked.

"It's simple, Pumpkin Flower," he said. "Believe!"

"Believe what?" I asked.

He looked at me hard. "*Awkuh!*" he said. "That's one of the things that is wrong. Everyone questions. Everyone doubts. No one believes in the old ways anymore. They want to believe when it's convenient, when it doesn't cost them anything and they get something in return. There are no more believers. There are no more warriors. They are all gone. Those who are left only want to go to the Moon."

A car drove up outside. It was Momma and Dad. Uncle Ralph heard it too. He slumped in the chair, resigned to whatever Momma would say to him.

Momma came in first. Dad then greeted Uncle Ralph and disappeared into the back of the house. Custom and etiquette required that Dad, who was not a member of Momma's tribe, allow Momma to handle her brother's problems.

She hugged Uncle Ralph. Her eyes filled with tears when she saw how thin he was and how his hands shook.

"Ralphie," she said, "you look awful, but I am glad to see you."

She then spoke to him of everyday things, how the car failed to start and the latest gossip. He was silent, tolerant of the passing of time in this way. His eyes sent me a pleading look while his hands shook and he tried to hold them still.

When supper was ready, Uncle Ralph went to wash himself for the meal. When he returned to the table, he was calm. His hands didn't shake so much.

At first he ate without many words, but in the course of the meal he left the table twice. Each time he came back, he was more talkative than before, answering Momma's questions in Pawnee. He left the table a third time and Dad rose.

Dad said to Momma, "He's drinking again. Can't you tell?" Dad left the table and went outside.

Momma frowned. A determined look grew on her face.

When Uncle Ralph sat down to the table once more, Momma told him, "Ralphie, you're my brother but I want you to leave now. Come back when you're sober."

He held a tarnished spoon in mid-air and put it down slowly. He hadn't finished eating, but he didn't seem to mind leaving. He stood, looked at me with his red eyes, and went to the door. Momma followed him. In a low voice she said, "Ralphie, you've got to stop drinking and wandering — or don't come to see us again."

He pulled himself to his full height then. His frame filled the doorway. He leaned over Momma and yelled, "Who are you? Are you God that you will say what will be or will not be?"

Momma met his angry eyes. She stood firm and did not back down.

His eyes finally dropped from her face to the linoleum floor. A cough came from deep in his throat.

"I'll leave here," he said. "But I'll get all my warriors and come back! I have thousands of warriors and they'll ride with me. We'll get our bows and arrows. Then we'll come back!" He staggered out the door.

In the years that followed, Uncle Ralph saw us only when he was sober. He visited less and less. When he did show up, he did a tapping ritual on our front door. We welcomed the rare visits. Occasionally he stayed at our house for a few days at a time when he was not drinking. He slept on the floor.

He did odd jobs for minimum pay but never complained about the work or money. He'd acquired a vacant look in his eyes. It was the same look that Sister and I had seen in the hobos when we were children. He wore a similar careless array of clothing and carried no property with him at all.

The last time he came to the house, he called me by my English name and asked if I remembered anything of all that he'd taught me. His hair had turned pure white. He looked older than anyone I knew. I marveled at his appearance and said, "I remember everything." That night I pointed out his stars for him and told him how Pahukatawa lived and died and lived again through another's dreams. I'd grown, and Uncle Ralph could not hold me on his knee anymore. His arm circled my waist while we sat on the grass.

He was moved by my recitation and clutched my hand tightly. He said, "It's more than this. It's more than just repeating words. You know that, don't you?"

I nodded my head. "Yes, I know. The recitation is the easiest part but it's more than this, Uncle Ralph."

He was quiet, but after a few minutes his hand touched my shoulder. He said, "I couldn't make it work. I tried to fit the pieces."

"I know," I said.

"Now before I go," he said, "do you know who you are?"

The question took me by surprise. I thought very hard. I cleared my throat and told him, "I know that I am fourteen. I know that it's too young."

"Do you know that you are a Pawnee?" he asked in a choked whisper.

"Yes, Uncle," I said.

"Good," he said with a long sigh that was swallowed by the night.

Then he stood and said, "Well, Sister, I have to go. Have to move on."

"Where are you going?" I asked. "Where all the warriors go?" I teased.

He managed a smile and a soft laugh. "Yeah, wherever the warriors are, I'll find them."

I said to him, "Before you go, I want to ask you . . . Uncle Ralph, can women be warriors too?"

He laughed again and hugged me merrily. "Don't tell me you want to be one of the warriors too?"

"No, Uncle," I said. "Just one of yours." I hated to let him go because I knew I would not see him again.

He pulled away. His last words were, "Don't forget what I've told you all these years. It's the only chance not to become what everyone else is. Do you understand?"

I nodded and he left.

I never saw him again.

The years passed quickly. I moved away from Momma and Dad and married. Sister left before I did.

Years later in another town, hundreds of miles away, I awoke in a terrible gloom, a sense that something was gone from the world the Pawnees knew. The despair filled days, though the reason for the sense of loss went unexplained. Finally, the telephone rang. Momma was on the line. She said, "Sister came home for a few days not too long ago. While she was here and alone, someone tapped on the door, like Ralphie always does. Sister yelled, 'Is that you, Uncle Ralphie? Come on in.' But no one entered."

Then I understood that Uncle Ralph was dead. Momma probably knew too. She wept softly into the phone.

Later Momma received an official call confirming Uncle Ralph's death. He had died from exposure in a hobo shanty, near the railroad tracks outside a tiny Oklahoma town. He'd been dead for several days and nobody knew but Momma, Sister, and me.

Momma reported to me that the funeral was well attended by the Pawnee people. Uncle Ralph and I had said our farewells years earlier. Momma told me that someone there had spoken well of Uncle Ralph before they put him in the ground. It was said that "Ralphie came from a fine family, an old line of warriors."

Ten years later, Sister and I visited briefly at Momma's and Dad's home. We had been separated by hundreds of miles for all that time. As we sat under Momma's flowering mimosa trees, I made a confession to Sister. I said, "Sometimes I wish that Uncle Ralph were here. I'm a grown woman but I still miss him after all these years."

Sister nodded her head in agreement. I continued. "He knew so many things. He knew why the sun pours its liquid all over us and why it must do just that. He knew why babes and insects crawl. He knew that we must live beautifully or not live at all."

Sister's eyes were thoughtful, but she waited to speak while I went on. "To live beautifully from day to day is a battle all the way. The things that he knew are so beautiful. And to feel and know that kind of beauty is the reason that we should live at all. Uncle Ralph said so. But now, there is no one who knows what that beauty is or any of the other things that he knew."

Sister pushed back smoky gray wisps of her dark hair. "You do," she pronounced. "And I do, too."

"Why do you suppose he left us like that?" I asked.

"It couldn't be helped," Sister said. "There was a battle on."

"I wanted to be one of his warriors," I said with an embarassed half-smile.

She leaned over and patted my hand. "You are," she said. Then she stood and placed one hand on her bosom and one hand on my arm. "We'll carry on," she said.

I touched her hand resting on my arm. I said, "Sister, tell me again. What is the battle for?"

She looked down toward the fence where a hobo was coming through. We waved at him.

"Beauty," she said to me. "Our battle is for beauty. It's what Uncle Ralph fought for, too. He often said that everyone else just wanted to go to the Moon. But remember, Sister, you and I done been there. Don't forget, after all, we're children of the stars."

Okanogan Traditional

THE BEGINNING AND THE
END OF THE WORLD

V V V V
V

Scomalt, another warrior woman, a great sorcerer, the leader of a race of white giants, and a giant herself, is hardly an example of the gentle feminine. Stories about warrior women portray them as capable of exerting great prowess, ruthlessness, and willingness to use what might and power they possess. In other words, they are not helpless, meek, mild, or otherwise passive recipients of male domination — or of any domination. One of the marked characteristics of contemporary Indian women's stories is that their characters seldom display the attributes that are usually attributed to women in Anglo-European fiction. Women in tribal societies have a multitude of strong models to learn from and model themselves after so long as they are fed on the traditions of women of power that have long shaped and sustained tribal life.

LONG, LONG AGO, when the sun was young and no bigger than a star, there was an island far off in the middle of the ocean. It was called Samah-tumi-whoo-lah, meaning White Man's Island. On it lived a race of giants — white giants. Their ruler was a tall white woman called Scomalt. Scomalt was great and strong, and she had Tahmahnawis powers. She could create whatever she wished.

For many years the white giants lived at peace, but at last they quarreled among themselves. Quarreling grew into war. The noise of battle was heard, and many people were killed. Scomalt was made very, very angry.

"I will drive the wicked ones of these people far from me," she said. "Never again shall my heart be made sick by them. And they shall no longer trouble the peaceful ones of my people."

So she drove the wicked giants to one end of White Man's Island. When they were gathered together in one place, she broke off that piece of land

and pushed it out to sea. For many days the floating island drifted on the water, tossed by waves and wind. All the people on it died except one man and one woman.

They floated and drifted for many more days. The sun beat down upon them, and ocean storms swept over them. They became very hungry, until the man caught a whale. Seeing that their island was about to sink, they built a canoe, put the whale blubber into it, and paddled away.

After paddling for many days and many nights, they came to some islands. They steered their way through them and at last reached the mainland. Here they stopped. The mainland was not so large as it is now, because it had not grown much yet. Wandering toward the sunrise, the man and woman came to the country now known as the Okanogan country. They liked that best, and there they stayed.

By this time they were so burned by the sun and whipped by the storm winds that their whiteness was entirely gone. Their skins were tanned a reddish brown. That is why the Indians have that color. All the Indians are the children of this first grandfather and grandmother.

In time to come, the Okanogan Indians say, the lakes will melt the foundations of the world, and the rivers will cut the world loose. Then it will float as the island did many suns and snows ago. That will be the end of the world.

THE CASUALTIES

Warriors on the warpath contend with other Native people who share an understanding of what they are doing; all Indian people, however, have been coerced into a kind of war that seeks to destroy rather than enhance spiritual power. The Anglo-Europeans who came here had one goal: destruction of life. That may sound extreme, but one of the best ways I know to discover purpose is to examine outcome. Now that we have reached a point where earth, air, water, and animal life of all kinds, including the human animal, have sickened unto death as a result of Western progress, it doesn't seem so extreme after all.

Indians have been one target of the overall destruction, perhaps because we have been seen as natural beings rather than as fully human. (If you want to learn about Indians, you go to the museum of natural history.) Indian affairs are regulated by the Bureau of Indian Affairs, part of the Department of the Interior, which oversees rivers, animal and plant life, forestry, parks, and other natural features, entities, and concerns. (Formerly, the Bureau had been in the Department of War.) Until the 1950s a number of tribal people (among them the Navajo) were designated prisoners of war. In a situation like this the casualties are high. Yet what awes me even more than the devastation is the ability of people devoted to the old ways of kinship with the supernatural to endure. The strength that that ability rests on is the main theme of the stories in this section.

Okanogan Traditional

COYOTE KILLS OWL-WOMAN

V V V V
V

This account of an Okanogan story forms the basis of the novel Cogewea, the Half-Blood, *from which "The Story of Green-blanket Feet" is taken. Humishima collected the story from Okanogan people and recounted it in her collection,* Tales of the Okanogans. *The main character in her novel, Cogewea or Chipmunk, has her heart stolen by a greedy philanderer, a white man from the East. Her plight is not new. Not only is it reflected in the original Cogewea's story, set in the early twentieth century, but occurred two times in the nineteenth century, once to the ill-fated Green-blanket Feet and another time to Cogewea's own mother.*

Because of this recurrence, "Coyote Kills Owl-woman" is a story about archetypal patterns. As such, it is a prime example of the oral tradition and the laws governing both that tradition and the written fiction of Native writers. In choosing to publish this story in her collection, Humishima provides us with the kind of clue that excites the literary detective. She clarifies the relationship between the oral and written traditions as these are practiced by tribal writers.

CHIPMUNK [*Cogewea*] was a little girl who lived with her grandmother. She had a special *ol-la-la* bush that she visited every day to see how many ripe berries she could find. She would climb on the tree and count the berries one by one as she ate them. She would say, "One berry ripe. Two berries ripe. Three berries ripe."

One day while in the tree counting and eating the berries, she put none in the basket that hung at her side. This basket was made out of the hoof of a deer. Chipmunk heard noisy footsteps beneath her. Looking down, she saw Owl-woman [*Sne'-nah*] with her big basket on her back. In this basket were many little children whom Owl-woman had stolen from their parents. These children she would eat as she grew hungry. Owl-woman traveled from camp to camp, from village to village, in search of children. She was the fear of both parents and children. She was the child-eating Owl-woman.

Chipmunk was very much frightened, but she knew that Owl-woman could not reach her up in the tree. The big woman coaxed her to come down. She said to Chipmunk, "Your father wants you."

Chipmunk replied, "I have no father. He died long ago."

Then Owl-woman lied, "Your mother wants you."

Chipmunk spoke back, "My mother died many snows ago."

Owl-woman still lied, "Your aunt wants you home."

Chipmunk laughed, "Ha! ha! My aunt never lived."

Owl-woman lied the more, "Then your uncle wants you."

Chipmunk again laughed, "Ha! ha! I never had an uncle."

Owl-woman coaxed her further, "Your grandfather wants you."

Chipmunk sauced back, "Ha! ha! My grandfather died before I was born."

Then Owl-woman said, "Your grandmother wants you home."

Chipmunk was silent, then spoke, "I will not come down from the tree unless you hide your eyes."

Owl-woman made the pretense of hiding her eyes, putting her hands over them but slightly. But Chipmunk was not easily fooled. She said to Owl-woman, "I can see your big eyes blinking! I will not come down the tree unless you hide all your eyes."

Owl-woman then hid her eyes almost entirely, only leaving a small space through which to watch Chipmunk come down the tree. Chipmunk jumped from the top of the tree, over the Owl-woman. Owl-woman tried to catch her, but only raked her back. The long fingers with their sharp claws left scratches the full length of Chipmunk's back, which she carries to this day.

Running to her grandmother, Chipmunk tried to talk but was so frightened that all she could say was, "*Sing-naw! Sing-naw!* (Owl! Owl!)"

The old grandmother with deafened ears misunderstood. She asked Chipmunk if she had stepped on a thorn. All the answer she received was, "*Sing-naw! Sing-naw!*"

At last the old grandmother understood. She tried to hide Chipmunk in her bed, but Chipmunk ran around under the robes so much with fear that her movements could be seen. The grandmother then put her in the berry basket, but Chipmunk was too noisy. The grandmother tried to hide her in the soup, where poor Chipmunk nearly drowned.

Meadowlark [*Wh-wet'-kula*] flew to a nearby tree and sang,

> "Two little oyster shells
> Hide her in!"

The old grandmother then put Chipmunk between two oyster shells where she was well hid. The grandmother took the necklace from her neck and gave it to Meadowlark that she would not tell where Chipmunk was hid. She knew that Meadowlark was a tattler. Meadowlark flew away.

Owl-woman followed Chipmunk's tracks to the grandmother's tepee. Going inside she asked, "Where is the hunted child that I am tracking?"

The grandmother denied that she knew. Then the mean Owl-woman began hunting for Chipmunk. She looked in the bedding, in the basket, and in the soup. At last she gave up hope of finding Chipmunk when Meadowlark flew back to the tree and sang,

> "I will tell you if you pay me!
> I will tell you if you pay me!
> Where she is! Where she is!"

Owl-woman went outside the tepee and threw Meadowlark a yellow vest. Meadowlark, the tattler, sang,

> "Two little oyster shells,
> Take her out!
> Two little oyster shells,
> Take her out!"

Meadowlark flew away with the necklace and the yellow vest which she had earned for befriending and then tattling on Chipmunk. She wears them to this day.

Owl-woman went back into the tepee. With all the begging of the grandmother, poor little Chipmunk was taken from the oyster shells. She was cut open by the sharp claws of Owl-woman and her heart taken out. Owl-woman swallowed it and said, "Yum, yum-yum! It is good. Little girls' hearts are the best." Owl-woman then went on with her big basket filled with children.

The grandmother cried for some time when she again heard the song of the Meadowlark from the tree,

> "Put a berry for a heart!
> Put a berry for a heart!"

At this, the grandmother put a half-ripe *ol-la-la* berry in the breast of Chipmunk and sewed it up. She then stepped over her work when Chipmunk jumped up, alive.

Owl-woman had not gone far from the grandmother's tepee when she met the cunning Coyote [*Sin-ka'-lip*]. Coyote knew Owl-woman. He said to her, "I love to eat all bad little children. If we travel together, we will have better success finding children." Owl-woman agreed. She was glad, for she knew the trickery of Coyote. Because of Coyote's evil powers, she thought that they would be greater than all the monsters of the earth. The two went traveling together.

They had not gone far until Owl-woman grew hungry. Coyote said, "We will stop and make a big fire. We will roast the children. They will taste better roasted than eating them alive and uncooked." Owl-woman consented. She praised Coyote for his wisdom, while Coyote flattered Owl-woman with good words. Coyote told her to let all the children out of the basket so they could do the work. Coyote and Owl-woman would oversee the work, that it was done right.

By Coyote's orders, the children gathered much pitchwood, piling it high. When Owl-woman was out of hearing, Coyote said to the children, "Gather the wood with most pitch. Gather the solid pitch in plenty if you wish to return to your parents." The children took spirit. They worked hard. Soon they set the big pile on fire.

Coyote said to Owl-woman, "This is to be a big feast. To make it what it should be, you had better blacken your face with charcoal. To make the charcoal stick good, you must rub your face over with pitch." This Owl-woman did, Coyote and the children helping. Coyote covered her arms with their many bracelets with pitch, then painted them with charcoal. They danced around the fire, singing and shouting for the roast-feast. They danced while waiting for the coals to grow hot.

When Owl-woman grew anxious to roast the children, Coyote told her that the pitch smoke would spoil the meat. Coyote said to her, "Let the children all get sticks, and we will pretend to dance the sun dance. We will roast the children afterwards." Owl-woman readily consented. She was flattered. Coyote instructed the children to get forked sticks.

Owl-woman asked Coyote, "Why forked sticks?"

Coyote replied, "We will use the forked sticks in turning the roasting children."

It was not long before Owl-woman grew tired of dancing. But Coyote insisted that the coals were not ready. They danced on, Coyote flattering her on her knowledge of dancing. She danced till she staggered, when Coyote purposely went against her. She fell, Coyote laughed and danced the harder. Owl-woman got up and began dancing again. Coyote danced around the fire a few times and then, pretending to stagger, fell against her again. Owl-woman was knocked into the blazing fire of pitchwood. Her pitch-covered face and arms blazed. Coyote told the children to help him with all their forked sticks to keep Owl-woman in the fire. They did so, and at last she was burned to death. She was roasted instead of the children.

Coyote then sent all the children back home. After Owl-woman's eyes burst, from them flew a small owl, alighting on a tree where it hooted its night call. Coyote told the bird, "In the future, Owl-woman's remains will only be a thing to scare a bad child into sleep. You will only travel by night because you will be blind in the daylight, only able to see in darkness, because your eyes were burnt out with the pitch." So it is to this day. Indian children are still afraid of Owl-woman.

Humishima

THE STORY OF
GREEN-BLANKET FEET

▼ ▼ ▼ ▼
▼

"The Story of Green-blanket Feet," excerpted from Cogewea, the Half-Blood, *takes place during an earlier period of contact with whites. In the story, Green-blanket Feet, an Okanogan woman, makes the same mistake Cogewea is making. The Stemteemä (Cogewea's grandmother) tells the story hoping that Cogewea will get the point and turn aside from her collision course with disaster. It doesn't work, but novelistically it points to traditional ways of using narrative to admonish, illuminate, and maintain personal identity within the traditions of the people. In the old times (before the coming of the Shoyahpee, the whites), Ogre Woman or other spirit people stole and murdered innocents, and one such story underlies the novel; in modern times that function was taken up by whites. The survival value of alertness, awareness, and connection to others is the same in both cases, and that alertness and wisdom can only obtain for those who hear and follow the messages and significances of the stories.*

> And he wooed her with caresses,
> Wooed her with his smile of sunshine,
> With his flattering words he wooed her,
> With his sighing and his singing.
> — *Hiawatha*

COGEWEA SOON RETURNED to the tepee in dry habiliments and with a show of her old gaiety. Seating herself on the vacant buffalo robe, she spoke:

"Well! my little Stemteemä, what is it to be — praises or a scolding? The Shoyahpee did not know that turning the *Swa-lah-kin* would bring a storm and when I told him what he had done, he pitched the thing into the river hoping to stay the Sun's anger."

The aged woman made no reply, but drew assiduously at the little stone pipe which Mary had filled for her. She continued in silence until the *kinnikinnick* was exhausted and then stowing the pipe away, she began impressively:

"My grandchildren! I am now old and cannot stay with you many more snows. The story I am telling is true and I want you to keep it after I am gone.

"*Green-blanket Feet* was my best friend and she told me this tale after she came back to our tribe from the Blackfeet. I remember her as a girl. How comely! how graceful. Eyes clear as the mountain stream; reflecting innocence and the dreamer. Cheeks blooming as the dusky wild flower of spring, with hair in two braids, reaching to her knees. Her feet were small and shapely. The pride of every Indian woman is the gift of a small foot. Hers was a generous heart and a confiding nature. But wayward, of adventures in the deep forest she had many. Her father and mother had died, leaving her no other protector but an old aunt, with whom she lived. This aunt could not compel her to stay in the tepee and sit on her feet like the other maidens of her tribe. She was trouble-free until she met her fate in the false Shoyahpee.

"My friend was at the spring in the woods, when she first saw the pale face. He carried a gun and had killed a deer. He spoke with a soft voice, but the tongue was strange. His words she could not understand, but the signs he made were pleasing. His eyes were afire with greed, but the young is ever blind. The buttons on his *capo* blazed as the sun. She brought him to the lodge of the aunt, where he left the deer as a gift and then went away.

"The following sun the white man came to visit at the lodge near the spring, and many more sundowns was he there. He planned until the girl gave her heart to him. She soon deserted her aunt, her people for the Shoyahpee, who lived at the fort.

"Yes, my friend left her own kind to dwell with her white husband among the pale faces. After many moons, a papoose came, a girl. She was glad to see the little Shoyahpee, nearly as white as its father. A snow passed and another papoose came; this time a boy. The mother was now wearing the white man's manner of clothing and was eating his food. She often longed for her people. She sometimes visited them in their lodges and her children kept warm her heart.

"The blow fell when her youngest child was two snows old. The white husband came to her while she was making moccasins for her little girl and said:

" 'Woman! listen well my words. I am called away; far towards the rising sun. It is from my Chief, whom I cannot refuse. It is at his bidding that

I go. If you want to care for our children, you can travel with me, but you may never see your own people again. You can stay here, but I will take the papooses and go. I am not coming back.'

"My friend's head drooped and tears visited her eyes, the first since childhood. She now realized the true gravity of taking a man not of her own kind, what it really meant to her life. She must make choice between him and her own race, desert or cling to her own children. He was not good to her, but her little papooses! She could not let him take them from her. She would go with him as far as he would permit.

"It was only a few more sundowns when the Shoyahpee with his wife and papooses rode away accompanied by another pale face with a cayuse pack train. The woman had promised her people that she would never forget them, that some day she would return. Her voice trembled as she said good-bye, then she rode swiftly away. The youngest papoose, Robert, was laced on his cradle-board and hung to the horn of the saddle. Kitty, the oldest, sat behind her mother, secure in the binding folds of a shawl. The names were those given the children by their white father. I saw this mother ride away without once looking back. It was many moons before I beheld her again and this is what she told me:

" 'When I went with my white man, I felt as if I were dying. Leaving my people was harder than had I let him go back alone to his kind. Only for my children did I go. I was heart-sick! Every tree, every little bush spoke to me; every stone called to me as I passed the nooks where I had first met the Shoyahpee. The birds sang in tones of sadness and the water's fret was wailing. But I clung to my little ones and followed my hated husband from sundown to sundown; camping on the trail. I watched closely and learned the country as we passed. I might come back to my people.

" 'We traveled till the big mountains were crossed and we reached the wide, flat lands where there are no trees and but little water. We were among strange tribes, enemies of the Okanogans. We saw buffalo roaming in great herds. There was other wildlife which reminded me of the land of the Okanogans. Every sun, my mind grew heavier until I could hardly endure to go farther. But when I looked at my papooses, I could not leave them alone with their white father.

" 'The Shoyahpee grew meaner to me as we trailed. He beat me! kicked me out from the night camps. One sun I made my mind brave to turn back and I lingered behind the pack train. When he saw this, he called me to hurry! I thought: 'What shall I do?' I whirled and rode hard back over the trail. I was flying to my people with my little ones. But not for long was the race. The pale face followed, shooting. My cayuse fell, shot through the body and killed. I pitched to the ground, stunned by the shock and unable to rise. The pale face came up and beat me with his quirt. He kicked me where I lay and called me vile names. This made me hate him as a reptile of the dust.

" 'I now had to walk, carrying my baby on my back. Kitty rode behind her father and sometimes slept, bedded and tied on one of the horse-packs. I was watched in every movement. I was made to walk ahead on the trail and at night do all the work about camp. A few sundowns more of this, when I determined to run away in the dark with my baby. I grieved to leave my little girl, but what else could I do! I had noticed the eye of the Shoyahpee and he meant thus to treat me after bringing me from my distant home. He intended killing me when near the journey's end. Better to live with one of my children than die and leave them both. I could carry my baby.

" 'I remember the time! It was clear and hot, as we resumed our travel. Over the plain which seemed to have no end, we hurried. I was tired when the evening came. I was glad for the chance to rest.

" 'I have wondered if other than the squaw mother can know the heartache and yearning for her young. I knew that this was to be my last sundown with my oldest child. I talked to my papooses, talked in our native tongue. Although Kitty, the oldest, had seen but three snows, she seemed to understand me. In her baby way, she cooed, nestling on my bosom. I tried to impress her that whatever might come in the snows ahead while with her white father, she should ever remember her Indian mother. I knew that it was not for me to attempt stealing her from the pale face. I never could carry both children back across those wide, desolate plains. I feared for him to keep me and the papooses. Bad tempered, he carried a gun and he slept but little at night. He forever watched until he thought I was asleep.

" 'I recall the night! The evening was starlight, no moon in the sky. I lingered long at the campfire, playing with my oldest child as a farewell. Kitty appeared to comprehend and clung to me as never before. I had settled my mind to take my youngest papoose no difference what might come. At last Kitty fell asleep from exhaustion and I sat holding her in my arms. Her father called to me angrily to bring her to bed which I did. I hugged her and kissed her brow, although this is not the custom of our race as with the whites. I whispered in her sleeping ear: "Oh! my little child! Life from my own being! do not forget your Indian mother." Kitty murmured in her sleep; I could not catch the words. Was it a spirit's voice? I gazed at her longingly for a moment, then went out from the tent; dropping the door-flap behind me.

" 'I walked to the fire where lay my youngest papoose, ready wrapped on his cradle-board. He was sleeping! Once more I turned hungrily to the white man's tent — not for him — but for the child I loved as my life. But my people! They were calling! as I stood by the dying embers out there on the boundless plain. I could hear their voices coming to me from the Westland. I would go! for I was not wanted by the white man, who would sometime kill me if I stayed.

" 'I had some food tied in a handkerchief, a very small amount. I took up my papoose and walked slowly out from the dim firelight. When hidden by the shadows, I placed him on my back and threw my green blanket over him. Then I ran swiftly away. Halish, a wolf breed dog that we had with us, came to me from hunting on the prairie. I glanced back to see the two pale faces bounding from the tent, each with a gun. They made after me and the fright, I think, caused me to drop into a badger hole large enough to shield me from sight. The dog stopped over me and I pulled him down close to me. I was glad that he was the color of brown. Though half wild, he appeared to know, for he lay perfectly still. The two men passed by, cursing loudly. I could have reached out and touched my white husband, nor did he suspect my place of hiding. The Great Spirit must have favored me, for my papoose did not move nor make a sound. I think, too, that he was awake.

" 'The pursuing pale faces fired their guns into the night darkness and threatened me, but to no effect. Then they coaxed for me to come out from the shadows, but I was so afraid that I hardly breathed. Twice the wolf-dog showed his gleaming fangs, but he did not growl. I did not tremble, but I knew what it meant should my Shoyahpee husband find me. I had long known that he was keeping me only to care for our children and not that he had love for me. I was told by the other pale face that he had a white squaw far away, who bore him no papooses. I had been lured from my own kind by this stranger with the voice of the wood-bird, but whose tongue, like that of the serpent, was forked and false.

" 'The two men kept stirring all night and it was nearly coming day before I dared move. The great dog still lay guarding me. My little papoose awoke at times, but I hushed him by taking him to breast and covering his head. I partly raised from my crouched position and looked towards the tent. The Shoyahpee father was sitting by the fire, rocking Kitty in his arms. Just then she put her little hand to her eyes and I knew that she was crying. I lifted myself and thought to go back to the camp. But as I drew near, I heard the mean words of the man, concerning me, what he meant to do should he ever catch me. I had lived with him long enough to understand his language in part, and to know what he was saying. I was afraid to go nearer.

" 'I gazed yearningly at the group, then turned to the sunrise. I did not dare look back. I would fail, my heart would grow weak in the resolution to leave if I again saw my child crying. The grave, faithful Halish was with me as I tramped. The sun rose high and gleaming before I stopped to rest and watch back over the trail. The white men might follow me, I thought; but I never saw them more.

" 'I walked and camped for many sundowns, till I came to a small bush, where we had stopped before and where I knew to find water. I drank! as did the dog. It was so cooling from the hot sun. I determined to stay and rest for a while. I spread my blanket and stretched in the shade. I bathed my papoose and self in the water. I thanked the Great Spirit that He had protected me so far.

" 'But my food was gone. Ofttimes I was hungry and would have starved, had not Halish caught rabbits and brought them to me. I made sage brush fires by striking flints which I had found on the plain. At this bush camp, I was roasting a rabbit on a stick stuck in the ground by the fire, when suddenly the wolf-dog jumped up and looked keenly in the direction that I was to go. That made me look also and I saw a thick cloud of dust coming towards me; a big cloud. As it drew near, I heard a deep rumbling roar like a storm and at once I knew my danger. Halish barked, then lifted his head and howled mournfully. I snatched up my papoose and ran out from the way of the stampeding buffaloes. My breath was almost gone before I cleared their way. With lowered heads they passed so close that I could have struck them with my hand. Halish, leaping, ham-strung a young bull and soon had it killed. Amid the turmoil and dust, I saw the half naked Blackfeet riding hard upon the flanks of the herd; shooting and thrusting with the spear. I threw myself down quickly, but Halish, who stood snarling with the front feet on his kill, was seen. I prayed to the Great Spirit but He seemingly had forgotten me, for the Blackfeet came riding towards me. Halish sprang in front of me, his back bristling and teeth bared. The leader of the Blackfeet raised his gun but before he could fire, I was shielding the dog with my own body. The gun was lowered, when I had quieted my protector, and I was made prisoner. When my captors saw the young bull killed by the wolf-dog, they were pleased and this, I think, caused them to spare his life. I was surprised to see so many hunters. It was an annual hunt and their camp was not far away. They took me! and I rode one of the ponies. I could not understand their language. Their tongue was different from that of the Okanogans.

" 'I was brought to the Chief's lodge, which was made of tanned buffalo skins, painted and decorated with *tul-le-men*. The Chief, an old man, had seven wives, the youngest a mere child of fourteen snows. He called his warriors and they had a council over me. This lasted for some time, but at last through signs, they made me to comprehend my fate. A prisoner for life, I was consigned to the Chief's lodge to wait on all his wives and relations. I was a slave.

" 'I stayed with the Blackfeet one snow, till the sun shone warm again and the prairie grass was green. My papoose was now walking, running about the doorway of the lodge. He resembled his sister and I loved him the more for it. But I hated the memory of his white father, who had lured me from my people; who had brought me all this trouble. To think of him was bitter.

" 'I was treated badly by the women of the Blackfeet. A slave for all of them, ofttimes I had not enough to eat. I used to steal *pemmican* for my papoose, when he would be crying with hunger. Much of this hardship, I think, was because I had chosen a Shoyahpee husband instead of one of my own kind; that my child was half white. The Great Spirit must have been displeased with me.

" 'One sundown when my child was playing in the tepee, he fell into the fire. His clothing, which I had brought from the Okanogan country, was of the white man's make and burned more quickly than buckskin. He fell! I ran to him but it was too late. His hair was blazing and his little moccasined feet were roasted as meat. For only one moment he clung to me, and then was gone forever.

" 'My heart was broken. I could have borne to live with the Blackfeet the rest of my life, if only my baby had been spared to cheer my days. For, were they not of the same race as myself? Though enemies of the Okanogans, they were Indians and far different from the hated Shoyahpee, whose very touch was taint to our blood. Then I reasoned that it was better that my child go, than to grow up a despised breed and a slave to an enemy tribe.

" 'Only a few sundowns passed after I had buried my papoose — buried him alone under a clustering thorn — when I determined to leave the Blackfeet. All the young warriors were out hunting the buffalo and only a few old men and women left in the village. There was one aged woman, the mother to the Chief's favorite wife, who was very cross to me. She usually sat on the opposite side of the doorway from me. I saw my chance. The sun had passed the center of the sky, was on the downward trail and it was hot. All the women but this one were outside the lodge shading themselves while I worked. I noticed my old enemy sitting across the way. She was nodding in her sleep, a *la-quhia* in her hand. She had been eating dried meat soup. I glanced to the doorway before stepping around the fireplace in the center of the lodge. I slowly took the *la-quhia* as she held it. I picked up her pot of soup and ate as fast as I could. I was hungry! almost starving. Finally I left the *la-quhia* and drank from the pot. When it was empty, I replaced it at her side, leaving the *la-quhia* as if she had dropped it. I then went back to my own place.

" 'The old woman awoke to find her soup all gone. She looked at the pot, then at me; but she seemed not to understand what had become of the broth. Soon she was again nodding. I reached to the back of the lodge where were kept the Chief's bow and arrows. His *tokee-sten* hung by he side of the war pipe. I threw the *tokee-sten* to the ground. I stepped on it! Then I drew one big breath through the sacred pipe, but left it hanging where it was. I took the bow and arrows for future use. Slinging the quiver over my back, I placed an arrow to the bowstring and came out of the tepee painted with the Chief's own *tul-le-men*. I ran for the river, then deep, swift and muddy from heavy rains. I was a good swimmer and did not fear the water.

" 'The distance was not far and I heard the war whoops of the old warriors in pursuit and the women calling as they followed after. Even the dogs joined in the chase. Turning, I let fly an arrow at the foremost man, striking him in the shoulder. This checked the hunt and being a fleet runner, I kept well ahead of the enemy. I flew down the slope as light-footed as the deer in our Okanogan forests. Gaining the river, I dashed into the flood. I was not afraid! Brush was overhanging the current under a low bluff and I made a hurried dive for it. My Spirit protector remembered me. I caught a limb and held there with the grip of renewed hope. I brought my head out of the water under the bushes for breath. Three Blackfeet were standing on the bank above me talking. I was now able to understand most of their language and I could hear them well. One said that I must be drowned, while another one thought that I was hiding under the bushes. He walked onto the bush, almost over me, but it bent to the water and he drew back. I do not know! Maybe he did not want to get his moccasins wet or was afraid of being drowned. He backed up the bluff where they all sat down and watched for me till the sun was hidden in darkness.

" 'I was glad when nightfall came to my rescue. My hands were numb and my limbs stiff from the chill of the water. My strength almost gave way but I called on my secret powers to aid me. I must reach my people, calling to me from the land of the Okanogans. I drew myself from the flood by the bushes, but I lost the bow and arrows. I was defenseless as I started for home, guided by the stars. I was off the trail that I had followed with the Shoyahpee a snow before. I walked all night and all the next sun, before stopping to camp and rest. I traveled suns and suns over the great plain and was often very hungry. Losing the bow in the river, I could shoot no game.

" 'I wished for Halish, but the mighty wolf-dog was dead. Some of the Blackfeet had gone far to hunt the woods-deer and took him with them. A mountain lion attacked a young hunter and the dog fought for him. Both dog and lion were killed, but the Blackfoot escaped, disabled for life. I missed my old companion's help and watchful guard.

" 'It was too late for the eggs of the prairie birds, but I dug roots and sometimes found a few berries. Once I saw a great eagle swoop down and kill a young antelope not far from me, but could not fly with it. I fought the savage bird and took the fawn of goodly size. It furnished me with food for some days. My moccasins were worn out and I made new ones from the skin, cutting it with a sharpened stone. My awl was a pointed bone and the sinew was thread. But the hide was tender and the jagged rocks often passed over, cut them to pieces. I was now glad that I did not leave my green blanket behind when I escaped from the Blackfeet. I tore strips from it with which to wrap my feet. I passed the tribes of the Pend d'Oreilles, Kootenais and the Flatheads. All were good to me. They supplied me with dried berries and meat and I traveled on. I was going home!

" 'I was glad when I came in sight of the big river we love so well. I like the salmon better than I do the meat of the buffalo. I love the wooded mountains more than I do the treeless plains so endless. The land of the Blackfeet is not so fair as that of the Okanogans.

" 'But my heart is buried with my little papoose in the wakeless sleep; and I long for the child who went with her white father. But I am to blame! I preferred him to my own people and he drove me away. I pray to my Great Spirit to favor me in seeing my child again. I now have children of my own kind, but they do not take the place of my first born with its unknown fate.

" 'When I reached my people, they were all glad to see me. My feet were bare except for the worn strips of my once fine four-point Hudson's Bay blanket. This is why I am called by my tribe, *"Green-blanket Feet."* The name connects me with the false-tongued Shoyahpee of other snows. It is the strong, clinging memory — hated thing — which recalls the face of the one I once loved; whose words I believed. The blanket was his gift when I first went to him. Let the maidens of my tribe shun the Shoyahpee. His words are poison! his touch is death.' "

The Stemteemä's story was finished; her audience had listened in rapt silence to the end.

Mary TallMountain

THE DISPOSAL OF
MARY JOE'S CHILDREN

V V V V
V

Mary Randle TallMountain, born about the time Humishima completed
Cogewea, began to be published in the early 1970s, as did most of the other
writers contained in this collection. "The Disposal of Mary Joe's Children"
is an autobiographical work that revolves around the insidious (and invid-
ious) effects of colonialism in tribal affairs, represented by Sister Anne
Celesta and the Roman Church and by the tuberculosis that has so dev-
astated Indian populations for several centuries, and the communality of
decision-making that characterizes tribal life. Mary Joe Bolshanin can assert
her autonomy by choosing to be lovers with Clem though she is married,
by Catholic rite, to another man. She can bear Clem's children, and neither
she nor the children are outcasts in Nulato society. But the children are
part of the village, of the fragile psychic web that composes tribal intelligence.
The fate of Mary Joe's children is everyone's fate, and their welfare is
everyone's concern. The old way of determining community action is upset
because Sister Anne Celesta, a colonizer, uses the democratic bias of the
people to wreak vengeance on Mary Joe.

> Thou hast kept me to be head of the heathen; a people which I
> know not shall serve me. Strangers shall submit themselves unto
> me; as soon as they hear, they shall be obedient unto me.
> — 2 Samuel 22:44

REVEREND MOTHER ANNE CELESTA closed the old Bible on the page,
softened and curled with innumerable fingerings. She performed this action
each morning. The passage seemed to embody a cryptic message which
still baffled her after five years of pondering it in an urgency to discover

its relevance to her vocation. "But the heathen are not obedient." She was unsure whether she spoke to herself or to a familiar presence. Again in bitterness she tasted the words: "They are *not* obedient."

The people had appeared docile. At first she considered them ignorant and slow of intelligence. Gradually, she perceived that behind their apparent taciturnity there lay an indecipherable and ancient essence of spirit. She sensed it would remain an enigma. It was exasperating. "A people which I know not shall serve me." She had chosen the boy Innokenty to "serve," after long reflection and with subliminal purpose. His stolid, somehow vulnerable person had come to represent this multifaceted people whose meaning was so elusive.

And still she knew them not.

Into this restive moment she permitted the disorder of her memories. She had arrived at her first mission, far downriver at Holy Cross, wearing the immaculate, long, flowing garments, the white starched coif of the Rule of the Sisters of Saint Anne, unsuited to the rude land where dust, mud, and mosquitoes beset the nuns in summer, paralyzing cold in winter. Her mien was high and proud, befitting the Bride she had been chosen; she carried the idealism of her twenty years like a pennon. She embraced missionary life with ardor. The savage land and the Rule, like stern taskmasters, soon subordinated her young zeal to grueling labor and the demands of hard-won convent ritual. She learned the habit of discipline slowly, harshly, doing herself violence, striving toward perfection. Custody of eyes and tongue — and more particularly, of thoughts and senses. Almost twenty-five years ago, now . . .

Long before, the first nuns of Holy Cross had been hardy women. They had wrested the mission out of the wild new country of Alaska. In a cluster of brown tents they celebrated Mass with the pioneer priests and brothers, said devotions, made their cells. They were forced to wrestle with the emerald-green earth for their meagre garden harvest. The people observed, and sent the children. Then commenced the work for which they had come. By the time Sister Celesta arrived in 1890, there was a completed dormitory building and some eighty children from the river villages, running and shrieking in a makeshift playground. She taught them religion, the Baltimore catechism, and the three R's. Her chief task was the instruction of the older girls in domestic chores: scrubbing, cleaning, waxing; cooking and canning; washing and ironing. She worked side by side with Native children from villages up and down the Yukon. She grew robust of mind and body.

At first it was exciting. She listened to the keening subarctic night song of malamutes and learned to detect their separate personalities, as diverse as the brown, muscular men who drove them. She knew the smells of smoke and salmon. She studied a leaf of alder, knew its green lacquer surface, the veins of its pale, sticky underside. She imagined the powerful presences of wolves circling the great moving dun-colored caribou herd beyond the purple Kaiyuh Mountains. Her eyes reveled to see the harsh, burnt orange sun of spring after the long black winter. She stood whipped by rain, awaiting with fierce joy the monstrous rolling thunder.

Even now, old fragments of beauty returned in the night with such insistence that she wakened with a startled cry, and found the wetness of tears upon her face.

Time brought authority and the blooming of a natural administrative talent; in 1918 she came to Nulato as Reverend Mother Superior. She was in command of the four Sisters and the education of the children. It was, however, her prime duty to serve as exemplar to some 150 Natives. She knew her duty familiarly; she knew their obdurate resistance to duty and to rules.

Now that she lived closer to them, there came on a silent tithing. No fish was caught or game trapped of which a portion did not go into the Mission larder. In lean times, benefactions were given to hungry families. But the proddings of conscience were faint; her mind grew yet more adamant with the intent to carry her vocation to its ultimate perfection.

At last the endless dark days of winter, the paralyzing cold, the enduring toil, entered her very spirit. The pangs were edged bitterly. She gritted her teeth and muttered: "I will not yield," as to a creature locked fast with her in mortal combat. The land had become her personal enemy. There was one solitary outlet. If she became nettled by Father's reticence, surmised a critical flash in a Sister's glance, if she found a child obstinate, the choler lying thin beneath her veneer festered until she found subtle means to mock Innokenty and impress harshly upon him some new bidding. Occasionally a fleet thought struck through: I am unfair to this witless boy. He is my scapegoat.

Even her Sisters did not suspect her strange discontent, and she took great care not to speak harshly to Innokenty in their hearing, so that she thought no one was aware of her strange perversity. In this close proximity, her strong habit of firmness and discipline ensured her safety. She was above reproach.

Now she heard impatiently the shuffling approach of Sister Mary Pacifica in her house slippers. She recalled complaints of a painful old bunion. Sister entered the office, rapping playfully on the door frame. She is remiss in discipline, thought Reverend Mother. Her lips firmed into a thin line, even as she relented, Ah, I am petty. Her fine hazel eyes lifted, and she waited with an air of patience. It was lost on Sister Pacifica.

Sister Mary Pacifica's short figure and wry face affected a look of domesticity. She said, "Little Jim brought up a brace of mallards. You ought to see their glorious green-blue and bronze necklaces!"

"Fine . . . fine . . . How many ducks did he shoot this trip?"

"Why, I don't know. Shall I bake these for Sunday dinner?"

"Cook both, and open two jars of canned duck besides." Why did I ask how many he shot? she thought. We don't need more — thank heaven we've got six dozen jars put by. She determined to curb her curiosity and observe more perfect charity thereby.

"Father Frank will relish it too," Sister said, going out.

Father Frank Galvan. Admittedly, he was a thorn in Reverend Mother's side. His presence filled her with a vague edginess. She had never understood why. To give him his due, he was a rare good man and priest. Ah, his humility, and he with that fiery shock of red hair! Sometimes she believed he saw her clearly, just as she was, from a place far behind his steadfast amber eyes. She felt like a housekeeper, with a clutch of keys at her belt. But I am a good steward, she thought — I have served well these children of God. Why am I constrained to dissemble, to hide my thoughts from him?

Discipline. It was the byword, implicit in the severity of their lives. Such enforced discipline was one matter. The habit of discipline was another, completely different. By now Reverend Mother knew intimately the nature of both. She thought of the coming winter. Wind howling with an obstinate life of its own about the eaves, whining at the white lacery of frost that covered the thin windowpanes, crawling across the Sisters' huddled forms in the ascetic cells which were the only privacy they possessed. It penetrated every crevice with its nagging voice, that voice of loss and want. The voice of discipline.

"And now at last my habit of discipline is beginning to fray," she said aloud. "All because I have not come to know the strangers."

She had closely observed Mary Joe Bolshanin, a most promising pupil at Holy Cross, and was positive the girl would attend normal school after graduation. But in the summer of 1909 when Mary Joe was fourteen she came home to Nulato and her family arranged a marriage to Taria, an older man of the village. She would not graduate. When Reverend Mother went to talk with her mother, Matmiya, she was met with courtesy, a cup of hot tea, and an impassable wall of reserve.

"We have always gotten husbands for the girls. It is the custom," Matmiya said firmly. The tone of her voice ended the discussion.

These were the strangers she had believed she sought to know.

Winged shadows moved over the papers on the desk. She looked out and saw a pair of bank swallows spiraling up from their summer nest under the eaves, tiny bundles of sepia-colored feathers tousled by the wind. Beyond, the river was whipped into a dark green smother, needled with spray. The swallows knew it was time. They spiraled in greater and greater circles, hovered once, and rose high over the village, fluttering and tossing on the vast channels of air. Their courage, their trust in God, she thought, letting themselves ride out on a journey perhaps endless, unknowing, their hearts tiny within them, yet sturdy. So was I once, she thought. The young Celesta would have run and danced in the river wind, celebrating with the swallows.

She shivered. The day had chilled. "They are the last to go," she said.

Ah, yes. Then something had happened. Mary Joe left Taria and returned to her mother's house. After Matmiya's death from consumption, for six years Mary Joe flaunted her affair with Clem Stone, the soldier, appearing with him in the village, he so jaunty in his sauntering manner, she with her black mane of hair tossing under a scarlet band. They were an impudent challenge.

Reverend Mother moved abruptly in her chair. Disturbing images floated out of the deep shadows of her mind: a young girl's forbidden yearnings, slow whispered secrecy in the black folds of confession, earnest repentance, certainty of forgiveness, urgent hasty penance, breathless retreat, dizzied into the light oh free — the child — ah! the chastened children — the children grown, yet fearful — vast nothingness, retribution, dark wings beating — the children . . .

She passed a hand over her eyes. What had she been thinking? Oh. Mary Joe and Clem Stone. It was true, after the first child was born they sought out Father to discuss marriage. He could not request a dispensation. The marriage to Taria had produced a boy, now living with his father in another village. There was no chancery cause for dissolution. Mary Joe was bound. Sister moved jerkily in her chair. Her fingers tapped the arm. Father should have ordered Mary Joe at once to end the impenitent affair. But he would not. He had some strange notion about conscience . . .

Now the people said that because Mary Joe had contracted consumption, the agnostics Doctor and Nellie Merrick would adopt her two children. For Sister, this completed the page of transgressions.

Suddenly she said aloud, "I will put a stop to it."

Quelling her anger with a determined act of the will, she laid her hands upon the breviary. It was the hour of tierce. She would place this knotted sin again into the hands of the Lord. A random page caught her gaze. She was unable to turn it. Her eyes moved inexorably through the passage.

> He that ruleth over men must be just, ruling in the fear of God. And he shall be as the light of the morning, when the sun riseth, even a morning without clouds; as the tender grass springing out of the earth by clear shining after rain. — 2 Samuel 23:4.

She read intently and slowly; she read again.
There was no doubt.

Innokenty's flat eyelids oozed open. Like black olives rolling in oil, his eyes shuttled toward the paling square of window. His mind stirred dully, prodded by the knowledge that he had to go again today to council.

It didn't occur to Innokenty to wonder why things were the way they were. Yesterday Big Mike had told him to go to the Dance House. He went. Again today, the other men would talk, going over and over this strange thing about Mary Joe's children. He, Innokenty, would be silent. He hoped the men would believe him wisely thinking.

There was only one reason for him to go there. Sister Celesta wanted him to be there. He never disobeyed her. It had started a long time ago, when he had first seen her in the village. He had been awestruck by her. Over the years, piecemeal, the people had told him he was Eskimo, and that in 1908 when he was a baby he had been bought by a Nulato Indian in a fur deal with an Eskimo trader from Kvih-pak. Later orphaned, he remembered no place besides this village. His life revolved around the Mission, that cluster of buildings between the river and the army barracks, on the land where *Gisakk* lived, a little separate from the native cabins. He did chores for Sister Celesta and gave her his game and fish. Every day at dawn he went to Mass. He was used to her tall muffled presence alone in the front pew. Yesterday morning she had followed him out after Father Galvan's *Ite, missa est.*

She didn't hesitate. "You're going to council today."

His black-olive eyes said yes, he was.

There was a heavy silence.

"Something important is happening." Intently she examined a long splinter at the edge of the last pew. "You're going to help me, Innokenty." She pried away the splinter. "They will ask your opinion. Whatever they say, you must answer *no.*" She looked at him and away; it was as if her face hid behind a thin curtain; and with the word *no,* her hand raised in a cautioning gesture. It clasped again around her shabby black prayer book. He stretched a finger toward the hand. It held steady; his finger moved closer. Then she was gone in a whirl of icy air. The door closed without sound. He peered at it, his look questioning.

The Dance House aroused a different emotion in him that afternoon: the bumpy wooden floor, the four-triangled log roof slanting to the bell tower, noon light lying through to the octagonal, bench-lined wall, dark yet not quite: sparked here by a flash of bright shirt-sleeved arm raised in emphasis, bulked there by the shapes of the others seated in their places in varying attitudes of thought, now and then leaning imperceptibly to each other, closing some intangible separation. The smells of the blue tobacco haze; of garlic on spent breaths; of dead sweat molded into the shapes of pants and jackets; of autumn-ripe forest through the open door; and knifing through it a sometime odor of dissension, wholly living and sharp: these smells distilled and flattened by the sharp-edged and squared spaces of air into the one smell he truly knew: the smell of loneliness.

Himself alone. There had never been anybody else to lean toward, to talk to, to sniff the human odor of, to gaze at, to feel easy with. Around him the talk of the others trickled lazily, exclaimed and surged, rose in agitation, relaxed into slow judicial accents.

He held one idea: Sister had told him to say *no.*

The day stretched into the early dark of fall, and still they talked. It was as if he waited in a hidden place for an animal whose exact whereabouts he knew, as if there were great reaches of time in which to await the animal in patient silence; sensing the least motion of its leisurely approach, whether it was weary or angry, ran or slept, feeling the presence of each insect that disturbed it, each wind that stirred its fur, while he ingested the flow of the oncoming flood of sky and earth curved into vast half-shells: the one brushed by southward wings of geese whose clamor was muted by height; the other belled in colossal rhythms of earthen waves clotted with ancient shining trees and sliding away on the distances to the pale thread of its interface with the first; both speaking in enigmatic tongues born through centuries of unfamiliar dark time — and balancing the movement of these, the reassuring grip of his still tension.

The tension was jolted.

Big Mike rasped, "You ready for the vote?"

Obal Manuska rumbled, "Yes."

"All right, we put it one man at a time. If you want the kids to go, say yes. If not, say no. You got that?" Big Mike spoke as nominal chief of the village, who traditionally acted as mediator at matters of council.

The men nodded in unison. One by one:

Little Jim said quickly, "No."

Steve hung back. "No," he said at length.

Ivan and Floyd's voices in unison said a fast "Yes."

Obal said loudly, "Yes."

They stared at Innokenty. He brushed away a cascade of hair from his face and looked up at the last slim pencils of light lingering in the bell tower. "No," he said.

"Well, God damn it," Big Mike growled, "you men got it all tied up. What the hell."

Everybody talked at once. A nervous laugh was quickly stifled. "Why don't we do it again," someone suggested. The second vote was identical.

Obal frowned directly at Innokenty. "It's late," he said.

"We can't change it tonight," Big Mike said, sending Obal a warning glance. "We'll sleep over it."

The men relaxed. Rising stiffly, rolling cigarettes in their rough fingers, stretching and yawning, they idled out the door and along different paths home. Under the bantering laughter was a sense of the suspension of common matters. They walked with a certain dignity.

Big Mike clasped Innokenty's shoulder. "Come on, young fellow. It's gonna be all right. You get some rest and come back tomorrow." They filed along the boardwalk. Innokenty drifted away to his shack. He wondered what it was that Big Mike had said was all tied up, and whether it could be got loose.

Big Mike and Madeline sat on the ground outside his cabin in the half-light of the crisp early evening.

"Olinga looks good," Big Mike said.

Madeline wrinkled her nose. "Sure — for her age. She was a good-looking woman one time, I guess."

"She still is," he said.

"Oh, Papa, you like all the women."

"Nobody can beat you for looks, daughter."

Olinga came toward them, setting her scruffy boots demurely on the boards. Wisps of bone-colored hair drifted into eyes made ashen by sun and wind. Her face was a red-brown chunk of dry riverbed netted with cracks. Three ample skirts belled out with each of her steps, exhaling the smoky smell of furs and hides that after a lifetime was part of her. She arced a long easy stream of brown Snoose to a hummock of dry grass five feet away. Looking at them humorously she said, *"Do-eent'a."*

"Aszoon," Madeline said.

Big Mike stood up with a single muscular lunge. Olinga's pale eyes found his face. Clutched under the wrinkles, the cage of bone appeared, clean as a young girl's. Her smile was the color and texture of old ivory. The two stood watching each other with deep and familiar comfort.

"Papa has troubles," Madeline said.

"I know," Olinga said.

Madeline grumbled, "Everybody knows. Now they've got the votes tied up."

Big Mike said, "Them boys — Ivan, Floyd — they're never gonna change. They stick behind Mary Joe a hundred percent." He scratched his chin. "Jimmie and Innokenty won't move an inch either, I know that."

"Never Innokenty," Olinga said. "He'll die to obey Sister, poor dumb child." Faint contempt twisted her lips. "How it happen he got on council anyway?"

"I got to try and keep people peaceful around here," Big Mike answered. "Them boys can't hurt nothing, they balance up . . . This way, we don't shut Sister Celesta out." He grinned.

"Pretty smart, old man," Olinga said. "I hear she want to put Mary Joe and the babies out of the village."

"Hah, shit! not a chance," Big Mike hissed.

"Those boys can't do any harm, least not Innokenty. He have no brains."

"Naw, it's them other two that can't make their mind up," Big Mike grumbled.

"What you think? Steve going to vote no again?" Olinga asked.

"He talks all the time about *Gisakk* ways, education, hygiene," he sniffed, "medical care, new tools and traps and boats. Don't mean a damn thing. It's only in the voice he says it. Him and Missa, they want to stay the same as we are."

Olinga said, "Maybe we won't worry about him." Her lips moved for an instant, and she looked narrowly at Madeline. "I guess it's Obal we're worrying about."

Madeline frowned. "He's got his own mind. Don't you think he loves those kids? His own niece and nephew."

"I know," Big Mike soothed. "He don't want you to get sick, daughter, that's all."

She tossed her long straight mane of hair. "You mean I can't take care of my own sister."

Olinga squatted on the dirt that was stamped solid as a block of stone. She laid her hand on Madeline's knee. "Everybody knows you can," she said. "Obal like Mary Joe's kids same as you do. But he want things right for everybody."

Big Mike said, "It don't mean Mary Joe's not gonna have plenty help," Big Mike said. "She trusts in that. She trusts in that better than anybody else does." He chuckled.

Anger formed behind Madeline's eyes. She got up, brushing away Olinga's hand. "Nobody listens to me. My husband won't let me do anything for Sister. I'll shut up. Let it go the way it wants to go. Always it's that way, no matter what I want."

"Hey, daughter, wait a minute." Big Mike sat back down as she walked fast away, stiff and solitary.

"She's too proud," Olinga murmured.

"Sick with nerves," Big Mike said. "What can I do. We got to move on."

Nokinbaa, the Snowy Owl, his feathers already spotted with winter white, flew in silence across Mukluk Creek. His wings lay in a long, still curve. Through the darkening air, the river shone like poured balm. Patterns endlessly formed, dissolved, and re-formed. A tranquil watchfulness grasped the two, a waiting ancient as the land.

Tentatively, Olinga said in a half-whisper, "You ever think about giving one child only?"

Startled, Big Mike turned. His teeth gnawed at the edges of his coarse mustache. He pushed back his cap.

"They ask first for Lidwynne. They want her bad," she said.

"Whew!" he breathed.

"Think on it, Mike," she said.

Noon light, sifting through the mist that had swirled all night in the upper air, now paled the open square of the bell tower. Obal, looming tall on the center floor, set a green-enameled gasoline lantern on the floor. He laid a match against the cotton mantle and a mass of glowing specks poured up around it. Flame and fuel hissed steadily together. Brilliance flared on the intent features of the men.

They inspected this new object.

Round-shouldered little Jim Yap stood fascinated. His jaw clenched a wad of Snoose. Inside the sagging seat of his overalls, his buttocks stood loose and skinny. A fringed hole bared his knee, leathery as old moosehide.

He blinked at the lantern with the flat, pale-coffee eyes that gave him an incorruptible appearance. "Gee! You got one," he breathed.

"Came in from Sears Roebuck on the barge today," Obal said proudly.

Little Jim's chin sank further into the vee of his wool shirt.

"What's the matter, Jimmie?" Steve asked.

He hawked a lump of phlegm. "No sleep," he said hoarsely. "My woman talks too much."

Innokenty giggled. His front teeth knifed down through a slab of white-fish and his tongue rolled the stony oblong back lumpily in his cheek to the spaces between his molars. Five minutes of slow grinding reduced it to a juicy wad. Smoke oozed around his taste buds; a streak of spit drizzled down his chest.

Floyd muttered, "Always suckin' that goddam fish," and Big Mike lifted a quick palm. Floyd elbowed Ivan. "Lucky we got no woman hollering around like Jimmie's got."

"She's pestering me to death," Little Jim said huskily.

"Talk-talk, they drive you crazy," Ivan agreed, although neither of the young men were yet married.

The other men glanced at Big Mike where he sat a little separated, but he was gazing at the floor and chomping his mustache. They grew serious as they saw that he was preparing to say something.

"Time to go to work," he said, eyeing each man in turn. "You wasted a whole day yesterday. You didn't get no solid opinion. Everybody's too stubborn. How can you men run a village if you can't make up your mind?"

"This one is a big problem," Obal protested. "We can't work it out in a couple days." The other men nodded.

"All right, cancel the whole thing. What I mean, that vote yesterday, it never happened."

They looked questioning at each other and at him. Steve said, "What should we do?" He had a permanent look of worry on his face, its wrinkles deepened now.

"You could start all over again," Big Mike suggested. Seeing their puzzled faces, he grinned. "I got a new idea." He hesitated and took a deep breath. "You should think about separating the two kids. That's what you better talk about today."

"Mike, Mike! Wait a minute," Obal said. "You mean let Doc adopt one and leave the other with Mary Joe?" He rubbed a hand over his chin. "Hell, I never thought about that . . . But which one, which way?"

"That's what I mean. Nobody thought about it, but it might work. Which one. You should talk about that plenty. It's up to you." He looked relieved. There was a jumble of voices and Big Mike leaned back, muttering, "Sweet Jesus. I don't know which one, or how to do what, neither." He had paced the floor of his cabin all night and his face was a mass of tense muscle.

With a grunt, Obal turned off the Coleman lantern. The men's expressions turned harsh in the cold light; sternly facing each other, they seemed to agree that they had reached a point where they might be better able to deal with the matter at hand.

Steve voiced his chief concern: "Lidwynne and Michael are smart kids." He darted a look at Big Mike, who was staring at a point high on the wall. He appeared not to be listening, but the angle of his head said that he would miss nothing. "Both parents come from smart people," Steve said. "Look at Mary Joe. She still remembers how to read."

Obal agreed, "Matmiya done that. She never let up on them kids. Maybe because she didn't learn it herself . . . I remember how she made all her kids, my cousins, go to school and study every night — It was no easy thing. Nobody else much around here bothered."

A smile spread on Big Mike's face.

"Hey, Mary Joe's oldest boy's a smart one, too," Floyd said. "I heard he's good in school down at Kaltag, sings and plays fiddle down there for dances. Ten years old now, that boy. Gee, she got married to Taria young, she was just out of school . . ."

"He's too old for her," Ivan interrupted.

"But she was always like she was on her own," Floyd went on. "She acted different than us, cared about schooling. Even read books when she didn't have to. Old Taria had no care for none of that."

Little Jim said, "*Gisakk* use books to make medicine like shaman. Those books got lot of power."

Obal mused: "It wasn't all work, she had a good time too. Those days she was always laughing, and how she danced."

Steve said, "Clem gets along good with her, he plays his fiddle and makes her dance. I hear them laughing a lot with the kids. Baby Michael has that music in him, he bounces all around and grins when Clem plays the fiddle."

Obal observed, "You can't tell so soon. He might get it from Clem though . . . That Clem's been a good man from the start. Little, but tough. Only *Gisakk* I ever took into Kaiyuh Flats. Made him swear to never tell no other *Gisakk* where our secret hunt grounds was."

Little Jim said, "That poor damn Taria. He tried to get her back, but he was too late."

"Too late? You mean too old," Ivan said.

Big Mike stirred himself and yawned. Warmth of the sun seeped into the chill hall as the men talked.

"What about Sister Celesta?" Ivan said. "She never spoke up till Doc wanted the kids. Right away she runs over to Merricks, wants them herself. Mary Joe refuses, and Sister is her enemy now."

Innokenty threw off his mackinaw and slouched, one boot up, along the bench.

Obal, glancing at the silent Eskimo, said softly, "You know. Grabby, like she's nervous. She wants too much."

"You lie," Innokenty said.

"No, he don't lie," Big Mike said in his calmest voice.

Steve said, "*Gisakk* don't know how to wait, they're not easy in this country. Work too hard when they don't need it. *Gisakk* don't understand Yukon time."

Obal, lighting his corncob pipe, murmured, "That's sure true."

Steve said, "We got to respect the church. Even when the Jesuits want to take away our medicine men, our *yega*, all the old things. But we know they don't mean bad so we go along with that and still follow our ways. It worked out, you bet."

The men nodded; their eyes shone with a tolerance born of years of habit.

"They're not all that way," Steve concluded. He leaned back against the wall, his nervousness settled now that the conversation was going easy.

Little Jim said resentfully, "Mary Joe got Father to baptize them kids when she couldn't stick with the church and Clem both . . . She did what she had to, I don't put no blame on her. Too bad Sister shamed her in front of her little girl, yelling at her in the yard. You ever notice another thing, Sister's got a bad habit, she never look at anybody. People get nervous when some *Gisakk* stare too long or don't look at all."

"All right, now," Innokenty growled, flinging an arm over his eyes and lounging full length on the bench.

"You like Sister real good, don't you," Obal said to him. Innokenty's eyes wavered dreamily. "She's my friend," he muttered, and dozed off.

Obal said, "Some people don't go to Mass regular every day. But we work hard, give Father what help we got. We split his wood, give fish and meat to him. He pays what cash he can turn loose of, he's got the Sisters to feed. Sister Celesta don't do that way. She takes it and offers nothing, like she's entitled. That's all right too, I figure we do the best we can. But if it wasn't for the village, that Mission would starve."

Big Mike rumbled, "Wasn't for the village, that Mission wouldn't be here."

Steve said, "The church expects the missionaries to live off the land, but they don't know how. They're like a bunch of children."

"I thought they were rich, same as Doc," Floyd said.

Obal asked, "What you mean, Doc's rich?"

"Doc's got plenty."

"Hey, he's not rich. Doc and Nellie got enough to eat but he only gets two hundred dollars a month for both of them, place to live, and wood. Fifty cents a day for food. Everything comes in by boat from Uncle Sam, outside. They never want free meat from us, they always buy it, what little fresh meat they get. Most of their meat's in tin cans. We live better than them."

Steve asked, "How long's Nellie been taking care of Mary Joe's kids? I can't remember."

"Off and on maybe three years. When Michael was about a year, she started it. Lidwynne was two then. Doc offered to help Mary Joe. They kept Lidwynne a while, and then kept Michael too. In good weather Mary Joe could get outdoors and fish around here close. She got better and that summer she took Lidwynne to camp at Four Mile, but Nellie sure didn't want to give her up after that. Soft-hearted, that Mary Joe, she let her take her then, right away." Obal laughed self-consciously. "I'm doing all the talking around here."

"Well, you know Doc Merrick better than us," Steve said.

Little Jim said quietly, "Remember they're *Gisakk*. The kids are mostly Indian."

"That's right," Steve said. "It's been on my mind." Worry returned to his face.

The men shuffled their feet and yawned.

Squaring his shoulders, Obal said, "They want those kids bad. They should have my three. Some winters it gets tough, feeding us five."

"I wouldn't care too much," Steve said. "But Missa's crazy for them."

Ivan asked, "You think Nellie could raise them?"

"I'll bet on it," Obal said.

"They'd get education, eat good, and there's Doc right there so they don't get that T.B." Floyd enumerated on his fingers.

"I know, you and Ivan voted to let them both go away," Obal said, "but we got to think about this other. Maybe we got to send one of them kids away." Steve watched Obal intently, the lines deepening in his cheeks.

Innokenty sat up, alert. "Mary Joe gonna be sick a long time?" he questioned.

No one moved.

"Who knows," Obal said at last. "T.B., consumption they call it. Goes different with each person. Might last a year, might be five years. She's a strong woman, she come from good blood." He nodded toward Big Mike, his sturdy Russian body sitting as erectly as any of the younger men.

"Who's gonna take care of her?" Innokenty persisted.

Floyd and Ivan darted looks at each other. A shade of eagerness rippled over Ivan's lean hunter's face. "We already figured that out," he said. "We'll feed her long as she needs, we'll bring wood, sweep her house. Whatever she wants." The young men and Mary Joe were long-time friends; it reached back to babyhood.

"Count me in too," Little Jim said.

"Big Mike knows where I stand," Steve remarked, still carefully observing Obal.

"Now everybody get this straight one time." Obal moved uncomfortably, now being forced into a statement. "I won't let Madeline do it, it's the wrong time, our kids are too young . . . She wants to help Mary Joe, fine, but it's too much work for Madeline, and damn, I — " His bluff voice trailed away.

Quickly Steve said, "It's all right. When the time comes, we can all take care of her, and we can take the kids and raise them . . ." His mouth worked as though he would say more, but he refrained.

"Mary Joe's *kid*, you mean," Obal said. "*One kid.*"

Steve's expression went bleaker than ever. "That's right. We have to split up the children, maybe." He continued to look at Obal covertly, remembering Missa pleading angrily and added, "Big Mike promised those kids to us, long time ago. *Gisakk* can't take them away."

The men eyed each other. They had almost forgotten the old binding promise made by Big Mike, how much depended on keeping promises made. Breaking it this way might bring on the enmities of *yega*, and bring bad luck on everything they tried to do, the whole village. It was as if Steve had thrown a rock at them.

Steve thought he saw why Big Mike had changed things. His son Andy's death last spring had hit hard. He wanted to keep his own family together now. He couldn't take away two of his grandchildren that way, it must be tough, he was so crazy about them. But where had Big Mike got the idea of splitting them up? He had only come up with it this morning. Something had happened during the night, Steve thought. Smart, that Mike, pulling the switch early today so nobody in the village could get to them. Because the people were stirred up and trying to pull council every which way. Like always, Big Mike wanted to please everybody. For him, it was a hell of a spot.

Obal focused on the heart of the problem. "Now, Steve, what if Mary Joe keeps one? It could help her get over losing the other. She could raise the one who stays for a while, anyway."

"What about the agreement, the promise from Big Mike? We can't go against it. It's bad luck, you know that."

Obal frowned. "But this means three lives, you see that. I know, Steve, it's a strange thing all the way. We got to bend somewhere, and I got to vote to keep Michael with his mother. Steve, when she gets so she can't look after him you can step in and *then* be keeping the agreement. I know, it's around the bush, but this is a heavy thing."

Steve nodded slowly. "She needs him too. Yeah." Something in the shaping of this idea made some sense to him. It boiled down to a simple thing: the kids had to be separated. Obal wanted to keep Michael and let Lidwynne go. But if he, Steve, let Missa have her way and Steve voted on keeping both, council would be tied up again and they'd be back where they started and likely both kids would have to stay. So he would vote with Obal. He would have to help send Lidwynne away. He felt as heavy as a loaded barge.

His voice was heavy, too, saying, "If we have to pick one, looks to me like Lidwynne should go, I guess. She's used to *Gisakk* ways." This bald utterance already placed a distance between themselves and Lidwynne, a distance which had already entered the hearts of the people, whether recognized or not. They had known that the time of separateness had arrived.

"That's right," Obal said flatly. "It's for everybody's good. There's no way we can help it."

Big Mike's stiff new pants creaked as he crossed his legs. "You men want to talk to my daughter," he stated.

"I guess we should ask her a couple questions," Little Jim said.

It was nearly dark inside. Mary Joe stood against the door, her vision adjusting until she saw the figures and faces of the men. Big Mike pointed to the bench which abutted the one where they sat in a row. She sat down, moving back until she sat erect against the wall, the angle of her body fitting snugly into the corner formed by its jointure with the bench. She glanced quickly at the men and, looking straight ahead, waited.

Their faces turned to her. Innokenty sat up and leaned forward, chin propped on his fists.

"*Snaa'*, they have to ask questions," Big Mike said.

Her head bowed briefly, acknowledging his words. Her look lingered on his face a fraction beyond custom, then turned back.

Each man was reluctant to be the first to speak. Time stretched in a simple waiting. At length Obal broke the pause. "You know what we came here for."

"Yes," she said in her faintly hoarse voice.

"You been sick a long time. You can't take care of the boy and girl. You let Merrick take care of them because you can't."

Her glance flicked over him from the corner of her eye. "He said it was better for me."

"Merricks want to adopt your boy and girl. Yesterday this council couldn't make a decision on that. Now we are thinking it could be done different."

Her eyebrows went up in a question.

"We talked about you giving them one child and keeping one." The words were immovable, hanging on the unmoving air.

Her sharp knuckles pressed each other white. Her face drained to the color of ashes.

"Would it be better if you don't lose both of them?"

"How can that be?"

"It depends on how long Doc Merrick says you will be sick," Obal said.

She moved abruptly. "How can I tell you, he doesn't know, nobody knows. I have to wait." She took a handkerchief from a pocket of the skirt, turned and coughed into it. Returning to him in a long gaze, her eyes were black counters, the lashes ticking off a remote rhythm.

"Doc never told you how long?" Obal asked insistently.

"He said I'm final."

The men turned their dim faces to each other, and heads were shaken.

"How bad is it now?" Steve asked.

"It comes, it goes. When I have hemorrhage I let Merricks keep Lidwynne. She's big. But Michael's still pretty small."

"He depends on you. Now he's running around, you got more work," Big Mike pressed, alert on the edge of the bench.

She didn't answer.

"You hear me?" he questioned.

"Yes, I hear you, Papa."

"Doc don't know how long he gives you," Obal said harshly.

"He can't say. Sometimes I'm strong for work, that helps me. Fresh air, moving around. I might go fast, or I might be a long time."

"Well, I ask you three times how long. Three times you say you don't know. That's enough." Obal's voice softened.

"Could you take care of them by yourself?" Steve asked.

She shuddered lightly. "If I think that, why did I listen to Merrick's wanting to take them?"

"You could handle Michael only?" he asked.

"Maybe so. For a while yet."

"We're going to help you, you understand that."

Her eyes glistened. "I may last long enough so Michael could have a chance — "

Eagerly Floyd interrupted. "That's right, Mary Joe. We bring you what you need and you don't fish, trap, nothing. All you do is keep Michael."

Ivan's large clear eyes bored straight into Mary Joe's, and he nodded, reassuring. Little Jim held out both hands, smiling.

Obal said, "These boys are hunters. Plenty luck. Some other people around here could help out. We'll stick together."

Mary Joe slid to the edge of the bench. "Something I don't understand," she said. "How is it so easy for these fellows to tell me I have to split up my babies. First, I heard they were talking about giving both of them away. That's how I thought it was going to be."

Big Mike cleared his throat.

"Now, I hear these fellows talking about splitting them up," she said, looking intently at the wall.

Big Mike said, "Council couldn't break the tie, *snaa'*, nobody would change their mind. So we had to do something. You have a right to say no. In that case, we can't do nothing. Both kids will stay in Nulato."

"Ahh, already they made up their mind," she said. "Nobody asks me, nobody asks my girl, the whole village decides. I was willing to let them both go. Now my own papa says I can't." Her glittering eyes mirrored the men's faces, looking everywhere except at her. It was the traditional women's scolding, addressed to everyone and no one.

"Now, Mary Joe," Steve said.

"Already Uncle Steve, my friend, is talking too that I should break up my family."

"What do you want, nobody care?" Obal said.

"The people talk about it and don't bother to ask me what I want. Even these men here, I know since I'm a baby."

"You see how it is," Obal said.

"Now what can I say. Have I got a right to say which one stays with me?" she asked Big Mike directly.

"Damn right, you got a right," he said.

She rested her face in her hands for a moment, and they waited. Her arms dropped, palms forward, open. Her eyes were distant, without emotion.

"What are you going to do?" Big Mike asked.

"What am I going to do, he says," she said, stressing each word and examining the ceiling. "What is there to do? My boy is too young. He needs me more than my girl."

"You sure about that?" Obal asked.

She leaned toward the men in a movement of deep reluctance.

"Then you got your mind made up . . . You know we have to vote on it again just the same," Obal said.

"That's right," Big Mike said huskily.

There was no sound as Mary Joe rose and went out.

Vicki L. Sears
GRACE

▼ ▼ ▼ ▼

▼

The workings of racial memory are truly mysterious. No Cherokee can forget the Trail of Tears, the time when entire Indian nations were abducted and held captive in strange lands by force of arms. Vickie L. Sears's stories about child abuse connect a modern problem with the historical treatment of her people, the Cherokee, by the "Great White Father."

I THOUGHT WE WERE GOING to another farm because it was time for spring planting. But the lady, she said we were going to be her children. You know how it is grownups talk. You can't trust them for nothing. I just kept telling my brother that we best keep thinking on ourselves as orphans. Our parents got a divorce and we don't know where they are, so we need to keep our thinking straight and not get fooled by this lady. I don't care if her skin is brown just like us, that don't mean nothing.

I hear my brother dozing off to sleep and I want to shake him, wake up, but these people are driving this truck and they can hear everything I say anyhow, so I just let him sleep.

This is the second time we've been riding in this old beat-up green pickup. The first time they came and got us from the children's home they took us down to Pioneer Square. I could see right away they was farm people by the truck having straw in the back and them not having real good clothes, like they wear in the city. City people talk more too. These people were real quiet right off. They answered the questions the orphanage people asked them but they didn't tell them much of anything. I guess I liked that some, but I wasn't going to tell them nothing about me. Who knew what they'd do? We never went nowheres before with brown people.

The man, he had on bluejeans and a flannel shirt and a jean jacket. His hat was all sweaty and beat up like his long skinny face. His boots was old, too. I guessed they didn't have much money and were needing to get some kids to help them with their work. Probably we'd stay with them until harvest time and then go back to the orphanage. That happened before, so it didn't matter much anyhow.

The woman was old and skinny. She had hands what was all chewed up and fat at the knuckles and she kept rubbing them all the time. She had white hair with little bits of black ones popping out like they was sorry to be in there by themselves. She had a big nose like our daddy has, if he still is alive, that is. She and the man was brown and talked like my daddy's mother, Grandmother, she talks kind of slow and not so much in English. These people, though, they talked English. They just didn't talk much.

When they said they was going to take us downtown I thought they was going to take us to a tavern because that's where the orphanage lady took me real late one night, to show me where all the Indian women was and what kind of people they are, always being drunk and laying up with men. That woman said that is all us Indian girls like to do and I will be just like that too, so I thought that's where these people would take us, but they didn't. They took us to dinner at this real nice place and let us have soda pop and even bought us a dessert. Me and Brother both got us apple pie, with ice cream, all to ourselves. I started thinking maybe these people are okay, but a part inside of me told me I best not get myself fooled. So I told them they wouldn't want us to live with them because my brother is a sissy and I'm a tomboy. But the lady said, "We like tomboys and Billie Jim looks like he is a strong boy. You both look just fine to us." Then they took us to walk in the square and we stopped by this totem pole. The orphanage lady told me that pole was a pretend God and that was wrong because God was up in heaven and the Indian people was bad who made the pole. This lady, though, she said that the totem pole was to make a song about the dead people and animals and that it was a good and beautiful thing. She had Brother and me feel the inside of the pole. Like listening to its belly. I don't know what she meant by that, but the wood was nice. I liked better what she said about the pole.

We walked around for a while and then they took us back to the orphanage. The lady said they would come back, when all the paper work was done, to get Brother and me, but I thought she was just talking big, so I said "Sure," and me and Brother went inside. We watched them drive away. I didn't think they would come back, but I thought about them being brown just like my daddy and aunts and uncles and Brother and me. They were more brown than us, but I wondered if they were Indian. They didn't drink, though, so maybe not.

We didn't see those people for a long time. Brother and me went to a big house to help clean for spring coming. I don't see why you clean a house so good just because the seasons change, but we done that anyway and then went back to the orphanage. I kept thinking on how nice those farmers were and how they might be Indians, but I didn't want to ask anybody about them. Maybe, if it was for real that they were going to come back for us, it would spoil it to ask about them. Seems like you don't ever get things just because you want them so it's better not to ask.

Then, one day, one of the matrons comes to tell me to find Billie Jim because there are some people come to visit.

My brother was up in a tree hiding from some of the big boys. First, I had to beat up Joey so's he would let Billie Jim come out the tree. We rolled in the dirt fighting and I knew I was going to be in trouble because I was all dirty and there was blood on my face. I thought I would get whomped too for getting in a fight. I spit on my hand to try to clean up my face, but I could see by the scowl on the matron's face that I didn't look so good. I pushed Brother in front of me because he was clean and maybe the people wouldn't see me so much. We went into the visiting room and I saw it was those farmers whose names I didn't remember. They asked the boss man of the home if they could take us now. He said, "Yes. It's so nice to place these 'special' children. I hope they'll be everything you want."

The man reached out his hand and the farmer brought his long arm out his sleeve. The orphanage man pumped his arm up and down, but the farmer just held his still. It was funny to see. The woman, she just barely touched the hand of the man. She was not smiling. I thought something was wrong, but I knew we were going with these people anyhow. I never cared much about where I went, long as the people didn't beat on us with sticks and big belts.

We didn't have to do nothing to get ready because we found our suitcases in the hall by the bottom of the stairs. The boss man gave Brother and me our coats and said, "You be good children and perhaps we won't have to see you here again."

I wanted to tell him I didn't like him, but I just took Brother's hand and we went out the door.

The people went to lots of stores downtown and then we went to lunch again.

I asked them, "Do you use a stick or strap for spanking?"

The man said, "We don't believe in spanking."

Before I could say anything, Billie Jim pinched me under the table and I knew he had to go bathroom. So I said, "Excuse us," and we got up to leave. The lady, she asked Billie Jim, "Do you have to go to the bathroom?"

Brother just shook his head and the woman said, "Paul, you take him."

They left and I worried about Paul messing with Billie Jim. My stomach felt all like throw up. When they came back, I asked Billie Jim, in our secret way, if something happened and he whispered no.

I wondered if these people were going to be all right, but I kept on guard because grownups do weird things all the time, when you never know they're going to.

After we ate, we walked and stopped at this drinking fountain what is a statue of Chief Sealth. Paul, he told us what a great man Sealth was and Billie Jim asked, "You know him?"

Both Paul and the woman laughed and Paul said, "No. He lived a long time ago. He's a stranger with a good heart."

Then the woman reached down to take my hand, but I didn't want her to get me, so I told her I had to take care of my brother and took Billie Jim's hand.

So then we were riding in this truck going to some place I never heard of, called Walla Walla. Grace, that's the lady's name, said they lived on a farm with chickens, pigs, a horse, and lots of things growing. She said we can have a place all our very own to grow things. When I sat down next to her, she let me ride by the window. I seen how my legs didn't touch the floor and how long hers were. She wasn't as long as her husband, but way bigger than me. She put my brother in her lap where he went to sleep, with his chubby fingers in her hand, but I stood guard just in case things got weird. Paul said I should help him drive home by looking at the map so he'd know the roads he was going on. I thought that was dumb because I knew he came to the city lots and must know how to get hisself home. I went along with him though, because he seemed to be nice and it was easy for me. I can read real good cause I'm nine years old. I told him that and see that Grace is smiling. She's got wrinkles that come out the corners of her eyes and more that go down her cheeks. She has on a smelly powder that reminds me of cookies. She says that there are lots of other children in neighbors' farms and that they have grandchildren who visit them lots. I guessed I would have to do lots of babysitting.

It's a long long ways to where they live and I couldn't stay awake the whole time. I woke up when Grace said, "Come on, sleepy heads. It's time to go to bed."

She gave my brother to Paul to carry, but I walked by myself, up one step into the house. We went through the kitchen, up some stairs, to the second floor with four bedrooms and a bathroom. She asked me if I have to go to the bathroom and I said yes. She showed me it and then closed the door. That's funny because she didn't stay. After a while, she came to knock and say, "There's a nightgown on your bed. I'll show you where you will sleep."

She took me to a room with only one bed with nobody else in it. I asked her, "Where's Brother going to sleep?"

Grace tried to take my hand to go with her, but I put it behind my back and followed her. She led me down the hall to a room where Billie Jim was already in a bed, all by hisself, sound asleep. Then we went to a room Grace said was for her and Paul and said I could come there if I'm scared or having a bad dream.

I told her, "I don't never have bad dreams and can take care on myself."

She asked me, "May I help you with your nightgown?"

Then I knew she was going to do bad things like the orphanage woman and I wanted to grab Billie Jim and run, but I didn't know where I was. I started to back down to where she said to sleep and she said, "It's all right if you don't want any help. Have a good sleep."

She went into her room and I watched until she closed the door. There was a lamp beside the bed and I slept with it on.

The first thing I did the next morning was check on Billie Jim. I asked him if they messed with him and he said no again. Nobody came into the room I was in either. We got dressed together and then went downstairs. Already Paul and Grace were up and at the breakfast table.

Grace asked, "What would you like for breakfast? Pancakes or bacon and eggs?"

Billie Jim said, "We can pick?"

"Sure," Grace said, "all you have to do is to wash your face and hands before coming to table. Can't have you start the day with a dirty face."

We looked on each other and saw we was dirty.

Grace said, "There's a pump here, if you want, or you can go upstairs to the bathroom."

We wanted to use that red pump with the very high handle. I tried to make it give water, but Grace thought she had to help push it down. She put her hand over mine but I moved mine. She smiled though, so I let her pump the water into a tin basin and give me a big brown bar of soap. She said she made it out of pig fat. It smelled icky but it made lots of bubbles.

After we ate, Paul said, "Come on, kids. I'll introduce you to our animal friends."

He put on his hat and opened the green screen door. There wasn't no grass nowhere. Just dirt, except where there was tall stuff growing. Paul told us it was alfalfa and wheat and that it got really high before you cut it. He took us into the barn to show us Henry, who was this old horse what lived there forever.

Out back of the barn was a pen with big fat pigs and a mommy one with some babies. I didn't like them much, but Billie Jim asked if he can touch them and Paul said, "Sure," so Billie Jim went into the pen and one of them pigs ran after him so Billie Jim screamed and the pig pushed him up against the barn wall so Paul had to chase the pig away. Billie Jim done good though and didn't even cry.

Paul walked us to the chicken house and showed us Rhode Island Reds and bantams. He taught us how to fill a basket with eggs by taking them out from under the chickens. I thought the chickens was mean, though, because they tried to bite us. Paul laughed and said as how it will get easier to do. Then we met the cows and Paul tried to teach us to milk them. I couldn't make nothing come out, though Billie Jim got a little. The warm milk tasked icky. We walked all over the place that morning and then we got to ride on a tractor with Paul for a long time.

I was sleepy, but Billie Jim wanted to do more things, so we went down to this wooden bridge which went over this river that Paul showed to us. He said we should be very careful to not fall into the river because it was very fast and we would be drownded.

Down to the bridge, I layed on my tummy and Billie Jim was on his and we poked at knotholes in the wood. The water was so fast it went around and around while it was going all wavery at the same time. When we put sticks through the knotholes, the water would just pull them right away like it was never going get fed another stick. We did that a long time until we heard Grace calling us to lunch.

At the lunch table I asked, "When will we start doing the work we came to do?"

Paul and Grace looked on each other as though I had asked something stupid and then they smiled.

Paul said, "You came to live with us to be just like one of our children. You will have lots of time to play and go to school. You'll have some chores because everybody on a farm has to work. One of you will help feed the chickens. One of you can care for the pigs. You can both help with Henry, and there'll be times when you can ride Henry, all by your-selves, into the woods or across the fields, after you learn to ride him. Other times we will all go to town or picnics or pow-wows or rodeos. Everybody has to have time to play. That's the way it is."

Then Grace said, 'I'll teach you how to sew and can and cook, Jodi Ann. You and I will go on special walks and plant a garden together. You too, Billie Jim, if you want. I want us to be friends and happy together."

I heard everything they had to say, but I was waiting, too, for the strange things I was sure they would do. I meant to keep my ears and eyes open just in case we needed to run somewheres.

About three days after going to her house, Grace tells us at breakfast table that, "Today is a good day to plant the garden. What would you like to grow, Billie Jim?"

"Potatoes an' rhubarb!" he says, all excited.

Then she asks me and I said, "Carrots and string beans, ma'am, because they're red and green. It'd be pretty."

She patted my shoulder and said, "Yes, it would be lovely. That's nice you can see that, Jodi."

I put my head down so she wouldn't see me smile.

Grace got this basket with lots of little envelopes and told us, "Come on."

We went outside, round to the side of the house. Paul was waiting, sitting on his tractor. He said, "It's all turned over for you."

Grace said, "Thank you, Paul," to him, and to us she said, "Here's two places for each of you. I'll go down to the other end."

She moved to her place and went down to the ground on knees and hands. Billie Jim and me just stood there because we never planted nothing before. She gave us some envelopes which shook with stuff, but they didn't mean nothing to us. Grace saw us standing and asked, "Have you children ever planted things?"

We shook our heads no so she came over and give us little shovels, like spoons, and took hers and made a little hole and put in a seed and covered it over with dirt. Then she put water on the place. She said, "You just do it like that, all in rows. Then you put the envelope on a stick here at the back of where you're planting. Then we wait for the rain and sunshine to help them grow."

She patted Brother on the hand and went back to where she was working.

We spent a long time doing gardening. The dirt felt good, like stored-up rain smells. We ate lunch by the garden and Grace said, "I think we deserve a walk. Let's go down by the river, kids."

Down to the river, Grace showed us different plants and birds. She knew a lot about birds. She told us the songs by making whistles through her teeth. She tried to show us how to do whistles with grass between her thumbs, but I think my teeth weren't big enough. Billie Jim didn't have a tooth in front, so he couldn't do it either. She showed us these grasses, too, that she said made baskets and we picked some. When we got back to her house, she put them in a big round pan, like for taking baths, and filled it up with water. That night she bit some grass apart with her teeth and showed me how to weave them in a basket. She thought I didn't know how to do this, but my grandmother already showed me before. I forgot some though, so my basket wasn't so good. She said, "You'll get better."

Grace read a story to us, then Billie Jim and me went to bed. When I was going to sleep, I thought on her telling about the birds.

One morning time I woke up extra early. The house was all quiet and I thought to go see some birds. I got dressed and went, real soft, down the stairs. I stopped on hearing noises in the kitchen. I crept up to the door and saw Grace putting water in the coffee pot, then poking embers in the stove. She went back to the sink and stood in the new sun coming in the window. She took one hand in the other and she rubbed on her swollen-up knuckles and all up and down her fingers. She put some stuff, what smelled like Vicks, all over her hands and slow rubbed her knuckles. Then she opened and closed her hands lots of times and rubbed more. She looked out the window the whole time, making a little smile all the time she was rubbing on her fingers. It looked like she done that lots of times before, so I stood still, so she didn't see me because the sun is so nice on her skin and shining in her hair, kind of like baby rainbows. I just wanted to watch. I did that for a long time and then made sounds like I was just coming down the stairs.

Grace said, "You're up very early, Jodi."

I said, "I wanted to go see birds and stuff."

She said, "If you want to come with me, I'll show you something magic."

She reached out her hand, but I put both arms behind my back and took hold of my own hands. She smiled and opened the door.

"We'll just take a walk over to the alfalfa. I want to show you some colors."

We walked between the wheat and alfalfa, the air all swollen up with their sweetness. Grace pulled down a piece of alfalfa and said, "Smell."

It was all sharp and tickled inside my nose, kind of like medicine. It got dew on it and it landed on my cheek. Grace got some on her nose. I wanted to touch it, but didn't.

Grace said, "See the different colors?"

She ran a finger down the alfalfa and I saw there was places where it was real dark then lighter then sort of like limes are colored. I always thought it was all one color, but I was fooled. Grace did the same thing with the wheat and said, "And here's something else that's wonderful. Look what happens when the sun comes to the plants."

Grace moved them different ways and I saw the light changes the colors, too. It's almost like you can look right through them.

She said, "If we come back at lunch and suppertime, when the sun is in a different place in the sky, they'll be different again. Do you want to?"

"Yeah!" I answered.

"Okay," she said. "It's just for you and me, though, Jodi."

Grace told me about the red-winged blackbird, what I never saw before, while we went back to the house.

Later, Grace called me and we went to see the colors again. They were changed. This time I saw, too, the little hairs each one had, what makes a wheat kernel, all full of lines and different parts just like people.

Then Grace said we had to go get a chicken for dinner. In the chicken yard, there was chickens scratching at the ground and picking in it for bugs. Their heads bobbed up and down and jerked from side to side. It was funny to watch them. Then, all of a sudden, they all ran to the coop. I didn't see no reason for it, but Grace pointed up in the sky and told me, "They see the shadow of the hawk. They're afraid, so they hide because they know hawks like to eat chickens."

The hawk circled awhile but went away and the chickens came back into the yard, scratching and clucking like nothing ever happened. Grace walked around in the yard, looking at all the birds, and finally spied one she liked. She chased it until she caught both the wings flat, with the chicken squawking the whole time we was walking to the clearing between the barn and house, to a stump where I had seen Paul split the kindling. Grace said, "You hold the chicken by the feet and give it a quick clean cut with the ax. Do you want to try it?"

I didn't never think on killing nothing to eat and didn't want to do it. I remembered the wild kitten I made friends with out in the tall grass back at the orphanage. I thought about how one of the orphanage matrons killed the kitten and hung it round my neck and told everybody I killed it. All day I had to wear the kitty, but I didn't cry. I just pretended like the kitty never was important. Now Grace wanted me to kill the chicken and I didn't want to, so I tried to back away, only she said, "I know you are strong enough to do this, Jodi."

She stuck out the handle to the hatchet, but I couldn't take it. I shook my head no and said, real quiet, "I don't want to, ma'am."

I backed up more and she said, "Well, we need supper. You watch and perhaps you'll be able to do it the next time."

Grace took that chicken and held it on the chopping block and chopped off the head so quick I almost didn't see her do it. I jumped back when the blood went flying everywhere, all hot-smelling in the sun, and making dark plops in the pale dust. She let the chicken go and picked up the head and threw it in the garbage. There wasn't no noise except chicken toenails making little scratches in the dry hard dirt and wings trying to fly when the chicken ran around and around. I didn't want to see it do that, but it was hard to stop looking. It ran in circles whole bunches of times and then just fell down, sort of jerking, till it stopped. That's when its eyes looked just like Popsickle kitty and my stomach felt like throw up and I wanted to run. Grace pulled out a big piece of string from her apron pocket and I knew it was going to be just like before, when she said, "Jodi, come on over. We'll string the chicken upside down and take off the feathers."

But I couldn't go near her. I yelled, "No!" and ran into the barn. I climbed the ladder and went behind some hay and pulled it all over me till nobody could see me and stayed real quiet. I sucked in air and didn't give it back. Grace came and called out, "Jodi, I'm sorry if I scared you. It's all right if you don't want to help. Jodi? You don't have to hide. It's all right."

But I was thinking on how I told a grown-up no and didn't do what she said. I knew I was going to get whipped. Paul and Grace would send me and Brother back because I was bad. Billie Jim was going to be all mad with me because we had to leave. Didn't nobody want to keep us if I'm bad and Brother and me most always went to places together.

I stayed in the hayloft a long time. Then I heard Paul and Brother calling me. They was yelling it was suppertime like nothing was wrong. I peeked through the slats of the door to the hayloft and saw Grace standing in the kitchen doorway. She didn't look mad. Paul and Billie Jim was holding hands, walking toward the fields, calling my name. Grace looked up to the barn like she knew I was there and started out to the barn.

I heard her shoes scrape on the rocks in the barn doorway, when she stopped walking. She said, "Hello, old Henry. You need some water, friend?"

The bucket handle squeeked and there was walking. The yard pump handle went crank crank crank and then water gushed into the bucket. Footsteps came back and there was horse tongue slurping, like Henry was real thirsty.

Grace said, "You know, Henry, when I was little, I used to do some of my best thinking sitting in the grass up on a hill behind my house. I guess the best place now would be up in the hayloft. It's the most like a grassy hill right around here."

Then I heard the dry snaps of weighted wood as Grace bent the ladder steps coming up. She was puffing a little when she came to the loft ledge and climbed over. I peeked out the hay and saw her dangling her legs and making a hum.

"Yes sir, Henry, old friend," says Grace, "this feels almost like my hill. If I were little and scared, this might be just the place to come think. I guess I'd know I was in just about the safest place in the world. Everything would be all right up here. After I had things all sorted out, I could come down and run on home to Momma and know she loved me, no matter what."

That was the most I ever heard Grace say in one mouthful of talking. I still didn't make noise, though. She was talking big, but she was still a grown-up. She sat there awhile, swinging her legs and humming. Then she said, "Well, Henry, guess I'll go into the house. I'm getting cold and hungry."

Grace climbed down and I saw her go to the screen door. She stopped and called out, in a loud voice, "Jo-o-o-d-d-i-i!" She waited a little bit then went in the house.

I wanted to think nothing was going to happen, but I knew I was going to get whomped. I had been spending most of the day in the barn but couldn't think on nothing to do, except face the punishment. I went down the ladder and out the barn. I peeked around the corner of the parlor window. Billie Jim was listening to Charlie McCarthy on the radio. He was sitting in Paul's lap while Paul read the paper. Grace was rocking in her chair, knitting. She looked like my really grandmother except my grandmother is short. I missed my grandmother only thinking on her won't do no good so I went around to the back door and slammed it real loud, when I came into the house, and marched right to the living room. Billie Jim jumped up and ran to me and said, "You made us real worried. Where was you?"

He grabbed my arm, but I pulled away and said, "I don't know why you were worried. I was only up to the top of this grassy hill, what I found, thinking about things."

Grace put down her knitting and looked at me. I felt my heart running fast when she looked at Paul. He looked back on her for a little then said, "Was it a nice hill, Jodi?"

I knew I couldn't say no more lies without making spit in my mouth because my throat was all dried up and my tongue would stick and not make words, so I just shrugged a shoulder. Grace stood up and started coming toward me. I figured to just stay where I was to take the hit so I was getting ready. Instead, she said, "I'm glad you're home so we can eat supper. I hope you had a nice adventure too."

She reached me and my body was stiff with waiting, but her arms was out like she was going to hug me. I didn't back down and she closed her arms around me and hugged. I just stood there, still stiff, and she bent down to whisper in my ear, "You've got straw in your hair, Jodi." Then she patted me on the shoulder and we went to the kitchen.

While she was putting food on the platters, Grace said, "Jodi told me she doesn't like fried chicken much, so she doesn't have to eat any if she doesn't want. We even have two nice pork chops here, with mint jelly, just in case Jodi would rather not eat the chicken."

She turned around with a platter filled up with chicken and on the end was the pork chops. They tasted good with jelly. We never got that in the orphanage.

I watched Grace real good the rest of the time before bed, but she never said nothing about the chicken or me not being good. She never said nothing about it ever again.

The April we came in, turned into July with everybody just doing their work and playing too.

We met Jim and Sara and Crystal, Paul and Grace's kids. Between them three, they had twelve kids and, sometimes, everybody came over at once and cousins and other people too. Lots of times we cooked outside and sometimes we ate things we growed in the garden. It was just like at our Daddy's house a long time before, except there weren't no grandparents because Grace and Paul were the grandmother and grandfather. Their parents was dead.

We did lots of things together. Paul taught Brother to fish and both of us to swim. When Brother and him went away for fishing, Grace and me did beading. She showed me how to do beads in a circle. We made lots of things to take to pow-wows. I sold one I made, but Grace sold lots. I made two baskets I liked, but I kept them. We went to a pow-wow over to the reservation and one at White Swan and down to Oregon. Everybody in the family went, in all the trucks, lined up on the highways and we all stopped together to eat.

One day, Paul said to Grace, "Their hair is long enough now. I guess it's time."

Billie Jim looked at me across the table and motioned at me to come with him. He took his short legs up the stairs, as fast as he could, to the bathroom and said, "Hurry up, Jodi."

He only left the door barely open enough for me to squeeze after him and slammed and locked it.

He whisper-yells, "They're gonna cut our hair, Jodi! Don't let 'em do it! Please make 'em not do it, Jodi!"

I asked him, "How come you think they're going to do that, Billie Jim? This ain't the orphanage. They won't cut it off like there. Grace and Paul and everybody, almost, gots long hair."

"But Jodi Ann, didn't you listen when Paul said it was long enough? It means a cutting!"

I started to say more, but Paul called us to, "Come on downstairs, kids, and meet us outside."

We went downstairs and out the door and walked slow to where Grace was standing. She had her hands behind her back. Paul was rolling a big log from the woodpile toward where the chopping block was. Paul set the log up like the block and said, "Okay, kids, we have a surprise for you. Take your seats and face each other."

My stomach was sick and I started to think Billie Jim might be right. When we sat down, I looked on Billie Jim and knew how much of a little kid he was and how I was supposed to take care on him, but it felt like the best thing was to just run away.

Grace stood by me and Paul was by Billie Jim. Paul said, "Okay, Grace, count with me. Ready? One, two, three, now! Surprise!"

When they yelled surprise, all their arms go up and I jumped and grabbed Billie Jim, pulling him off the log, and we ran backwards.

Grace said, "Wait, Jodi! Look!"

In each of their hands were ribbons, streaming out in the breeze.

Paul said, "It's time to teach you how to braid your hair. Come on over."

We walked over, still holding hands, and Paul said, "Okay, now Jodi, you watch me while I do Billie Jim. Then Billie Jim can watch Grace and you."

They slow weaved the ribbons in the shiny black of our hair. In and out go hair and ribbon until the end, when there was just enough to tie the braid tight. We did it to each other until we was real good at it and sometimes Paul and Grace let us braid their hair. We all went to the next family picnic with ribbon braids.

Paul showed us how to ride and take care of Henry, too. We went lots of places all by ourselves on Henry. He never went too fast, but sometimes he tried to scrape us off on trees. Sometimes he liked to go through the barn door with the top part closed. One time he knocked me off and I didn't want to ride no more, but Grace said I got to because Henry would think he won something and wouldn't let me ever ride him again, so we got the box for me to stand on and I got back up.

I got to spend lots of time with Grace. Many mornings I watched her doing her finger rubs while seeing the morning coming, by peeking around the doorway. We went on walks together all the time. She taught me lots about flowers and birds. Most of the time just her and me went, but sometimes we let Brother come. I let her hold my hand sometimes too because it seemed like the bumps in her fingers felt better. Least she always smiled when I let her. She didn't squeeze my hand or put it in her tee-tee. She didn't never put her fingers in mine or play with Billie Jim's pee-pee. Neither did Paul. Brother and me both liked that.

One day, Billie Jim and me was brushing Henry when Grace yelled, "Oh, Jodi and Billie Jim! Come see what Pickles is doing!"

We ran to the other side of the barn by the door, where hay was stacked. There was a big pile not in a bale, so Billie Jim and me could feed the cows and Henry, and there, in the middle of the pile, was Pickles, the cat. She was laying on Paul's bathrobe, sort of all crookedy on her side and making funny noises. Rufus the dog was sitting by her and sometimes Pickles hissed at him when he stuck his nose near her. That was funny to see cause they were friends.

I asked Grace, "What's the matter with Pickles?"

Billie Jim said, "She's sick, you dummy!"

I wanted to pinch him, but Grace took our hands, pulling us into the straw. She said, "You watch and something amazing is going to happen. Pickles is having babies."

We sat forever, but nothing happened except Grace talked real slow and stroked Pickles. Pickles made funny noises and her stomach swelled up and down and moved and she licked her bottom, but that's all. The screen door banged and Billie Jim jumped up, yelling, "I'm gonna get Paul!"

When he was gone, Grace asked, "What are you thinking, Jodi?"

I said, "I don't see how Pickles can make babies and, besides, it's boring."

Grace pulled me up to her lap and told me about how the babies got inside and growed and I thought it was icky and she said, "It takes a long time and lots of hard work to make something as special as a baby. Someday you might want to do it. Here, you pet Pickles too."

It felt good in Grace's lap and we stuck our arms out at the same time to pet Pickles.

Just about that time we heard a squishy noise with a grunt from Pickles. Then this icky stuff came squirting out and then Pickles acted like she couldn't get no air and was panting and then this kitten popped out in a white sack and Pickles bit it open and ate it up and licked the sticky stuff off the kitten. I heard what Grace said, but was thinking on not having no babies if I have to do that.

Billie Jim came back with Paul and Paul said, "Aa-a-y, that's where my bathrobe went. I couldn't find it this morning. You're doing a nice job, Pickles."

He pats her head and she meows to him.

Grace said, "Paul, you take Billie Jim for a walk and tell him some things."

Paul said, "We did that before we came out, Grace."

He put his arm on Billie Jim's shoulder and my brother was smiling like he was all full up with something nobody ever knew before.

Paul said, "Let's all sit down together here."

All of us watched Pickles have two more kittens and then Grace said, "Well, it's time to give our new momma a rest. Billie Jim, you bring her some water. Jodi, you run get an egg and put it into a bowl. Rufus, you come inside with me before you get your nose scratched."

Billie Jim and me went lots of times to see Pickles that night. The kittens were all crawling on Pickles' tummy and pushing for milk and making soft cries while Pickles was licking their fur all soft clean. Grace was right that they were beautiful.

In August, everybody in the family came around every day for the harvest. It was real hard work. Brother and me helped too, but mostly the grown-ups did it. Grace and Sara and me cooked lots. Outside the air was all pale green and sort of fuzzy with little pieces of the cutted stuff filling the wind. It smelled real clean and wet even though it was hot days. I liked it except it made me sneeze. Grace said, "It's best if you stay inside, Jodi, and help with cooking. You can make your biscuits."

I made good biscuits. We all worked really hard.

One harvest day, it was after a big rain in the night, Billie Jim and me were playing Huckleberry Finn on these boards we made into a raft, in a pond in the bend of the road. All of a sudden, there was this high screaming sound and a long white ambulance coming down our road. It ran fast by us making mud fly all over. We ran after it, up to the house. Jim said, "Stay back kids. Give them room."

Some men went into the house and came back with Paul sleeping in this bed they carried. Paul had a thing on his face with a bag going in and out like wind. Grace came behind him and she looked like she was going to throw up. They speeded away. Everybody else got in the green truck and we went to the hospital where we sat in a hall. Then came a medicine man who sang songs with his rattle, but the nurse people made him sit in the hall too. He didn't care though because he still sang real soft and, whenever there wasn't no nurse around, he went back in the room. After a long time, a doctor came to say, "Each of you can go in, two at a time." Then he went away.

Sara took me in and I see Grace was looking really sad so I look on Paul and knew he was dead. His skin felt all cold and he didn't have no smile. I couldn't think on what it meant. I wanted Grace to make it not be, but she just patted my hand. I wanted to hold hers, but she didn't do nothing but pat me.

A long time later, we went back to the house with Sara. Grace didn't come home for three days. When she saw Brother and me, she said, "Come into the living room, children. I need to talk with you."

Me and Billie Jim went in and Sara and Jim and Crystal were there too. Everybody was all quiet.

Grace said, "In a little while the county car will be here to pick you up because you are going back to the orphanage. They say I'm too old to keep you children by myself. I told them we would be just fine together, but they tell me a woman alone isn't enough. So you have to go."

Billie Jim asked, "Didn't we do enough work?"

I pinched him and he yelped so Grace took my hand and Billie Jim's too, then she said, "You're wonderful children, but they just won't let you stay. But you be strong an' make us all proud of you."

I wanted to run, but I didn't know how come.

Then Grace said, "Let Sara and Crystal help you while I rest here."

Nobody said nothing while we packed up. I saw a car coming what had writing on it. It was the kind that most always takes and gets us from foster homes. It stopped and the driver started honking. Billie Jim and me didn't walk too fast going downstairs, but didn't no one say we were bad because we were slow. Everybody walked by us to say a goodbye except Grace. She took our hands to go out the back door. She knelt down and said "Ouch."

I asked her, "You hurt?"

She just said, "I knelt on a little rock, but it's okay. You be good children. Listen to the Creator like Paul told you and you'll stay strong."

Grace took Billie Jim in a hug and kissed him too. He squeezed her neck and I saw he was crying, but he didn't make no noise. Then she took both my hands. I looked on her big brown knuckles and didn't want to leave watching her in the sun. She hugged me real hard an' I hugged her too. We didn't say nothing and she stood up really slow.

The county man put us in the back seat and started to drive, right away. We both begin to get up on our knees, to see out the back window, but the man yelled to us, "Sit down," so we did and we couldn't see nobody until we went over the bridge and turned onto the highway. Then we saw Grace, still standing still by the door, waving. Billie Jim and me held hands to wave too.

And that's the way it was.

Linda Hogan

MAKING DO

▼ ▼ ▼ ▼

▼

Linda Hogan's finely wrought "Making Do" opens our experience to the hurt of destruction, the finality of loss, the sadness of grief. The wooden birds in the story are a symbol of a better time, when the people put medicine power into what they carved. Yet the protagonist does so not out of a sense of power but of powerlessness. Still, the old ways, here strangely transformed, provide a kind of healing and a kind of grace: the woman with her birds learns to resist destruction and begins the painful journey toward becoming the kind of warrrior that this odd age we inhabit, as we approach the twenty-first century, requires us to be.

ROBERTA JAMES became one of the silent people in Seeker County when her daughter, Harriet, died at six years of age.

Harriet died of what they used to call consumption.

After the funeral, Grandmother Addie went to stay with Roberta in her grief, as she had done over the years with her children and grandchildren. Addie, in fact, had stayed with Roberta during the time of her pregnancy with Harriet, back when the fifteen-year-old girl wore her boyfriend's black satin jacket that had a map of Korea on the back. And she'd visited further back than that, back to the days when Roberta wore white full skirts and white blouses and the sun came in the door, and she lay there in that hot sun like it was ironed flat against the floor, and she felt good with clean hair and skin and singing a little song to herself. There were oak trees outside. She was waiting. Roberta was waiting there for something that would take her away. But the farthest she got was just outside her skin, that black jacket against her with its map of Korea.

Addie never told Roberta a word of what she knew about divided countries and people who wear them on their backs, but later Roberta knew that her grandmother had seen way down the road what was coming, and warned her in little ways. When she brushed Roberta's dark hair, she told her, "You were born to a different life, Bobbie."

After the funeral, Roberta's mother offered comfort in her own way. "Life goes on," Neva said, but she herself had long belonged to that society of quiet Indian women in Seeker, although no one would have guessed this of the woman who wore Peach Promise lipstick, smiled generously, and kissed the bathroom mirror, leaving a message for Roberta that said, "See you in the a.m. Love."

Grandma Addie tended Angela, Roberta's younger daughter. She fed the baby Angela spoonsful of meal, honey, and milk and held her day and night while Roberta went about the routines of her life. The chores healed her a little; perking coffee and cleaning her mother's lipstick off the mirror. She swept away traces of Harriet with the splintered broom, picking up threads from the girl's dress, black hair from her head, wiping away her footprints.

Occasionally Neva stopped in, clasped her daughter's thin cold hands between her warm ones, and offered advice. "That's why you ought to get married," she said. She wrapped Roberta's shoulders in a large gray sweater. "Then you'd have some man to help when things are down and out. Like Ted here. Well, anyway, Honey," she said at eye level to Roberta, "you sure drew a good card when Harriet was born. Didn't she, Ted?"

"Sure sugar, an ace."

But when Roberta wasn't looking, Neva shook her head slowly and looked down at the floor, and thought their lives were all hopeless.

Roberta didn't get married like her mother suggested. She did take some comfort on those long nights by loving Tom Wilkins. Each night she put pieces of cedar inside his Red Wing boots, to keep him close, and neatly placed them beneath her bed. She knew how to care for herself with this man, keeping him close in almost the same space Harriet had abandoned. She wept slightly at night after he held her and he said, "There now. There now," and patted her on the back.

He brought her favorite Windmill cookies with him from town and he sang late at night so that the ghost of Harriet could move on more easily, like he eventually moved on when Roberta stopped placing cedar in his boots.

"Why didn't that Wilkins boy come back?" Grandma asked. "Choctaw, wasn't he?"

Roberta shrugged as if she hadn't left his boots empty of cedar. "He was prettier than me." She pushed her straggly hair back from her face to show Grandma what she meant.

A month later, Roberta was relieved when the company summoned Tom Wilkins to Louisiana to work on a new oil field and she didn't have to run into him at the store any longer.

Roberta's next child, a son she named Wilkins after the father, died at birth, strangled on his own cord. Roberta had already worn a dark shawl throughout this pregnancy. She looked at his small roughbox and said, "He died of life and I know how that can happen."

She held on to her grandmother's hand.

Grandma Addie and Neva talked about Roberta. "A woman can only hold so much hurt," Grandma said.

"And don't think I don't know it," said Neva.

Roberta surfaced from her withdrawal a half year later, in the spring of 1974, when Angela looked at her like a little grandmother and said, "Mother, I know it is hard, but it's time for me to leave you" and immediately became feverish. Roberta bathed her with alcohol and made blessing-root tea, which she dropped into little Angela's rose-petal mouth with an eye dropper. She prayed fervently to God or Jesus, she had never really understood which was which, and to all the stones and trees and gods of the sky and inner earth that she knew well, and to the animal spirits, and she carried her little Angel to the hospital in the middle of praying, to that house made of brick and window and cinders where dying bodies were kept alive, carried the girl with soft child skin in a small quilt decorated with girls in poke bonnets, and thought how funny it was to wrap a dying child in such sweetness as those red-cheeked girls in the calico bonnets. She blamed herself for ignoring Angela in her own time of grief. Four days later Angela died, wearing a little corn necklace Roberta made, a wristlet of glass beads, and covered with that quilt.

"She even told Roberta she was about to die," Neva told Ted. "Just like an old woman, huh, Bert?"

Roberta went on with her silence through this third death, telling herself over and over what had happened, for the truth was so bad she could not believe it. The inner voice of the throat spoke and repeated the words of loss and Roberta listened hard. "My Angel. My Harriet. All my life gone and broken while I am so young. I'm too young for all this loss."

She dreamed of her backbone and even that was broken in pieces. She dreamed of her house in four pieces. She was broken like the country of Korea or the land of the tribe.

They were all broken, Roberta's thin-skinned father broken by the war. He and Neva raised two boys whose parents had "gone off" as they say of those who come under the control of genie spirits from whiskey bottles, and those boys were certainly broken. And Neva herself who had once been a keeper of the gates; she was broken.

In earlier days she read people by their faces and bodies. She was a keeper of gates, opening and closing ways for people to pass through life. "This one has been eating too much grain," she'd say, or "That one was born too rich for her own good and is spoiled. That one is broken in the will to live by this and that." She was a keeper of the family gates as well. She closed doors on those she disliked, if they were dishonest, say, or mean, or small. There was no room for smallness in her life, but she opened the doors wide for those who moved her slightly, in any way, with stirrings of love or pity. She had lusty respect for belligerence, political rebellion, and for vandalism against automobiles or businesses or bosses, and those vandals were among those permitted inside her walls.

And now she was broken, by her own losses and her loneliness.

Roberta cried against Addie's old warm shoulder and Grandma Addie stayed on, moving in all her things, cartons of canning jars, a blue-painted porcelain horse, her dark dresses and aprons, pictures of her grandchildren and great-grandchildren, rose-scented candles of the virgin of Guadalupe, even though she was never a Catholic, and the antlers of the deer.

Roberta ignored her cousins from the churches of the brethren of this and that when they came to comfort her in their ways, telling her that all things were meant to be and that the Lord gives and takes.

Uncle James was older and so he said nothing, and she sat with him, those silent ones together.

Roberta's mother left messages on the bathroom mirror. "There is a time for everything in heaven."

With Grandma there to watch over Neva and the house, Roberta decided one day to pack her dishes, blankets, and clothes into the old Chevy she had bought from Ted, and she drove away from the little square tombstones named Angela, Wilkins, and Harriet, though it nearly broke her heart to leave them. She drove away from all those trying to comfort her with what comforted them. The sorrow in her was like a well too deep for young ground; the sides caved in with anger, but Roberta planned still to return for Grandma Addie. She stopped once, in the flat, neutral land of Goodland, Kansas, and telephoned back.

"You sure you don't want to come with me? It's kind of pretty out this way, Grandma," she lied. She smelled truck exhaust from the phone booth and she watched the long, red-faced boys walking past, those young men who had eaten so much cattle they began to look like them.

"Just go and get settled. I'll be out to visit as soon as you get the first load of laundry hung on the line."

Roberta felt her grandma smile. She hung up the phone and headed back to the overloaded, dusty white car.

She headed for Denver, but wound up just west of there, in a mountain town called The Tropics. Its name was like a politician's vocabulary, a lie. In truth, The Tropics was arid. It was a mine town, uranium most recently. Dust devils whirled sand off the mountains. Even after the heaviest of rains, the water seeped back into the ground, between stones, and the earth was parched again. Still, *Tropics* conjured up visions of tall grasses in outlying savannas, dark rivers, mists, and deep green forests of ferns and trees and water-filled vines. Sometimes it seemed like they were there.

Roberta told herself it was God's acres, that it was fate she had missed the Denver turn-offs from the freeway, that here she could forgive and forget her losses and get on with living. She rented a cabin, got a part-time job working down at the Tropics Grocery where she sold single items to customers who didn't want to travel to town. She sold a bag of flour to one, a can of dog food to another, candy to schoolchildren in the afternoon. She sold boxed doughnuts and cigarettes to work crews in the mornings and 3.2 beer to the same crews after five. She dusted and stacked the buckling shelves, and she had time to whittle little birds, as her Uncle James had done. She whittled them and thought of them as toys for the spirits of her children and put them in the windows so the kids would be sure and see them. "This one's for Harriet," she'd tell no one in particular.

When she didn't work she spent her time in bed, completely still and staring straight at the ceiling. They used to say if a person is motionless, their soul will run away from the body, and Roberta counted on that. They say that once a soul decides to leave, it can't be recalled. Roberta lay in that room with its blue walls and blue-flowered blanket. She lay there with her hair pulled back from her round forehead. She held the sunbonnet quilt in her hands and didn't move.

To her disappointment, she remained alive. Every night she prayed to die and join her kids, but every morning she was still living, breathing. Some mornings she pulled at her flesh just to be certain, she was so amazed and despairing to be still alive.

Her soul refused to leave. It had a mind of its own. So Roberta got up and began a restless walking. There were nights in The Tropics that she haunted the dirt roads like a large-shouldered, thin-hipped ghost, like a tough girl with her shoulders held high to protect her broken heart. Roberta Diane James with her dark hair that had been worn thin from the hours she spent lying down trying to send her soul away. Roberta, with her eyes the color of dark river water after a storm when the gold stirs up in it. The left eye still held the trace of a wink in it, despite the thinness of skin stretched over her forehead, the smell of ivory soap on her as she tried over and over to wash the grief from her flesh.

2

When I first heard how bad things were going for Roberta, I thought about going home, but I heard my other voices tell me it wasn't time. "There is a season for all things," Mom used to say, and I knew Mom would be telling Roberta just that, in her own words, and that Roberta would be fuming inside as I had done with Mom's fifty-cent sayings.

I knew this much: Roberta would need to hold on to her grief and her pain.

Us Chickasaws have lost so much we hold on to everything. Even our muscles hold on to their aches. We love our lovers long after they are gone, better than when they were present.

When we were girls, Roberta and I saved the tops of Coke bottlecaps and covered them with purple cloth like grapes. We made clusters of grapes sitting out there on the porch, or on tire swings in the heat, and we sewed the grapes together. We made do. We drank tea from pickle jars. We used potato water to starch our clothes. We even used our skinny dark legs as paper for tic-tac-toe. Now the girls turn bleach containers into hats, cutting them in fours and crocheting them together.

Our Aunt Bell is famous for holding on and making do. There's a nail in her kitchen for plastic six-pack rings, a box for old jars, a shelf or box for everything, including all the black and white shoes she's worn out as a grown woman. Don't think those boxes or nails mean she's neat, either. She's not. She has hundreds of dusty salt and pepper shakers people gave her, and stacks of old magazines and papers, years of yellowed history all contained in her crowded rooms, and I love her for it, for holding on that way. I have spent hours of my younger life looking at those shakers and reading those papers. Her own children tell her it is a miracle the viruses of science aren't growing to maturity in there.

We save ourselves from loss in whatever ways we can, collecting things, going out to Danceland, getting drunk, reading westerns or finding new loves, but the other side of all this salvation is that we deny the truth. When some man from town steals our land, we say, "Oh, he wouldn't do that. Jimmy Slade is a good old boy. I knew his folks. I used to work for the Slades during the Depression." Never mind that the Slades were not the hungry ones back then.

Some of us southern Indians used to have ranches and cattle. They were all lost piece by piece, or sold to pay for taxes on some land that was also lost. Now and then someone comes around and tells us we should develop our land like we once did. Or they tell us just to go out in the world. We nod and smile at them.

Now and then some of us young people make a tidal wave in the ocean of our history, an anxiety attack in the heart monitor of our race. We get angry and scream out. We get in the news. We strip ourselves bare in the colleges that recruited us as their minority quota and we run out into the snowstorm naked and we get talked about for years as the crazy Indian that did this or that, the one that drove to the gas station and went on straight to Canada, the girl who took out the garbage and never turned and went back. We made do.

I knew some people from up north. You could always tell they were from up north because my friend's daughter had a wall-eye with a hook tattooed on her forearm. Once we went to a pow-wow together and some of the women of the People wore jingle dresses, with what looked like bells. "What are those?" I asked my friend.

They were snuff can lids. Those women of the forests and woodlands, so much making do just like us, like when we use silver salt cans in our dances instead of turtle-shell rattles. We make music of those saltshakers, though now and then some outsider decides we have no culture because we use store-bought shakers and they are not traditional at all.

I defy them: Salt is the substance of our blood, sweat, our secretions, our semen. It is the ocean of ourselves.

Once I saw a railroad engineer's hat in a museum. It was fully beaded. I thought it was a new style like the beaded tennis shoes or the new beaded truckers' hats. But it was made in the late 1800s when the Lakota were forbidden to make traditional items. The mothers took to beading whatever was available, hats of the engineers of death. They covered colony cotton with their art.

We make art out of our loss.

That's why when I heard Roberta was in Colorado and was carving wooden birds, I figured it made sense. Besides, we come from a long line of whittlers and table carvers, people who work with wood, including the Mexican great-grandfather who made santos and a wooden mask that was banned by the priests. Its presence got him excommunicated.

Uncle James carves chains out of trees. We laugh and say it sounds like something *they* would do.

Roberta was carving wooden birds, crows, mourning doves, and even a scissortail or two. She sent some of the birds back home to have Aunt Bell put them on the graves of her little ones.

I think she was trying to carve the souls of her children into the birds. She was making do.

THE RESISTANCE

The annals of Indian resistance to white encroachment since the seventeenth and eighteenth centuries are long and distinguished. Among the more renowned examples are Pontiac's War, the Cherokee Nation's heroic legal and congressional battles, Geronimo's long war, and the flight from persecution of the Nez Perce and the Oglala Lakota. In the contemporary era the resistance continues — mostly in the courts but also through writing, community organizing, and Indian social life. The fight of Ada Deer and the Menominees to regain federal recognition after being swindled out of it by the United States government in the 1950s under the provisions of the Termination Act is another major example. The Termination Act was designed to "get the government out of the Indian business," as President Eisenhower put it. Under its provisions federally recognized tribes, which had previously been entitled to a number of economic, educational, legal, and medical rights that were protected by federal statute, had their treaty relationships and rights with the federal government terminated, and the government no longer took any responsibility for the rights of these tribes.

This period also saw legal and bureaucratic battles over Indian Land Claims, Water Rights, Fishing and Hunting Rights, Indian Child Welfare provisions, control of and/or advisory input into Indian schools, on- and off-reservation health programs, and economic development programs. Since the 1960s, as more and more Native Americans receive college and graduate degrees, the economic and legal affairs of tribal people are being increasingly administered by Indians. These are all aspects of Indian resistance.

Elizabeth Cook-Lynn

THE POWER OF HORSES

▼ ▼ ▼ ▼
▼

"The Power of Horses" is about soul-theft, the theft of magic, of wonder, from the people. Without wonder, the lot of humans is indeed miserable, whether that misery is ensconced in a tiny, squalid house on the reservation or in a huge, split-level house in some splendid neighborhood. "The Power of Horses" is also about reclaiming the wonder that forms the weft of our traditions, and that gives human life its sublimity and significance. The bonding between mother and daughter in this story is not only a result of sharing tasks like canning beets, or sharing perspectives, as when they watch the men from the window, or sharing pain, as when the mother sends her daughter to confront a straying man. It is much more: it is the speaking of the truth, a truth that is part of our relation to the supernaturals; it is protecting their gifts from harm and thereby protecting the generations unborn; it is sharing responsibility for the life of the planet, its spirit's life, and thus our own. On the morning when Marteen goes with her father to take the "shota" horse to safety, she enters the tradition and becomes one of the people.

THE MOTHER AND DAUGHTER steadied themselves, feet planted squarely, foreheads glistening with perspiration; each grasped a handle of the large steaming kettle.

"Ready?"

"Un-huh."

"Take it then," the mother said. "Careful." Together they lifted the tub of boiled beets from the flame of the burners on the gas stove and set it heavily on the table across the room. The girl let the towel which had served as a makeshift pot holder drop to the floor as the heat penetrated to the skin, and she slapped her hand against the coolness of the smooth painted wall and then against her thigh, feeling the roughness of the heavy jeans with tingling fingers. To stop the tingling, she cupped her fingers to her mouth and blew on them, then raised her apologetic eyes and looked at her mother. Without speaking, as if that was the end of it, she sank into the chrome chair and picked up the towel and began wiping the sweat from her face. The sun came relentlessly through the thin gauze curtains and the hot wind blew across the stove, almost extinguishing the gas flames of the burner, making the blue edges turn yellow and then orange and then white. The towel was damp now and stained purple from the beets and the girl leaned back in the chair and laid the towel across her face, feeling her own hot breath around her nose and mouth.

"Your hands get used to it, Marleen," the mother said, not even glancing at the girl nor at her own rough, brown hands, "just have to keep at it," saying this not so much from believing it as from the need to stop the feeling of futility in the girl and the silence between them. The mother gingerly grasped the bleached stems of several beets and dropped them into a pan of cold water, rolling one and then another of the beets like balls in her hands, pushing the purple-black skins this way and that, quickly, deftly, removing the peel and stem and tossing the shiny vegetable into another container. Finishing one, she hurriedly picked up another, as if by hurrying she could forestall the girl's rebellion.

The woman's arms, like her hands, were large, powerful. But, despite the years of heavy work, her sloping shoulders and smooth, long neck were part of a tender femininity only recently showing small signs of decline and age. The dark stains on her dark face might have seemed like age spots or a disfigurement on someone else but on the woman they spread delicately across her cheeks, forehead and neck like a sweep of darkened cloud, making her somehow vulnerable and defenseless.

"Your hands'll get used to it, Marleen," she repeated, again attempting to keep the girl's unwillingness in check and an avenue to reasonable tolerance and cooperation open.

The brief rest with the towel on her face seemed to diminish the girl's weariness and for an instant more she sat silently, breathing peacefully into the damp towel. As the girl drew the towel across her face and away from her eyes, something like fear began to rise in her and she peered out the window where she saw her father standing with a white man she had never seen before. Her father was looking straight ahead down the draw where the horses stood near the corral. They always want something from him, she thought, and as she watched the white man put a cigarette in his mouth and turn sideways out of the wind, the flame of his lighter licking toward his bony profile, she wondered what it was this time. She watched the man's quick mannerisms and she saw that he began to talk earnestly and gesture toward his green pick-up truck which was parked close to the barbed wire fence encircling the house and yard.

The girl was startled out of her musings at the sound of her mother's, "Yu-u-u-u," softly uttered indication of disapproval, insistent and always compelling a change in the girl's behavior. And she turned quickly to get started with her share of the hot beets, handling them inexpertly but peeling their hot skins away as best she could.

After a few minutes, during which the women worked in silence, only the monotonous hiss of the burning gas flame between them, the girl, surprised, thought: Her sounds of disapproval aren't because I'm wasting time; instead, they are made because she is afraid my father and the white man will see me watching them. Spontaneously, defensively, she said, "They didn't see me." She looked into the brown stained face but saw only her mother's careful pretense of being preoccupied with the beets as she picked up a small knife to begin slicing them. All last winter, everytime I came home, I spied on him for you, thought the girl, even riding my horse over to Chekpa's through the snow to see if he was there. And when I came back and told you that he was, you acted as if you hadn't heard anything, like now. So this is not the beginning of the story nor is it the part of the story that matters, thought the girl, and she started to recognize a long, long history of acrimony between her parents, thinking, in hindsight, that it would have been better if she had stayed at Stephen Mission. But then, she remembered her last talk with Brother Otto at the Mission as he sat before her, one leg languidly draped over the other, his collar open, showing his sparse red chest hairs, his watery pale eyes looking at her searchingly, and she knew that it wasn't better to have stayed there.

He had sat quivering with sympathy as she had tried to tell him that to go home was to be used by her mother against her father. I rode over to Chekpa's, she told him, hating herself for letting out the symptoms of her childish grief, despising him for his delicate white skin, his rapt gaze, the vicariousness of his measly existence. Até was there cutting wood for the eldest of the Tatiopa women, Rosalie, the one he was supposed to marry, you know, but instead, he married my mother. My mother had sent me there and when I rode into the yard and saw him, he stood in uncertainty, humiliated in the eyes of Chekpa, his old friend, as well as all of those in the Tatiopa family. Worse yet, she knew, humiliated in the eyes of his nine-year-old daughter.

In her memory of that awful moment, she didn't speak nor did her father, and so she had ridden out of the yard as abruptly as she had come, standing easily in the stirrups, her face turned toward her right shoulder out of the wind, watching the slush fly behind the horse's hooves. She didn't cut across Archie's field as she usually did but took the long way, riding as hard as she could alongside the road. When she got to the gate, she reined in, dismounted and led her horse through the gate and then, slowly, down the sloping hill to the tack shed. She stood for a long time with her head against the wide, smooth leather of the stirrup shaft, her eyes closed tightly, the smell of wet horse hair in her nostrils. Much later she had recited the event as fully as she could bear it to the Mission school priest much like she had been taught to recite the events of her sinful life: I have taken the Lord's name in vain, I have taken the Lord's name in vain, I have taken . . .

Damn beets, damn all these damn beets, the girl thought, and she turned away from the table back to the stove where she stirred the second, smaller pot of sliced beets and she looked out through the gauze curtains to see if her father and the white man were still there. They had just run the horses into the corral from the small fenced pasture where they usually grazed when they were brought down to the place.

"He must be getting ready to sell them, is he?" she asked her mother.

Her mother said nothing.

"How come? I didn't know he was going to sell," the girl said slowly, noticing that her horse, two quarterhorse brood mares and a half-Shetland black and white gelding she had always called "shota" had been cut out of the herd and were standing at the far corner of the pasture, grazing. The heat shimmered above the long buffalo grass and the girl's thoughts drifted and, vaguely, she heard her mother say, "You'd better spoon those sliced ones into these hot jars, Marleen." And then, almost to herself, her mother started talking as if in recognition of what the girl did not know about the factual and philosophical sources from which present life emerges. "I used to have land myself, daughter," she began. "On it, my grandfather had many horses. What happened to it was that some white men from Washington came and took it away from me when my grandfather died because they said they were going to breed game birds there — geese, I think.

"There was no one to do anything about it," she continued. "There was only this old woman who was a mother to me and she really didn't know what to do, who to see, or how to prevent this happening.

"Among the horses there on my land was a pair of brood mares just like those two out there," she pointed with her chin to the two bays at the end of the pasture. And looking at the black and white horse called "shota," she said, "And there was also another strange, mysterious horse, Su'ka wak a', i-e-e-e." She used the word for "mysterious dog" in the Dakota language. And the mother and daughter stood looking out the window at the "shota" horse beside the bays, watching them pick their way through the shimmering heat and through the tall grass slowly, unhurried. The beets were forgotten, momentarily, and the aging woman remembered the magic of those horses and especially the one that resembled the "shota" horse, thinking about that time, that primordial time when an old couple of the tribe received a gift horse from a little bird and the horse produced many offspring for the old man and woman, and the people were never poor after that. Her grandfather, old Bowed Head, the man with many horses, had told her that story often during her childhood when he wished to speak of those days when all creatures knew one another. And it was a reassuring thing: I wish this tribe to be strong and good, the mysterious horse had told the old man, and so I keep giving my offspring every year and the tribe will have many horses and this good thing will be among you always.

"They were really fast horses," said the mother, musing still, filling in the texture of her imagination and memory. "They were known throughout our country for their speed, and the old man allowed worthy men in the tribe to use them in war or to go on a hunt with them. It is an old story," the woman concluded as though the story were finished, as though commenting upon its history made everything comprehensible.

As the girl watched her mother's extraordinary vitality which rose during the telling of these events, she also noted the abruptness with which the story seemed to end and the kind of formidable reserve and closure which fell upon the dark stained features of the older woman as she turned again to the stove.

"What happened to the horses?" the girl wanted to know. "Did someone steal them? Did they die?"

After a long silence, her mother said, "Yes, I suppose so," and the silence again deepened between them as they fell to filling hot jars with sliced beets and sealing hot lids upon them, wiping and stroking them meticulously and setting them one by one on a dim pantry shelf.

The girl's frustration was gone now and she seemed mindless of the heat, her own physical discomfort and the miserableness of the small squalid kitchen where she and her mother moved quietly about, informed now with the wonder of the past, the awesomeness of the imagination.

The sun moved west and the kitchen fell into shadow. The wind died down. The mother and daughter finished their tedious task and carried the large tub of hot water out through the entryway a few feet past the door and emptied its contents upon the ground. The girl watched the red beet juice stain the dry, parched earth in which there was no resistance, and she stepped away from the redness of the water which gushed like strokes of a painter's brush, suddenly black and ominous as it sank into the ground. She looked up to see the white man's green pick-up truck disappearing over the rise, the dust billowing behind the heavy wheels, settling gently in the heat.

The nameless fear struck at her again and she felt a knot being drawn tightly inside her and she looked anxiously toward the corral. Nothing around her seemed to be moving, the air suddenly still, the sweat standing out in beads on her face and her hands, oddly moist and cold. As she ran toward the corral, she saw her mother out of the corner of her eye still grasping one handle of the boiler tub, strangely composed, her head and shoulders radiant in the sun.

At the corral a moment later, she saw her father's nearly lifeless form lying face down in the dirt, his long grey hair spread out like a fan above him, pitifully untidy for a man who ordinarily took meticulous care with his appearance. He had his blue cotton scarf which he used as a hand-kerchief clutched tightly in his right hand and he was moaning softly.

The odor of whiskey on his breath was strong as she helped him turn over and sit up, and in that instant the silent presence of the past lay monumentally between them so that he did not look at her nor did he speak. In that instant, she dimly perceived her own innocence and was filled with regret that she would never know those times to which Até would return if he could, again and again. She watched as he walked unsteadily toward the house, rumpled and drunk, a man of grave dignity made comic and sad and helpless by circumstances which his daughter could only regard with wonderment.

"*Keyapi: Late one night when the old man had tied the horses near his lodge, someone crept through the draw and made ready to steal them; it was even said that they wanted to kill the wonderful horses. The mysterious gift horse called to the sleeping old man and told him that an evil lurked nearby. And he told the old man that since such a threat as this had come upon them and all the people of the tribe, the power of the horses would be diminished and no more colts would be born and the people would have to go back to their miserable ways.*"

As her father made his way to the house, walking stiffly past her mother who pretended to be scrubbing the black residue from the boiler, the girl turned and walked quickly away from the corral in the opposite direction.

I must look: she thought, into the distance, and as she lifted her eyes and squinted into the evening light she saw the Ft. George road across the river, beyond the bend in the river so far away that it would take most of the day for anyone to get there. I must look: at the ground in front of me where my grandmothers made paths to the ti (n) psina beds and carried home with them long braided strands over their shoulders. I must look: she thought, into the past for the horse that speaks to humans.

She took long strides and walked into the deepening dusk. She walked for a long time before returning to the darkened house where she crept into her bed and lay listening to the summer's night insect sounds, thinking apocalyptic thoughts in regard to what her mother's horse story might have to do with the day's events.

She awoke with a start, her father shaking her shoulder. "You must ride with me today, daughter, before the horse buyer comes back," he said. "I wish to take the horses away out to the far side of the north pasture. I am ready to go, so please hurry."

The girl dressed quickly, and just as dawn was breaking she and her father, each leading two horses with the others following, set out over the prairie hills. These were the hills, she knew, to which the people had come when the Uprising was finished and the U.S. Cavalry fell to arguing with missionaries and settlers about "the Indian problem." These were the hills, dark blue in this morning light, which she knew as repositories of sacred worlds unknown to all but its most ancient tenants.

When they reached the ridge above Dry Creek, the girl and her father stopped and let the horses go their way wildly. The "shota" horse led them down the steep prairie hills and into the dry creek bed and, one by one, the horses disappeared into the stand of tall cottonwood trees which lined the ravine.

She stood beside her father and watched them go. "Why were you going to sell them?" she asked abruptly.

"There are too many," he replied, "and the grass is short this summer."

"It's been too hot," he said, wiping his face with the blue handkerchief and he repeated, "The grass is short this summer."

With that, they mounted their horses and rode home together.

Cochiti and Laguna Pueblo Traditional
YELLOW WOMAN STORIES

▼ ▼ ▼ ▼
▼

"Evil Kachina Steals Yellow Woman" and "Sun Steals Yellow Woman"
are presented in close-to-literal translations, while the third, "Whirlwind
Man Steals Yellow Woman," is my own reworking of the story. The first
two stories were collected in the 1920s by the famed anthropologist Franz
Boas and his then student, Ruth Benedict. Benedict maintained that the
stories of the people — in this case, the Cochiti Pueblos — were inextricably
connected to everyday life. Of course this implies that the sacred and the
ordinary are perceived as a seamless whole.

The Yellow Woman[1] stories included here are to be read with that point
in mind. Far from being arcane (though they may seem puzzling at first)
they are about daily life, not merely because they speak to the concerns of
loss, persecution, rescue, and the relation of these to the sacred, but because
the Yellow Women stolen are Irriaku — sacred ears of corn that link persons
to our Mother, Iyatiku. The loss of these Yellow Women portends loss of
rain, of livelihood, and of connection between the people and the sacred
place where Iyatiku lives, Shipap.

This is not to say that the stories do not also inform listeners about
behavior. The behavior in question is that of the gods, the supernaturals,
the hocheni, and the people. For the people, it is a question of right
understanding of ritual events, of the ritual-daily calendar and the cycles
of plenty and famine, rain and drought.

Two versions of "Evil Kachina Steals Yellow Woman" were recorded,
one by Boas and one by Benedict. The Boas story had Kochinnenako (Yellow
Woman) finding and picking up a kicking stick, while in the Benedict
version she finds a crystal. Among the Keres, kicking sticks are used in
games (and games inevitably have their ritual counterparts), while crystals
are used to amplify inner perception. While the object she takes is bound
to have some bearing on the significance of her abduction, for the purposes

of this collection it is sufficient to realize that in either case she has taken something the Evil Kachina feels some claim to.

The introduction of Grandmother Spider into the narrative is a convention for this kind of story, which Benedict identifies as a "novelistic tale." Little happens in these stories without the intervention of Grandmother Spider, who is the overarching divinity of the Keres. (Her other name is Thinking Woman.) She is the force of magical or spiritual power that enables whatever happens to happen. The introduction of the husband going in search of his wife is another novelistic convention, although in the variant that Benedict recorded, he is Arrow Boy, a figure with his own supernatural connotations.

Yellow Woman, like the tradition she lives in, goes on and on. She lives in New Mexico (or that's what they call it at present), around Laguna and other Keresan pueblos as well. She is a Spirit, a Mother, a blessed ear of corn, an archetype, a person, a daughter of a main clan, an agent of change and of obscure events, a wanton, an outcast, a girl who runs off with Navajos, or Zunis, or even Mexicans. She is also mother of the little war twins, consort of the sun, granddaughter of the one who plays with stars, somehow (obscurely?) related to Grandmother Spider, the Woman Who Thinks Us As We Are Being. In the stories you'll find here, only the tiniest portion of her vast identity is revealed.

Evil Kachina Steals Yellow Woman

SHE WAS IN A TOWN. Then Yellow Woman went for water. With her jar Yellow Woman went for water. She reached the river. The girl was standing there. She saw a kicking stick. Below there was the kicking stick. Then Yellow Woman picked it up. She put it into (her dress). The Evil Kachina arrived. He told Yellow Woman, "Did you not pick up a kicking stick?" "No," said the girl. "Yes," said Evil Kachina to her, "yes," said he. "You have it somewhere," said he to the Yellow Woman. "It is so," said Evil Kachina. "I have not got it," said Yellow Woman. Then, "Yes," said Evil Kachina. "Somewhere," said he to her. "Give me the blue one (?)" said Evil Kachina. "Give me the kicking stick." "No," said Yellow Woman; "I shall keep it as my own," said she. (?) "I just might give you the kicking stick." Then Evil Kachina took away Yellow Woman. Evil Kachina took her to a place where he dwelt. Evil Kachina was bad. Evil Kachina arrived with her at his house. Evil Kachina carried her on his back to where he dwelt above, where a rainbow stands on Evil Kachina's house. Then he made Yellow Woman arrive. Early he went hunting deer. Then Evil

Kachina ordered the girl to grind corn. When she was ready to grind corn, Yellow Woman ground it. Then she put the flour of the corn into a basket. Then Yellow Woman was to make wafer bread. Then she gave Evil Kachina wafer bread to eat. He arrived in the evening. Then Evil Kachina told her that he had killed a deer which he had brought to his house. Then Yellow Woman went out and took the deer. He gave it to Yellow Woman to eat. Then she put it down in front of the fireplace and Yellow Woman took sacred corn meal. Then Yellow Woman gave sacred meal to the deer to eat. Yellow Woman inhaled. "Thank you," said she, "you killed a deer, thank you," said she to Evil Kachina. He was eating wafer bread. "Eat wafer bread!" said she to Evil Kachina. He was eating. Then Evil Kachina finished eating. "Thank you," said he. "I have eaten wafer bread," said Evil Kachina. "Put the deer down here." Then Yellow Woman put down the deer.

Right here in the town was Yellow Woman's house. Then her husband came home. Then Yellow Woman was not in her house. He had lost his wife. She was not there. Then he searched for his wife. He searched at the river; he was searching for her where his wife Yellow Woman had drawn water. The jar was at the river. Then her husband found the jar. Then (he said), "Where did my wife go? Where did she go to?" Then he was searching for his wife. Then Old Spider Woman told him. "Where are you going, grandson?" said Old Spider Woman to him. Then he spoke thus, "I am searching for my wife," said he. Then Old Spider Woman spoke thus to him, "Poor grandson," said she to him. "Evil Kachina has taken her away," said Old Spider Woman to him. She told him that Evil Kachina had taken away his wife. "He took her eastward," said she. "Poor grandson," said Old Spider Woman to him. "Come in, grandson," said she to him. "How can I go in?" said the husband of Yellow Woman. Then he entered Old Spider Woman's house. "Sit down!" said Old Spider Woman, "my grandson." Then he sat down. Then, "Eat, grandson!" Old Spider Woman cooked a snowbird head. Just one was there. Then she served it to him. He was eating. He ate the head of the snowbird. He broke it to pieces. Then Old Spider Woman spoke thus, "Oh my," said she, "grandson! you have broken the snowbird head," said Old Spider Woman. "We had only one to serve, grandson. The poor one! My poor grandson killed one. He always goes hunting snowbirds. My poor grandson never kills any more (?)" said Old Spider Woman. Then her grandson spoke thus, "Do not say so. I shall go hunting, grandmother, I shall hunt snowbirds for you." Then he killed snowbirds. He arrived below at the river. Then he went hunting snowbirds for her to serve. Then he made traps for the snowbirds. He made snares. Then he hunted the snowbirds with snares, and he killed many. Then Old Spider Woman took them to her house. Then he arrived at Old Spider Woman's house. Then, "Grandmother," said he to her, "there below!" said he. "That is good!" said Old Spider Woman. Then her grandson entered downward. He was in search of his wife. He had been hunting snowbirds for Old Spider Woman. "Thank you," said Old Spider Woman. "Grandson, I want to take you to where your wife is. Evil Kachina took her away. Will you go after your wife?" said she to him. "Yes; I will go after my wife," said he. "Let me take you there, grandson!" Then Old Spider Woman made medicine for him. Then they went. Old Spider Woman took him to Evil Kachina's house. He arrived there. Then he arrived at the town. Then, "Woe!" said the people of the town. "Woe! He is mean. He has taken your wife. Woe! Evil Kachina is mean. He will kill you. Nobody stays there. Evil Kachina has gone hunting," they said. "Right there in the town, there is your wife," they said. "Evil Kachina has stolen her. He is very mean. Did he take your wife?" they said to him. "Yes," said he. "I came to get her, because Evil Kachina stole her from me. I came after her. I must get my wife back." Then he entered Evil Kachina's house. He went in. Then his wife was there. Then he found his wife. Then his wife jumped toward her husband. She hugged him. "My poor husband," said she to him. "How did you come here?" said she to him. "I have been searching for you," said he to his wife. "Poor one," said he to her. "Old Spider Woman brought me here," said he. "Evil Kachina stole you from me," said he. "I came to get you," said he to his wife. "Now let us go, I'll take you to our home," said he to her. Then he took her back. Old Spider Woman was waiting for them. Then he took her there. Old Spider Woman said thus to him, "Are you coming, grandson?" said she to him. "Yes," said he. "Now I brought my wife here," said he. "Poor one," said Old Spider Woman, "grandson. Let us go!" said she. Then Old Spider Woman and his wife (and he) went together. He took his wife back. They went back from the east. They had been in the east. There in the east dwells Evil Kachina. Far away he had taken Yellow Woman. Here from the east he took her. Together from the east came they, the three together. Way over there in the east dwells Evil Kachina. Then he arrived at his house. Yellow Woman was no longer there. Now her husband had already taken back Yellow Woman. Then Evil Kachina arrived. No more did he find Yellow Woman. Already her husband had taken her back. Then Evil Kachina became angry. Then Evil Kachina pursued Yellow Woman. Evil Kachina came from the east. Already Yellow Woman had arrived at her house here. She had arrived at her husband's house. Evil Kachina was pursuing them. Then Evil Kachina came out from the east thundering. He was about to shoot them, both her and her husband, (but) Evil Kachina shot beside (the mark). Evil Kachina is mean. Then Evil Kachina arrived at Yellow Woman's house. Then he said to him thus, "Why did you take her back?" said Evil Kachina to him. Thus he said to the two, "If Yellow Woman were not pregnant, I should kill you." Thus he said to both Yellow Woman and her husband. Then Evil Kachina said to him, when the pregnant Yellow Woman would give birth to a child that would be Evil Kachina's child. Then she gave birth. Evil Kachina came after his child. Yellow Woman being pregnant, therefore Evil Kachina did not kill the two. Then Evil Kachina said it was his child. Then Yellow Woman gave birth to a child. Then Evil Kachina went to where he dwelt. There somewhere on the northeast side far away he came out. Evil Kachina had taken away too many Yellow Women. He had already taken many. Those who did not make wafer bread quickly enough Evil Kachina threw down from the north side. He is mean. The poor girls, he threw them down upon the ice. Many he had taken. He is too mean. They all died below on the north side on the ice, the poor ones. Nobody went after the Yellow Women, the poor ones, and they froze to death there below. He is too mean. He never forgave them. Evil Kachina had no consideration. Whoever did not grind flour quickly enough and had not made wafer bread when he came home from hunting, and they had not made the wafer bread, then he threw them down, the Yellow Women, on the north side. Then there below they died. They froze to death on the ice, the poor Yellow Women. Down below there they died. No one went after the Yellow Women. Then Evil Kachina threw them down. Evil Kachina did not forgive any one of them. Therefore they abused Evil Kachina below in this town. He would take any Yellow Woman. Therefore they abused Evil Kachina. "Oh, poor ones," they said. "Now he has again taken from somewhere a poor Yellow Woman." Oh, dear, Evil Kachina is mean, the poor Yellow Women. He fooled the poor Yellow Women. The poor ones! Evil Kachina took them along. "Oh my! He is mean," they said, "Oh my! The poor ones, he fools the poor ones with the kicking stick. Therefore he always takes away the Yellow Women. He has fooled many poor Yellow Women. They all died there below on the ice. He threw down the poor Yellow Women and their sisters. Evil Kachina is mean. Oh my! Evil Kachina comes after them this way, with the kicking stick. Then he takes the Yellow Woman away. The poor ones! He kills them. Evil Kachina asks them too urgently to work for him. A Yellow Woman that does not agree to do so when he has taken the Yellow Woman, then that one he throws them down on the north side. Evil Kachina is too mean. When he has taken a Yellow Woman and anyone goes after the

Yellow Woman then, when he arrives in the evening and does not find the Yellow Woman, then Evil Kachina knows about it. At once he pursues the Yellow Woman (and the one who took her back). Now Evil Kachina kills them. He always kills them. He walks with much noise. Nobody lives there, but Evil Kachina lives by himself. He is all alone. He is very bad. — That long is the bald tail. That is all.

Sun Steals Yellow Woman

AT OLD COCHITI (Tiputse) lived a man and his wife. His name was Stilina (dance shells). His wife went for water and Sun came and stole her. Her husband didn't know where she had gone. He mourned for her and tried to follow her tracks. He was lying in a muddy place and something crawled on his neck and spoke to him. It was Spider Woman. She said, "What are you doing here?" "I'm mourning for my wife who was stolen from me." "Don't think of her, my son, and keep wondering where your wife is. Your wife is where the sun comes up. There are two roads to that place, a new and an old. Don't follow the new road; take the old. On the new road a dangerous person will kill you. So go the old road."

He started on his journey. When he came to the two roads, he wondered why Spider Woman had said not to go by the good road, so he took the new road. He came to the house of Whirlwind Man. He was out hunting, only his mother was at home. She set out food for her guest. He was still eating, when he heard Whirlwind Man coming. He came in. They fought. The mother tried to separate them, but Shell Man killed Whirlwind Man. His mother was frightened. She said, "Hurry, hurry, press his stomach. See if you can make him alive again." Then Shell Man pressed him, and he came to life. Then his mother said to her son, "Don't fight with this man any more, my son. It is because of Shell Man that you are alive again." She put food out again.

Whirlwind Man said to Shell Man, "I will take you where you wish to go." So he took him where Sun rises. Whirlwind Man picked him up and took him to the top of the high cliffs where his wife was. Whirlwind Man said to Shell Man, "Go over yonder, you will find her alone. Sun is out hunting." He went into Sun's house, and he found his wife grinding. She was frightened. "How did you get here, my husband? Nobody comes here, it is too dangerous." "I've come to get you. Before Sun comes home from hunting I will take you back." She got ready. They went out before Sun came home. When they got where Whirlwind was waiting, he started homeward with them.

Sun came home and the woman was gone. He shot an arrow after them but it fell to one side. They were safe, no man can harm a woman while she is carrying his child. They reached Whirlwind Man's house. "We have to go on to our home," they said. They came to their own house. While they were coming along the road, Sun shot another arrow. Shell Man cried, "Hurry up, we must go faster, the man who stole you is coming after us!" Sun was shooting. When they got to Tiputse, Sun was right behind them, but the woman was safe. Sun said to Yellow Woman, "You shall have a child and he shall be chief of this people."

Whirlwind Man Steals Yellow Woman

KOCHINNENAKO, YELLOW WOMAN, was grinding corn one day with her three sisters. They looked into the water jars and saw that they were empty. They said, "We need some water." Kochinnenako said she would go, and taking the jars made her way across the mesa and went down to the spring. She climbed the rockhewn stairs to the spring that lay in a deep pool of shade. As she knelt to dip the gourd dipper into the cool shadowed water, she heard someone coming down the steps. She looked up and saw Whirlwind Man. He said, "Guwatzi, Kochinnenako. Are you here?"

"Da'waa'e," she said, dipping water calmly into the four jars beside her. She didn't look at him.

"Put down the dipper," he said. "I want you to come with me."

"I am filling these jars with water as you can see," she said. "My sisters and I are grinding corn, and they are waiting for me."

"No," Whirlwind Man said. "You must come and go with me. If you won't come, well, I'll have to kill you." He showed her his knife.

Kochinnenako put the dipper down carefully. "All right," she said. "I guess I'll go with you." She got up. She went with Whirlwind Man to the other side of the world where he lived with his mother, who greeted her like his wife.

The jars stayed, tall and fat and cool in the deep shade by the shadowed spring.

That was one story. She knew they laughed about Kochinnenako. Brought her up when some woman was missing for awhile. Said she ran off with a Navajo, or maybe with a mountain spirit, "Like Kochinnenako." Maybe the name had become synonymous with "whore" at Guadalupe. Ephanie knew that Yellow was the color of woman, ritual color of faces painted in death, or for some of the dances. But there was a tone of dismissal, or derision there that she couldn't quite pin down, there anyway.

No one told how Kochinnenako went with Whirlwind Man because she was forced. Said, "Then Whirlwind Man raped Kochinnenako." Rather, the story was that his mother had greeted Yellow Woman, and made her at home in their way. And that when Kochinnenako wanted to return home, had agreed, asking only that she wait while the old woman prepared gifts for Kochinnenako's sisters.

Ephanie wondered if Yellow Woman so long ago had known what was happening to her. If she could remember it or if she thought maybe she had dreamed it. If they laughed at her, or threw her out when she returned. She wondered if Kochinnenako cried.

Leslie Marmon Silko
YELLOW WOMAN

v v v v
v

Captivity narratives form an early part of American women's literature, but this form of narrative has a particular application to American Indian women's lives. Certainly abduction and captivity by spirit people preoccupied earlier tribal women, and, after the coming of the white man, narratives of that sort proliferated because abduction by Spaniards, Mexicans, Frenchmen, and Anglos, as well as by other Native people became a relatively frequent occurrence. The narrator's confusion in "Yellow Woman" reflects the confusion in the tradition, as spiritual and historical events blend into one another in American Indian life and consciousness.

My THIGH CLUNG to his with dampness, and I watched the sun rising up through the tamaracks and willows. The small brown water birds came to the river and hopped across the mud, leaving brown scratches in the alkali-white crust. They bathed in the river silently. I could hear the water, almost at our feet where the narrow fast channel bubbled and washed green ragged moss and fern leaves. I looked at him beside me, rolled in the red blanket on the white river sand. I cleaned the sand out of the cracks between my toes, squinting because the sun was above the willow trees. I looked at him for the last time, sleeping on the white river sand.

I felt hungry and followed the river south the way we had come the afternoon before, following our footprints that were already blurred by lizard tracks and bug trails. The horses were still lying down, and the black one whinnied when he saw me but he did not get up — maybe it was because the corral was made out of thick cedar branches and the horses had not yet felt the sun like I had. I tried to look beyond the pale red mesas to the pueblo. I knew it was there, even if I could not see it, on the sandrock hill above the river, the same river that moved past me now and had reflected the moon last night.

The horse felt warm underneath me. He shook his head and pawed the sand. The bay whinnied and leaned against the gate trying to follow, and I remembered him asleep in the red blanket beside the river. I slid off the horse and tied him close to the other horse, I walked north with the river again, and the white sand broke loose in footprints over footprints.

"Wake up."

He moved in the blanket and turned his face to me with his eyes still closed. I knelt down to touch him.

"I'm leaving."

He smiled now, eyes still closed. "You are coming with me, remember?" He sat up now with his bare dark chest and belly in the sun.

"Where?"

"To my place."

"And will I come back?"

He pulled his pants on. I walked away from him, feeling him behind me and smelling the willows.

"Yellow Woman," he said.

I turned to face him. "Who are you?" I asked.

He laughed and knelt on the low, sandy bank, washing his face in the river. "Last night you guessed my name, and you knew why I had come."

I stared past him at the shallow moving water and tried to remember the night, but I could only see the moon in the water and remember his warmth around me.

"But I only said that you were him and that I was Yellow Woman — I'm not really her — I have my own name and I come from the pueblo on the other side of the mesa. Your name is Silva and you are a stranger I met by the river yesterday afternoon."

He laughed softly. "What happened yesterday has nothing to do with what you will do today, Yellow Woman."

"I know — that's what I'm saying — the old stories about the ka'tsina [kachina] spirit and Yellow Woman can't mean us."

My old grandpa liked to tell those stories best. There is one about Badger and Coyote who went hunting and were gone all day, and when the sun was going down they found a house. There was a girl living there alone, and she had light hair and eyes and she told them that they could sleep with her. Coyote wanted to be with her all night so he sent Badger into a prairie-dog hole, telling him he thought he saw something in it. As soon as Badger crawled in, Coyote blocked up the entrance with rocks and hurried back to Yellow Woman.

"Come here," he said gently.

He touched my neck and I moved close to him to feel his breathing and to hear his heart. I was wondering if Yellow Woman had known who she was — if she knew that she would become part of the stories. Maybe she'd had another name that her husband and relatives called her so that only the ka'tsina from the north and the storytellers would know her as Yellow Woman. But I didn't go on; I felt him all around me, pushing me down into the white river sand.

Yellow Woman went away with the spirit from the north and lived with him and his relatives. She was gone for a long time, but then one day she came back and she brought twin boys.

"Do you know the story?"

"What story?" He smiled and pulled me close to him as he said this. I was afraid lying there on the red blanket. All I could know was the way he felt, warm, damp, his body beside me. This is the way it happens in the stories, I was thinking, with no thought beyond the moment she meets the ka'tsina spirit and they go.

"I don't have to go. What they tell in stories was real only then, back in time immemorial, like they say."

He stood up and pointed at my clothes tangled in the blanket. "Let's go," he said.

I walked beside him, breathing hard because he walked fast, his hand around my wrist. I had stopped trying to pull away from him, because his hand felt cool and the sun was high, drying the river bed into alkali. I will see someone, eventually I will see someone, and then I will be certain that he is only a man — some man from nearby — and I will be sure that I am not Yellow Woman. Because she is from out of time past and I live now and I've been to school and there are highways and pickup trucks that Yellow Woman never saw.

It was an easy ride north on horseback. I watched the change from the cottonwood trees along the river to the junipers that brushed past us in the foothills, and finally there were only piñons, and when I looked up at the rim of the mountain plateau I could see pine trees growing on the edge. Once I stopped to look down, but the pale sandstone had disappeared and the river was gone and the dark lava hills were all around. He touched my hand, not speaking, but always singing softly a mountain song and looking into my eyes.

I felt hungry and wondered what they were doing at home now — my mother, my grandmother, my husband, and the baby. Cooking breakfast, saying, "Where did she go? — maybe kidnaped." And Al going to the tribal police with the details: "She went walking along the river."

The house was made with black lava rock and red mud. It was high above the spreading miles of arroyos and long mesas. I smelled a mountain smell of pitch and buck brush. I stood there beside the black horse, looking down on the small, dim country we had passed, and I shivered.

"Yellow Woman, come inside where it's warm."

He lit a fire in the stove. It was an old stove with a round belly and an enamel coffeepot on top. There was only the stove, some faded Navajo blankets, and a bedroll and cardboard box. The floor was made of smooth adobe plaster, and there was one small window facing east. He pointed at the box.

"There's some potatoes and the frying pan." He sat on the floor with his arms around his knees pulling them close to his chest and he watched me fry the potatoes. I didn't mind him watching me because he was always watching me — he had been watching me since I came upon him sitting on the river bank trimming leaves from a willow twig with his knife. We ate from the pan and he wiped the grease from his fingers on his Levi's.

"Have you brought women here before?" He smiled and kept chewing, so I said, "Do you always use the same tricks?"

"What tricks?" He looked at me like he didn't understand.

"The story about being a ka'tsina from the mountains. The story about Yellow Woman."

Silva was silent; his face was calm.

"I don't believe it. Those stories couldn't happen now," I said.

He shook his head and said softly, "But someday they will talk about us, and they will say, 'Those two lived long ago when things like that happened.' "

He stood up and went out. I ate the rest of the potatoes and thought about things — about the noise the stove was making and the sound of the mountain wind outside. I remembered yesterday and the day before, and then I went outside.

I walked past the corral to the edge where the narrow trail cut through the black rim rock. I was standing in the sky with nothing around me but the wind that came down from the blue mountain peak behind me. I could see faint mountain images in the distance miles across the vast spread of mesas and valleys and plains. I wondered who was over there to feel the mountain wind on those sheer blue edges — who walks on the pine needles in those blue mountains.

"Can you see the pueblo?" Silva was standing behind me.

I shook my head. "We're too far away."

"From here I can see the world." He stepped out on the edge. "The Navajo reservation begins over there." He pointed to the east. "The Pueblo boundaries are over here." He looked below us to the south, where the narrow trail seemed to come from. "The Texans have their ranches over there, starting with that valley, the Concho Valley. The Mexicans run some cattle over there too."

"Do you ever work for them?"

"I steal from them," Silva answered. The sun was dropping behind us and the shadows were filling the land below. I turned away from the edge that dropped forever into the valleys below.

"I'm cold," I said, "I'm going inside." I started wondering about this man who could speak the Pueblo language so well but who lived on a mountain and rustled cattle. I decided that this man Silva must be Navajo, because Pueblo men didn't do things like that.

"You must be a Navajo."

Silva shook his head gently. "Little Yellow Woman," he said, "you never give up, do you? I have told you who I am. The Navajo people know me, too." He knelt down and unrolled the bedroll and spread the extra blankets out on a piece of canvas. The sun was down, and the only light in the house came from outside — the dim orange light from sundown.

I stood there and waited for him to crawl under the blankets.

"What are you waiting for?" he said, and I lay down beside him. He undressed me slowly like the night before beside the river — kissing my face gently and running his hands up and down my belly and legs. He took off my pants and then he laughed.

"Why are you laughing?"

"You are breathing so hard."

I pulled away from him and turned my back to him.

He pulled me around and pinned me down with his arms and chest. "You don't understand, do you, little Yellow Woman? You will do what I want."

And again he was all around me with his skin slippery against mine, and I was afraid because I understood that his strength could hurt me. I lay underneath him and I knew that he could destroy me. But later, while he slept beside me, I touched his face and I had a feeling — the kind of feeling for him that overcame me that morning along the river. I kissed him on the forehead and he reached out for me.

When I woke up in the morning he was gone. It gave me a strange feeling because for a long time I sat there on the blankets and looked around the little house for some object of his — some proof that he had been there or maybe that he was coming back. Only the blankets and the cardboard box remained. The .30-30 that had been leaning in the corner was gone, and so was the knife I had used the night before. He was gone, and I had my chance to go now. But first I had to eat, because I knew it would be a long walk home.

I found some dried apricots in the cardboard box, and I sat down on a rock at the edge of the plateau rim. There was no wind and the sun warmed me. I was surrounded by silence. I drowsed with apricots in my mouth, and I didn't believe that there were highways or railroads or cattle to steal.

When I woke up, I stared down at my feet in the black mountain dirt. Little black ants were swarming over the pine needles around my foot. They must have smelled the apricots. I thought about my family far below me. They would be wondering about me, because this had never happened to me before. The tribal police would file a report. But if old Grandpa weren't dead he would tell them what happened — he would laugh and say, "Stolen by a ka'tsina, a mountain spirit. She'll come home — they usually do." There are enough of them to handle things. My mother and grandmother will raise the baby like they raised me. Al will find someone else, and they will go on like before, except that there will be a story about the day I disappeared while I was walking along the river. Silva had come for me; he said he had. I did not decide to go. I just went. Moonflowers blossom in the sand hills before dawn, just as I followed him. That's what I was thinking as I wandered along the trail through the pine trees.

It was noon when I got back. When I saw the stone house I remembered that I had meant to go home. But that didn't seem important any more, maybe because there were little blue flowers growing in the meadow behind the stone house and the gray squirrels were playing in the pines next to the house. The horses were standing in the corral, and there was a beef carcass hanging on the shady side of a big pine in front of the house. Flies buzzed around the clotted blood that hung from the carcass. Silva was washing his hands in a bucket full of water. He must have heard me coming because he spoke to me without turning to face me.

"I've been waiting for you."

"I went walking in the big pine trees."

I looked into the bucket full of bloody water with brown-and-white animal hairs floating in it. Silva stood there letting his hand drip, examining me intently.

"Are you coming with me?"

"Where?" I asked him.

"To sell the meat in Marquez."

"If you're sure it's O.K."

"I wouldn't ask you if it wasn't," he answered.

He sloshed the water around in the bucket before he dumped it out and set the bucket upside down near the door. I followed him to the corral and watched him saddle the horses. Even beside the horses he looked tall, and I asked him again if he wasn't Navajo. He didn't say anything; he just shook his head and kept cinching up the saddle.

"But Navajos are tall."

"Get on the horse," he said, "and let's go."

The last thing he did before we started down the steep trail was to grab the .30-30 from the corner. He slid the rifle into the scabbard that hung from his saddle.

"Do they ever try to catch you?" I asked.

"They don't know who I am."

"Then why did you bring the rifle?"

"Because we are going to Marquez where the Mexicans live."

The trail leveled out on a narrow ridge that was steep on both sides like an animal spine. On one side I could see where the trail went around the rocky gray hills and disappeared into the southeast where the pale sandrock mesas stood in the distance near my home. On the other side was a trail that went west, and as I looked far into the distance I thought I saw the little town. But Silva said no, that I was looking in the wrong place, that I just thought I saw houses. After that I quit looking off into the distance; it was hot and the wildflowers were closing up their deep-yellow petals. Only the waxy cactus flowers bloomed in the bright sun, and I saw every color that a cactus blossom can be; the white ones and the red ones were still buds, but the purple and the yellow were blossoms, open full and the most beautiful of all.

Silva saw him before I did. The white man was riding a big gray horse, coming up the trail towards us. He was traveling fast and the gray horse's feet sent rocks rolling off the trail into the dry tumbleweeds. Silva motioned for me to stop and we watched the white man. He didn't see us right away, but finally his horse whinnied at our horses and he stopped. He looked at us briefly before he lapped the gray horse across the three hundred yards that separated us. He stopped his horse in front of Silva, and his young fat face was shadowed by the brim of his hat. He didn't look mad, but his small, pale eyes moved from the blood-soaked gunny sacks hanging from my saddle to Silva's face and then back to my face.

"Where did you get the fresh meat?" the white man asked.

"I've been hunting," Silva said, and when he shifted his weight in the saddle the leather creaked.

"The hell you have, Indian. You've been rustling cattle. We've been looking for the thief for a long time."

The rancher was fat, and sweat began to soak through his white cowboy shirt and the wet cloth stuck to the thick rolls of belly fat. He almost seemed to be panting from the exertion of talking, and he smelled rancid, maybe because Silva scared him.

Silva turned to me and smiled. "Go back up the mountain, Yellow Woman."

The white man got angry when he heard Silva speak in a language he couldn't understand. "Don't try anything, Indian. Just keep riding to Marquez. We'll call the state police from there."

The rancher must have been unarmed because he was very frightened and if he had a gun he would have pulled it out then. I turned my horse around and the rancher yelled, "Stop!" I looked at Silva for an instant and there was something ancient and dark — something I could feel in my stomach — in his eyes, and when I glanced at his hand I saw his finger on the trigger of the .30-30 that was still in the saddle scabbard. I slapped my horse across the flank and the sacks of raw meat swung against my knees as the horse leaped up the trail. It was hard to keep my balance, and once I thought I felt the saddle slipping backward; it was because of this that I could not look back.

I didn't stop until I reached the ridge where the trail forked. The horse was breathing deep gasps and there was a dark film of sweat on its neck. I looked down in the direction I had come from, but I couldn't see the place. I waited. The wind came up and pushed warm air past me. I looked up at the sky, pale blue and full of thin clouds and fading vapor trails left by jets.

I think four shots were fired — I remember hearing four hollow explosions that reminded me of deer hunting. There could have been more shots after that, but I couldn't have heard them because my horse was running again and the loose rocks were making too much noise as they scattered around his feet.

Horses have a hard time running downhill, but I went that way instead of uphill to the mountain because I thought it was safer. I felt better with the horse running southeast past the round gray hills that were covered with cedar trees and black lava rock. When I got to the plain in the distance I could see the dark green patches of tamaracks that grew along the river; and beyond the river I could see the beginning of the pale sandrock mesas.

I stopped the horse and looked back to see if anyone was coming; then I got off the horse and turned the horse around, wondering if it would go back to its corral under the pines on the mountain. It looked back at me for a moment and then plucked a mouthful of green tumbleweeds before it trotted back up the trail with its ears pointed forward, carrying its head daintily to one side to avoid stepping on the dragging reins. When the horse disappeared over the last hill, the gunny sacks full of meat were still swinging and bouncing.

I walked toward the river on a wood-hauler's road that I knew would eventually lead to the paved road. I was thinking about waiting beside the road for someone to drive by, but by the time I got to the pavement I had decided it wasn't very far to walk if I followed the river back the way Silva and I had come.

The river water tasted good, and I sat in the shade under a cluster of silvery willows. I thought about Silva, and I felt sad at leaving him; still, there was something strange about him, and I tried to figure it out all the way back home.

I came back to the place on the river bank where he had been sitting the first time I saw him. The green willow leaves that he had trimmed from the branch were still lying there, wilted in the sand. I saw the leaves and I wanted to go back to him — to kiss him and to touch him — but the mountains were too far away now. And I told myself, because I believe it, he will come back sometime and be waiting again by the river.

I followed the path up from the river into the village. The sun was getting low, and I could smell supper cooking when I got to the screen door of my house. I could hear their voices inside — my mother was telling my grandmother how to fix the Jell-O and my husband, Al, was playing with the baby. I decided to tell them that some Navajo had kidnaped me, but I was sorry that old Grandpa wasn't alive to hear my story because it was the Yellow Woman stories he liked to tell best.

Paula Gunn Allen
DEEP PURPLE

V V V V

V

The situations that face modern Native women differ in some ways from those that faced our elders, but most of the features in those situations are the same. In earlier times, the fact of inundation by white culture was not as stark as it is at present, so some choices that seemed possible then become improbable now. Resistance to colonization — to soul-theft, heart-theft, and mind-theft — takes a different tack in the late twentieth century. In our time, that resistance is expressed as often through the poetry, stories, and novels being published as it is in Indian activist movements. Indeed, the two go hand in hand. "Deep Purple" addresses the issue of colonization in the women's movement. In many respects, Leela's quandary is analogous to the one in which Yellow Woman, Green-blanket Feet, Blue Bird, Albertine, and Esther find themselves mired. Because she is a Native lesbian cast ashore on the beach of the white lesbian's world far from the sacred traditions of her people, because she loves a white woman, and because she is an urban Indian, Leela tries to reclaim connection to All That Is, to The Mystery, by means of politics and marijuana.

"Deep Purple" explores Leela's despair and sense of powerlessness, and indicates her growing awareness that The Mystery is present and powerful in her life. It is the Thunder Serpents and their earthly cousin who speak to her, the power of the old ways that surrounds her and all the women in the tale.

The final stories in this collection, "Deep Purple," "An American in New York," and "Stories Don't Have Endings" are ultra-contemporary in tone, content, and theme. They signal a shift in the kind of writing Indian women are engaged in. Rather than writing "Indian stories" as those have come to be defined in this century by non-Indian writers, editors, and publishers, these stories strike out and reoccupy territory stereotypically off-limits to Native writers.

The focus of these stories is American society. From the lesbian community in a southwestern American city to the ugly, bizarre, and terribly human world of Manhattan, issues of sexual identity, drugs, and their endemic presence in contemporary Native American life, and the right of Indian people to comment on and critique American society, are explored. In theme, style, and approach these stories rove far from the "drum and feathers" stereotype of Native people. They reflect the Native identity of Indian women while portraying them as an active participant in larger American society. No more to be seen simply as curio or victim, the Native woman emerges as a strong, doubting, curious, inventive, frightened, brave, confused, and very contemporary human being.

Certainly the stories in this book and the vast sky full of stories they arise from and return to testify that, for five-fingered beings, unfinished dialogue, a conversation that never ends, is as much the definitive characteristic of human life as laughter or grief.

IT WAS LATE. The meeting had gone on forever. Leela had to be up by six to make it to work. She was tired and stoned on the sensamilla she and Karen had smoked on their short, shivering walk home from the meeting.

The thunder and lightning that had played intermittently on the southern horizon all evening continued their display. Occasional bursts of sheet lightning illuminated the room briefly, while the flashes of thunder serpents marked their jagged trail through the dark ground with a distant crack. There was no rain expected. Only the gods conversing with one another, female to male, in noisy, ebullient exchange.

As from a far distance Leela could hear anger echoing. Her anger, that should have had her gut in tangles, her face muscles tight. But if tangled or tight she didn't feel it, floating as she was far from immediacies. She gazed at her face in the mirror, dim-lit from light in the hall. She hadn't turned the bathroom light on, fearing its shattering brightness.

"Man, what a trip!" she thought. Then corrected herself quickly, "I mean, gee, what a trip. No, not gee," she giggled silently, "gee is probably short for Jesus, and we want no hint of patriarchalism in this house. In this mirror. In this head. Both the one on the body and the one the body and head are standing in. You shouldn't even be living here!" she scolded herself.

The anger burst through her haze: "Goddammit, Karen Powers, I hate you for getting me into this! You tick me off, sweetie, you and your perfect politics. Damn you!" She seethed in a low mumble.

"I hate being used! Why oh why do I go to these damned meetings? Why do I love that damn woman? What do we have in common, anyway?" Feeling calmer, she squeezed toothpaste onto her purple toothbrush with exaggerated care. "The color purple? Purple prose, maybe. But, color? Naw. Too many of us don't have any, don't want any, and are sure as hell pretending we'd like to be close to some, like you, Karen dear, my one and only love."

She treasured the brush, felt triumphant in having found one in exactly that shade of deep purple. She had thought of it as a symbol of community, of belonging, of true love and commitment. For a second she recognized that the community she sought was made of the same stuff as the toothbrush.

She found an old old tune in the litter of her mind. *When the deep purple falls over sleepy garden walls.* She felt with a rush the feelings the song had long evoked, the longing, the sense of love, of closeness, the heat of a New Mexico July day giving way to the purple shadows of a cool, sky-brilliant night, the memory of rain falling in purple sheets from the bellies of great thunderheads. She was filled with a feeling of loss, of despair, as a sudden flash of lightning illuminated the great gulf between how she wanted her world to be, and how it was. "Yeah," she taunted the thunder serpents, "and it's not July, either. It's October and winter's a-comin' in. So you can stop with the fireworks, gang. You're out of time!"

Her thoughts drifted to the adobe-walled yard, the adobe house where she and her lover, Karen, had spent the evening. She was almost numb to the despair hovering in the shadowy spaces of the bathroom, her reflection in the mirror rebounding over the flat planes of her dark face, making it somehow darker.

"Let's see. There must have been thirty or thirty-five mostly standard American brand dykes and a smattering of deviants, which included me twice: two fatties — me and Isabel; five coloreds — me, Isabel, Gilda, Dorothy, and Trini; and a couple of leather dykes — Trini and the blonde woman whose name I forgot to get.

"Of course Trini would show up. She smelled blood probably. Drank herself silly. I was just as glad she was there in her slick d.a. hair style, her leather vest, heavy metal studded wrist band, her lined and scarred face. We're so few, and watching Julia and her gang get uptight as Trini got more and more blasted was a trip. Back in that loop again. The thing about sensamilla is that it gets you into the weirdest loops."

Leela had felt a warm sympathy with Trini, a tough-talking Chicana bull-dyke, and had wished that she, Leela, could be as bold and brazen as Trini, as direct with people and clear about her real position in the world of the mostly middle-class suburban-bred lesbians she hung out with. Trini seemed to know exactly what the white women Leela hung out with thought of her. Even Leela, so good at not noticing whatever might make her too uncomfortable, had noticed their patronizing friendliness, their self-conscious political carefulness masking the contempt that flickered in and out of their lips like snake tongues. Leela was reminded of the snake she had seen the week before. It had been strange, seeing a rattler this late in the year. She had been walking down the path toward her mother's apartment when she spotted a small snake slithering across it. She stopped, and so did the snake. She had said, "Hi, snake," and the creature had curled itself gracefully into a figure-eight then raised its head and flickered its tongue at her. She had wondered if it was trying to taste or sense her. She thought it might coil all the way into a spiral and strike at her, but it didn't. They had stood silently regarding one another for a time, until Leela took a small step forward. At that, the snake had fled into the bushes where it disappeared. "Bye," Leela had said as it disappeared.

In her present marijuana clarity, Leela wondered if her friends' contempt for men and maleness masked their contempt of women like Trini.

"For sure," she thought, "Trini makes me feel weird too. Scared. Ashamed. Of what, I wonder? Of looking like that? Of being seen like that? Of harboring a secret lech for her style, her bull-dyke type? A lech? Isn't *leche* the Spanish word for milk? *Leche* mama, milky mama, *leche* baby."

She wondered what Trini had in mind when she came to the meeting — something she'd only done once or twice before. Leela had the idea that Antonia Gracia and Imelda Chavez, the women Beau had thrown out, were buddies of Trini's.

The thunder serpents and sheet lightning played the role of chorus and commentator throughout the meeting at Kay and Julia's house, a few blocks from Leela's. There, brokers who denied they had any power planned an assault on the livelihood of a real, live, black bulldagger. In spite of the thunders' impressive efforts, nothing had been resolved.

Kay, the president of the lesbian feminist organization Leela and Karen belonged to, Kay's lover, Julia, and their cohorts had been determined in pursuing their argument. As nearly as Leela could tell, those intent on confronting what they termed Beau's racism in making a couple of *cholas* leave the bar didn't seem to notice that Beau was black.

Two of the black women there, Dorothy and Gilda, had tried to head off this organized attack on a black sister, and in the end Leela had doggedly sided with them. She had remained outwardly tactful, inwardly unsettled by the color lines suddenly drawn by a group she had thought of as her friends.

But the Organization's officers had stood unmoved by the colored women's detailing of Beau's contributions to the community. As far as Leela could see, the officers had a cause, and were swept up by the heady feeling of importance and power that went with it.

"They've got to have noticed that Big Beau is deep, dark gloriously black as the sky at midnight. Could that be what caused their attack?" she wondered.

"Or maybe what really gets them is that Bodacious Beauregarde Baptiste the Bad Black Bulldagger from New Orleans has the bad taste to own a jumping women's bar uptown. Maybe they're torqued that she wields so much power in our little woman's world."

Uneasy with her reflections, Leela wriggled uncomfortably in her place in a far corner of the crowded living room where shadows partially veiled her. Her thoughts were making her even more uneasy. She didn't like her suspicions, but the situation had brought them to a head.

From the way Trini stared coldly at Kay as she talked, from the way Isabel Mendoza seemed to almost disappear into her chair, from the way Dorothy and Gilda glanced at each other, Leela judged that her discomfort was shared by the other women of color at the meeting.

Kay, a slender, carefully groomed woman with luxurious light brown hair and intense eyes, had written up a formal grievance statement accusing Beau of racism, exploitation of women, and lack of concern for the women's community. She wanted Beau to admit to the charges leveled against her and to publicly apologize to the women she'd thrown out of the bar. If Beau failed to meet those demands, Kay said in her clear, well-modulated voice, the Organization for Women and Lesbians would stage a girlcott of Beau's bar, La Coatlique, which the women usually called the Snake Den.

Leela noticed that most of the women at the meeting didn't really agree to Kay's decisions. They simply said nothing, making it seem that they agreed with whoever had the floor. Leela knew they had come to the meeting mainly for something to do, that they would attend a few meetings over the year, attend the parties, and make some connections.

Leela's partner Karen and her closest friends, Jennie and Meg, had not been among the silent. But they had done little to clarify the situation. They were what they referred to as "the red diaper contingent," and their chosen mission in life was to promote class consciousness and get certain points into the minds of whomever was handy. While she felt deeply bonded with Karen, Leela never understood what the points were.

As she did at every meeting, Karen had taken up her cause. Leela had not listened. Gazing around the crowded room, she noticed the heavy stillness that had blanketed it as Karen spoke. It seemed everyone had abandoned their bodies, leaving only breathing corpses in their place. She noticed lovers who moments before had been leaning close and cuddling each other shifting their positions until they were turned away from one another, no longer touching, no longer linked.

Their faces, which earlier had been at least attentive, went slack and blank, as though the life had gone out of them. Even their posture was lifeless, sort of slumped and heavy. They reminded her of corpses she had loaded into her ambulance, of people suffering from massive strokes. She realized that she had seen the same thing happen a number of times in the five or six years she had known Karen, and wondered why she hadn't paid attention to it before now.

A burst of lightning closely followed by a crack of thunder interrupted Karen's monologue, and Kay used the lull to reclaim the floor. She stood for a moment, slim and compelling, and in a voice just loud enough to command attention, over the chorus of "oh's" and exclamations of "that was close!" she read from her typed statement.

"It is essential that we as lesbian feminists oppose patriarchy in all of its forms. That includes calling our sisters to account when they employ patriarchal methods in businesses that cater only to women."

She continued, shifting her weight so that her usually militaristic bearing more closely reflected her prep-school breeding. "As lesbians we commit ourselves to the dignity of women, and that means to the respectful and loving treatment of women in our enterprises, organizations, and relationships."

A few women murmured agreement, and Kay continued reading. "Our commitment to building a woman's community is both spiritual and political, and that includes watching over our economic base, and in accordance with that view it's crystal clear that our business must rest on the basic principles of feminist vision.

"Though she may not have done so maliciously, Beau Baptiste has betrayed those principles which we are committed to, and we ask that she issue a formal apology to the women she has barred from Coatlique, open her books and employee policies to public scrutiny, join with representatives of the women's community, including members of this Organization, to draw up policies concerning customers' rights and responsibilities, and agree to abide by the Association of Feminist Business Women's Resolution on Fair Business Practices."

She looked up from her papers, "Of course we'll supply her with a copy of them, in case she's mislaid the one we sent her last year after they were drawn up."

Another loud clap of thunder louder erupted, almost drowning Dorothy's loud protest: "You've gotta be kidding!" She stood abruptly. "What is this, the Feminist First Reich?"

"No," Gilda said, irony thick in her voice, "it's the New Women's Plantation. And what's going to become of Beau if she says no, Missy?" she challenged Kay.

Kay cleared her throat and replied in her coolest tone, "As I said earlier, we'll call for a community-wide girlcott of the Coatlique, the Snake's Den."

A number of women murmured their agreement. Some, who had been looking distressed with Dorothy and Gilda's protests, were beginning to shift about, as though preparing to get up and go in search of more relaxing entertainment. Gilda and Dorothy clearly were not among the content, but before one of them could say anything, Karen's buddy Meg cut in.

"It'd be better, Kay, if you included something about the structure of the Organization. I think we ought to stipulate that Beau reorganize the Snake's Den as a collective. I mean," Meg's voice took on a more pro-nounced twang, "as long as we're saying Beau should follow sound feminist business practices, we ought to make it really clear how a feminist enterprise operates."

"Right on!" Julia belted as she untangled herself from the cushion she was curled up on and stood, her lanky presence seeming to tower over the seated women. She paused for a moment, her eyes wandering over the faces of the women sitting and lying around the room, then said, "I mean, why should we just make a dent in what's basically a colonial situation? Thing is, we need to nip reverse racism in the bud, and make certain the community moves in a positive direction."

A loud crash of thunder greeted her words. The lamps in the room flickered a few times then steadied.

Falling abruptly silent, as though her power had been turned off, Julia caught Kay's impatient stare, and blinked rapidly, as though she'd suddenly awakened from a light doze. Someone responded to her point but she seemed not to hear. Instead she ducked her head and collapsed slowly to her cushion, eerily resembling an inner tube that had suddenly sprung a leak. Leela knew Julia and Karen had spent the afternoon together. Given

Julia's proclivity for taking on the opinions and attitudes of the strongest personality she'd been most recently influenced by, Leela was not surprised at her outburst or sudden deflation. "She's a sort of psychological chameleon," Leela thought. "Takes on the protective coloration of her surroundings."

Karen said, "I think we should give Meg's proposal careful consideration before we decide on a final draft. That means we need to take a long look at Kay's proposal. Anyone seriously against a couple of weeks' delay?" Pausing for the barest fraction of a breath to glance around the mostly silent room, she continued, "If we're agreed, let's appoint a small committee to get together after this meeting and work on it. Maybe Meg, Isabel, Julia, Dorothy, and of course Kay, and," she paused again looking quickly around the room, "how about you, Leela?" she asked.

"Uh," Leela began, "say what? I feel like I didn't hear the lonesome whistle blow!" Her face felt flushed. She didn't like being pulled out of the shadows, or being forced to take sides. She folded her arms tightly across her chest and drew a shaky breath, glancing at Dorothy, Gilda, and Trini. The reassurance she sought didn't seem forthcoming.

"Uh, well, I guess one color's same as another, right?" she grinned, lifting her hair out of her eyes. She glanced uncomfortably at Isabel, wanting to ask her if she was willing to be roped into Karen's ploy.

She took a breath. "Okay, I'll do it. But, if I'm gonna be on the committee, I'm gonna talk to Beau first. Maybe Isabel will talk to Imelda and Tonia. I don't really know what's happening, except for some gossip I heard and then what Kay said."

She was surprised when her offer was met by a loud chorus of agreement. One young stranger, her platinum hair framing her face in aggressive spikes, suddenly erupted into life.

"I've never been to one of these meetings before, and after what I've heard tonight I might never come to another one, but for what it's worth, that's the only plan I've heard yet that makes any sense," she said.

"I think that Leela — that's your name, right?" she asked, continuing when Leela nodded, "that Leela should not only talk to Beau but she oughtta report back to us at next month's meeting. And someone else oughtta talk to the other women, maybe get them to come and tell us what went down. Then, after we get some real information, maybe we'll decide to drop it. Which is what we probably oughtta do anyway. But let's take this one step at a time, gang."

Her voice had gotten louder as she spoke, and her pale, delicate features had turned red, whether from nervousness or fervor, but Leela warmed to the big woman who looked somehow fragile.

Everyone quickly agreed, Trini offering to join Leela to talk to Beau about the complaints. "Me and *mi carnal* Beau need a good rap, joo know?" Trini said in an exaggerated Mexican accent.

At that, the group dissolved into small groups of talking, laughing women. Relief flashed brightly through the room; raised voices rumbled into sharp laughter and exclamations of greeting as the women rose and began to move toward the kitchen for drinks or smokes and crowded around the dining room table for food.

Relieved to be out of the spotlight, Leela moved through the crowd to the kitchen, hoping for a sip of wine and maybe some weed. She figured somebody would be out there with a joint going by now. She was right.

She spotted the punk dyke who had spoken up earlier slouching against the refrigerator. The woman's costume included five earrings in one ear, smooth black leather pants, a heavy metal-studded belt, and a wristband on one arm. The other arm sported an intricate tattoo that climbed it and disappeared beneath the white thin cloth of her t-shirt. She was a large woman, tall as Leela and broad-shouldered. Leela pushed through the tiny room to her side. Sure enough, she had a joint in her hand.

As Leela took her place next to the woman their hands reached out automatically, one offering, the other taking, the socially sanctified weed. They stood companionably for a moment, and then the woman said, "You know that blond woman, the one in the radical chic blazer standing by the door?" She nodded in the direction of one of Karen's friends.

"Yeah," Leela said. "Megan. We call her Meg."

"Well," said her stoned companion, "I used to work with her. She ruined the gig for all of us, and I quit."

"Yeah?" Leela said, not as interested in the woman's story as in her stash. "Where was that?"

"At one of the big law firms downtown. I was working as a proofreader, you know, going over the documents checking 'em for mistakes. It was a cool job. We gals took care of each other, did as little as possible, got paid for it. Got paid pretty good, matter of fact. Came in late, left early, you know, just sort of messed around. It was a cool scene. The dudes we worked for were cool, acted like they didn't give a shit as long as we got the stuff to 'em in a steady stream.

"Anyways, that broad comes to work there and next thing you know she's trying to organize us, get us in some union, yammering about the dignity of the poor workers, the rights of the poor workers, the health of the poor workers. She kept sending off memos, agitating for phones, different lighting, better ventilation, you know, the whole nine yards.

"Next thing she's got the boys all riled, and they start clocking what time we come in, leave, take a shit, you know. Hassling us. About the time she was getting up a full head of steam around unionizing, I split. Wasn't worth working there anymore. No way."

The woman offered the roach to Leela. It was tightly held by a heavy paperclip, one of the extra large ones. "Some of my bootlegged treasure from that scene," the woman said, nodding at the clip. Leela declined the last toke.

The woman snorted in derision. "Working class, my ass. That woman never took a working class in her life, you know what I mean?"

Leela nodded. She knew what the woman meant.

Kay made her way through the crush to where Leela was standing. "Leela," she said, "I want to thank you for your offer to mediate this issue. It was a stroke of genius, offering to talk to Beau." She smiled warmly and placed her well-manicured hand on Leela's arm, drawing Leela toward her. "It's so pleasing to know that women of color are getting involved in issues that are important to the larger women's community."

Leela regarded her blankly. She never knew what to make of Kay. She felt wary, almost cold whenever she talked to her, but she also felt reassured, even comforted by the woman's seeming warmth and confidence. In her confusion she usually reacted with friendliness, as she did now.

She put her arm around Kay's waist and smiled down at her. "Not to worry, Kay old girl," she said. "Beau's surely gonna see that you don't mean any harm by all this," she waved vaguely in the direction of the papers Kay was holding, "and only have the best interests of our community at heart." She took the papers from Kay and leafed through them.

"Those are for you," Kay said, her voice tinged with confusing warmth. "You can take them and show them to Beauregarde, so she'll know what's being said. I don't want to seem underhanded," she added, gazing guilelessly into Leela's eyes.

"Tell her to call me if she wants to know any more about this. I'd be happy to chat with her and get her side of the story.

"You know, I tried to reach her," she confided, dropping her voice and leaning closer to Leela. "I called her a couple of weeks ago, right after those women called me about what Beau had done."

Kay sighed softly, holding Leela's gaze steadily for a moment. Looking away she raised her voice. "Apparently she didn't care to discuss it. She never returned my call." Her tone was carefully pitched to carry through the noise of the room. When Leela looked around she saw a number of women looking at them.

"You should know," Kay continued crisply, "that Imelda and Tonia were very upset. They said they hadn't been able to sleep or eat for days. Imelda took me aside and said she'd come home from work one day and found Tonia lying there unconscious. Evidently she'd taken a massive dose of tranquilizers in an attempt at suicide. Understandably, Imelda was frantic with worry, and convinced Tonia, after getting her cleaned out and more or less coherent again, to come and talk to us. She said it was the only way she could get Tonia to agree not to do anything so drastic again."

Leela stared at Kay, momentarily speechless. "Wow," she said finally, running a hand through her hair. "You sure about that? I have the idea that Tonia's a heavy user. Maybe she o.d.'d. One of the drivers at work told me he took her to the hospital on an overdose last year." Taking a small breath, Leela ploughed on, her neck flushing with warmth.

"I think Beau's okay. Really. I mean, a sister's a sister, eh? and she's had some pretty tough times herself from what I hear. I mean, Beau's older of course, and maybe she's not as political as some of us, but she's a good head. A woman named Allie works with my mom, and she's old friends with Beau. She's told me a lot about Beau's past. Besides, Beau's been real good to lots of us. I can't believe she'd try and kill someone, or not give a shit if she knew somebody had o.d.'d."

"Well," said Kay, drawing closer to Leela, "we can't know for certain until someone talks to her."

Leela drew imperceptibly away, impatient with the sparring, suddenly desperate to break free. In spite of the usually calming marijuana, she could feel her fear turning to anger, her sense of comfort turning to a powerful conviction that Kay was the enemy and she, Leela, was betraying someone or something unutterably precious.

"Well, maybe Beau won't agree that there's a problem, or maybe she won't feel responsible for Tonia's overdose since she's had the rules posted clearly for years now. Tonia and Imelda must have known they were breaking them and would be thrown out," she said, her heartbeat sounding painfully loud in her ears.

"On the other hand, I think it's some kind of betrayal when women trash a woman-owned business." She eyed Kay briefly to measure the effect of her words. "Especially one owned by a woman of color."

"Let's not think of it that way," the white woman said. "Even people of color can be backward in their politics. Look at the ones in the present administration! Trying to say affirmative action isn't necessary anymore, that comparable worth is a farce . . . I'm sure you don't agree with that, do you?"

Leela felt her stomach contract painfully. "Of course not, Kay," she replied, forcing her mouth into a grin. "I just think it'd be a good idea to get Beau's side of the argument before we go riding in like the cavalry to the slaughter."

Kay's eyes went distant and cold. "I'm sure you're right," she said. Her perfunctory smile did not warm the rest of her face. "I have faith in you, Leela," she said levelly. Withdrawing from Leela's arm, she moved away, disappearing quickly into the other room.

"Whew," the spike-haired woman said, glancing at Leela. "You sure got her riled!"

"Yeah, well, I guess I shouldn't have rubbed her fur the wrong way," Leela shrugged. Her stomach felt like an ant's nest, with all the creatures stinging her at once.

Her companion patted Leela's back. "Let's salute the girls who got free," she said, grinning, and turned sideways so Leela could see her tattoo, flexing her muscles so the snake on her arm sprang to life.

As she did so, the uncurtained window behind her lit suddenly with three successive flashes of brilliant blue light. It returned to blackness for a moment, then Leela saw four thunder serpents hurl themselves jaggedly groundward. The furious shock of sound that followed seemed to crack the pane. Someone screamed, then everyone laughed.

"What a weird night," Leela said.

"Yeah," the blond stranger said, nodding. "Awesome."

Leela contemplated her companion's tattoo. "Where'd you get that?" she asked suddenly.

"Actually," the dyke began, "in San Diego. Pretty boss, huh?"

"Yeah. Wish I had the courage to get one. How much did it cost?"

"Don't remember," the dyke said. "I was stoned. Probably a couple hundred, maybe more. A girl can't spend too much on her beauty, you know. You thinkin' 'bout getting one?"

"I dunno," Leela said vaguely. "Maybe. Maybe someday."

The gods were all around. And it seemed that last night they were aiming to be heard. Leela dressed in the predawn darkness, then turned on the kitchen light. Sitting at the kitchen table, she sipped herbal tea and munched rice cakes, her eyes nearly shut against the glare of the artificial light.

She was still caught in the rhythm of the dreams that had gripped her. The chime of the electronic alarm had scarcely turned her awareness dayward. She was barely awake enough to pull on her light blue uniform and tie her shoes.

Now, slumped over the table, she rolled a joint, her first of the day.

Flashes of her dream tumbled on her mind screen. Something about snakes falling through the midnight sky. Snakes that were starfires hurtling through the atmosphere to land far out on the western mesas in terrifying explosions. Snake egg fireballs, dozens of them, erupting all along the western horizon above Albuquerque. The total silence, the brilliant, blinding light.

In the dream she had been out on the west mesa at Volcano Cliffs, high above the western rim of the city. She had found a circle of stones on the southern edge of the southernmost cliff, and in it somebody had dropped a rubber floor mat from a car. Leaning down to get a closer look, she had seen a design in the black rubber. It was a jagged bolt of lightning surrounded by a circle. It was then that the firesnake bolts had plummeted from the sky and dropped their explosive eggs all along the slope behind her.

After that, she remembered trying to get home, to her mother's. Running in total, frightful silence. Running, but her feet not touching the ground. Running, not flying, but then riding in some sort of airborne vehicle. Not a helicopter, not a plane. Something like a car, like a science fiction hovercar.

Someone was sitting beside her, the pilot or driver. They were talking, but she didn't see his face. He told her to look below as they crossed the Rio Grande, heading northeast. The cottonwood trees of the bosque along the river turned into snakes, thousands of them, their black and gold bodies sliding over and under one another in a sea of orderly, almost beautiful motion. Oddly, she hadn't been afraid.

"Look up there," he commanded, pointing to the Sandias that rose stark and sheer above the writhing city. She followed his pointing finger and gasped. High above the eastern peaks she saw a giant white cloud mushrooming. It was filled with light. Light so bright it seemed she could see the bones of the great peaks below outlined in it.

As she watched in utter stillness the vast mushroom cloud took on the form of a giant woman, perfectly contained in the brilliance, perfectly, blindingly white.

The car she was in began to sink toward the valley floor as a thick, purplish mist surrounded it. The last thing she remembered seeing was her guide's right hand. It was pale and square, burnished with a light scatter of gold-red hairs. On his middle finger he wore a large ring, set with a round onyx stone engraved with a lightning bolt.

Recovering her wits, Leela sighed deeply and finished the last of her cold tea. "Sure wish I knew what was going on," she sighed again. "If this was the old times, or if Maggie had been a traditional, I could have gone to the medicine woman or someone and talked about this. As it is, I guess I better get to work."

She got up, picked up her warm jacket, and slinging it over her shoulder clicked off the light and shut the kitchen door.

"Rats," she swore as she started down the walk to her car. "Forgot to brush my teeth."

LeAnne Howe

AN AMERICAN IN NEW YORK

▼ ▼ ▼ ▼

▼

LeAnne Howe's family name is Anolitubbee, which means "One Who Tells and Kills." Her story, "An American in New York," is a quintessential example of what that name means. Only recently have Indian people been pushed into the constricting role of visitor and victim in what is, after all, their homeland. Howe's work definitively pushes beyond the prison bars, reclaiming an Indian voice that comments upon its world with humor, bitterness, sauciness, and compassion. She refuses to accept the limits imposed upon us by American expectations and requirements and, raising a clear voice, she sings the old-way songs, tells the new stories in their slangy reservation and urban ghetto entirety.

"An American in New York" takes a modern American Indian woman's story and, by means of style and content, tightly connects the narrator's journey to strange, exotic places with the oral tradition. It is a lively account of a Native traveler's experience, the kind that has been told since time immemorial during the meal the returned traveler shares with her welcoming kin.

"An American in New York" reminds me of some Laguna stories about travelers who went to a far-off land and encountered very strange people who had long tails and used them to swing from tree to tree. Ethnographic commentary on those stories holds that the Lagunas met monkeys in Central American jungles and didn't know it. But we have another interpretation, analogous to Howe's interpretation of New York, New York.

THE FIRST THING I REALIZED when I went to New York City was that everyone is something different from what they seem: JAPs are Jewish American Princesses; Arabs are Towel Heads, and Haitians are cab drivers.

I was sent to New York on financial business. The high-stakes bond business. There's something hypocritical about an Indian selling and trading U.S. Treasury Bonds. Even the word *bond* connotes servitude. To bond, to bind, to restrain, to obligate, to indebt, to enslave.

Bonds also help prop up, and perpetuate, the country's economy. They're printed on one-hundred-percent white bonded paper by the government, so the government will be able to pay interest on the other bonded pieces of paper they printed last year. The government's bonds are its words to its people. This is what we're worth. Our word is our bond.

"We're all bonded," said the head of government operations at Saloman Brothers. "When you're responsible for receiving and delivering four billion dollars a day worth of government bonds you have to be bonded."

I was sent to New York with a wad of expense money to entertain, beguile, and prepare the hogs (our operations people) for the slaughter. My boss gave me a pep talk before I left for the Big Apple.

"Show 'em a good time, take 'em out to eat, get 'em drunk, take 'em to a show. Do whatever you have to do to get 'em to handle our bond trades more efficiently."

Yes, Kimosabe. Me go to New York. Me make 'em like Indian.

I saw this assignment as a kind of reversal of historic roles. This time an Indian was going to buy immigrants. And I thought it a perfect opportunity to trot out my Tonto-with-tits garb. I'd learned a long time ago that even in Texas people don't recognize you as an Indian unless you're wearing a costume. They've seen too many Hollywood movies. So I packed my leather and feathers and flew back East.

For most of the three days I was in Manhattan, I wore my hawk feathers for protection from the enemy and as a way of advertisement. An American in New York. No one caught the irony.

Now that I put the whole episode in perspective, I think I saw myself as some kind of native sojourner on a vision quest, in search of that magical ambience Frank Sinatra sings about in *New York, New York*.

I wanted to see the Empire State Building, Fifth Avenue, the Garment District, Central Park, Broadway, Rockefeller Center, the World Trade Center, Radio City, the Statue of Liberty, and Hell's Kitchen.

No wonder we sold the whole place for twenty-six bucks and some beads. I wouldn't give you twenty-six cents for the entire island right now. It stinks. There's trash piled higher than your head on every corner. Old men and women are puking and peeing all over the place. You can't see the sky. Everywhere you look there's black grunge growing up the walls on the buildings, and there are rats the size of small coyotes climbing trees in Central Park. It's horrible.

Outside my hotel at the World Trade Center there was a young man who thought he was a bird. He ran day and night, up and down the concrete median between the streets, flapping his arms trying to fly away.

I asked the hotel doorman what was going to happen to the Bird Man. He told me when the Bird Man dies the city health department will pick up his body and bury it.

Sonofabitch. Those scenes from Woody Allen's film *Manhattan*, where he and Mariel Hemingway are taking a romantic carriage ride around Central Park, are as fabricated as those where Ward Bond is looking for smoke signals in *Wagon Train*.

I was as surprised by what I saw as the New Yorker who landed at Oklahoma City's airport and asked me where all the Indians and tepees were. I was working as a waitress at the airport coffee shop.

I stood there proudly pouring him a cup of coffee and said, "Right here, sir. I'm an Indian."

As I stood there in my stiffly starched yellow and white SkyChef's uniform, the New Yorker looked me up and down and asked, "You're it? I've come all this way to see Indians and you're telling me you're it? My God, darling, you mean you live in houses just like the rest of us?"

I said, "Well . . . I live in an apartment."

While I was working with the people in government operations during the day, my friend Sheree Turner, who'd flown to New York with me, was learning a lot about the city and its residents.

She told me that more than two million of the city's seven million residents are from overseas. There are more Dominicans in New York City, some 350,000, than in any city but Santo Domingo, more Greeks than anywhere but Athens, more Haitians than anywhere but Port au Prince. She told me most immigrants come to New York City because they know they can find fellow countrymen in this city, where everyone is an alien and no one is an alien.

On our last evening in Manhattan, Sheree and I decided to see a show and do some exploring on our own.

We dressed up like some kind of tourists in semi-evening clothes. Again, the victims of commercialism. We thought you dressed for the theater.

Sheree wore a backless dress with feathers and I wore a shirt that was slit down to my navel (sans feathers).

Most everyone else attending that evening's performance of A *Chorus Line* looked like they were going to a Texas Ranger baseball game, except two little old ladies from Kansas City who were wearing synthetic velvet.

After the show, I flagged down a horse-drawn taxi. A man steered his carriage toward us and stopped. Sheree jumped in back and the driver asked me if I'd like to ride up front with him. I was ecstatic.

As I was climbing into the coach, I realized why he asked me to ride up front. Both my tits were hanging out of my shirt as I'd flagged him down.

"Where you be wantin' to go, Miss?"

God! A real Irishman with a thick Irish brogue, complete with auburn hair and freckles. I imagined him a cross between Barry Fitzgerald and John Kennedy. (My faith in Woody Allen was restored.)

"We want to see everything, go everywhere, and spend some of my company's money."

He gave me a delicious grin and said to my tits, "Okay, Miss, we're off."

Seamus MacDonald was a wonderful guide. I loved the way he talked. He dutifully drove us around the Rockefeller Center and seemed to genuinely enjoy pointing out the sights. He told us where we could catch the Staten Island Ferry to see the Statue of Liberty after he dropped us off. He pointed out some hot night spots, and asked me where I was from.

We got on very well. I played the part of an investigative reporter, asking him everything from how long he had been in this country to what kind of girls he dated.

He was Catholic. His three older brothers were in this country going to law school. There were ten children in his family and his mother was still in Ireland raising the other six. His father worked in America and sent money to Ireland. Seamus said he was a boxer and eventually wanted to go professional. He planned to win the New York City Golden Glove Heavyweight Championship coming up in the fall. He said he loved to fight. (I knew we'd get along.) He dated girls who weren't Catholic. He was open-minded, but knew he would never marry outside the church.

I said I didn't believe he was big enough to be a heavyweight boxer.

"How tall are you? You don't look like you weigh enough to be a heavyweight."

I was baiting him. I like to symbolically challenge men. Whether it's a question of their manhood, their physical stature, strength, or just a game of trivia questions, they can never resist a challenge. Then, once they've proven they're stronger, taller, bigger, faster, or smarter, you have them hooked.

Women are no fun at this little ritual. They'll never meet a challenge head-on with another woman; they'll just go in another room and talk bad about you behind your back.

Anyway, Seamus fell for it. Putty in my hands. He laughed at me, gave me the reins, and stood up as we were going around 42nd Street.

He was big. (I'm attracted to big men.) Standing up in the carriage seat, his crotch was at eye level. He was also thick and very tall. He had a good size butt on him, too.

I bit my lip. My eyes glazed over and I swallowed hard. I began to struggle with my conscience. I was married. I was also averse to fucking someone only five years older than my son. (I wondered if my deodorant was still working? Was I wearing clean panty hose?) He probably had AIDS, or herpes. Besides, I hadn't lost that twenty pounds or so I was going to lose before coming to New York.

I looked around at Sheree sitting in the back seat of the carriage. I'd been ignoring her ever since I'd climbed in the driver's seat. She'd passed out with a grin on her face.

Just as I looked up at Seamus, our eyes met. He was still standing up in the carriage. His eyes were green and heavy-lidded. He smiled wide, revealing deep dimples and brilliant white teeth. I let my gaze match his and he said softly, "Your time's up. This is where you get off."

Oh shit. How humiliating. He'd just been playing the game, too. I wanted to kick myself. What am I going to be like in twenty years, a heavy-breathing old broad lusting after young boys with supple bodies?

"Wait a minute. I have more money and you didn't take us anywhere except around Central Park. I want to see things other tourists don't get to see. This is my last night in New York, and goddammit, I wanna see everything."

"Okay. For another twenty dollars I'll drive you places I don't take out-of-towners, then I'll drop you near a cab stand so you can get back to your hotel."

He headed toward streets partially lit by dim street lamps. We passed small, all-night coffee shops with outdated 10, 2 & 4 Dr. Pepper signs in the windows. Our carriage stopped behind a delivery truck and I watched a man with no shirt, and what looked like a dirty, wet towel on his head, rummage through piles of garbage. He picked up a crate covered with wilted lettuce leaves, shook them off, and carried it somewhere toward the dark end of the street.

"They are everywhere," said Seamus. "New York nobility used to bewail each succeeding wave of Irish immigrants. Now there's a lot of concern around here that the new immigrants, these Middle Easterners, these Haitian boat people, these wandering Hispanics, can't be assimilated into our society."

"Our society?"

"Yes, our society. I'm going to get my American citizenship one day soon. Most everyone wants the same things. We wanna eat hamburgers, and pizza, buy designer clothes, and Swiss-made watches. Maybe that's materialistic but that is why everyone comes here."

"But there's more to life, and more to America than just things."

"More to life than expensive carriage rides and Broadway theatre, you mean."

I shut up.

We continued our trip around a curve and slowed behind several cars that were in some kind of a line.

Standing on both sides of the street were women with strangely exaggerated facial expressions. Painted women. Women with day-glo faces.

"Whores," he said softly. "You wanted to see unusual sights. Here they are."

"Where are we?"

"We're close to what used to be Hell's Kitchen."

The whole scene became surrealistic. The women, some wearing bras and panties, some completely naked, reminded me of South African baboons I'd seen in film clips on Channel 13. Like wild animals running down from the hills to beg tourists for sweets, the women ran from behind massive iron trash dumpsters and empty warehouses to beat on the sides of the cars and throw themselves on the car hoods.

It was another kind of feeding frenzy. There were thin-lipped, gaunt, white girls; pregnant older women; kinky-haired Asians; flat-chested black/white girls with gray, anemic skin and bleached hair. They were pandering, competing, cajoling, and hustling up their dinner money from the car men in line.

When the Ford Pinto in front of us finally came to a dead stop, I grabbed Seamus's arm.

"Don't worry. They won't come over here, we're not customers."

The white man rolled down his window and the tall, black/white girl in a red garter belt, red hose, and heels with waist-length, mica-white hair leaned through the driver's window. I was drawn to her and the moment in a way I'd never felt before. My breathing quickened and my palms felt sweaty. I reckoned this was what it felt like to be a voyeur peeking into someone's night room.

All we could see were the buttocks and legs of the girl leaning through the car window. The engine sputtered for lack of gas. The whole car body shook for a brief instant, then went dead.

My eyes watered from staring at the girl's legs and then she raised up out of the car and looked in our direction.

Her mouth was open and she spit on the sidewalk.

I stood up. I was amazed. "God, she's spitting cum on the sidewalk."

Seamus pulled me down in the seat.

"Shut up."

The woman-whore met my gaze.

"You want some of this?"

She rubbed her stomach and then rubbed the wadded bills between her fingers. Her gaze pulled me into her circle. The Pinto engine started up and from the distance we heard an ambulance turn the corner. I looked toward the sound and then looked back toward the black/white girl. She was gone. They were all gone. There were only the cars in front of us pulling out one by one.

"Where'd they go?"

"They're like rats. They run and hide when a city car comes. If they get picked up by the police, their pimps pay their bond."

We spent the rest of the ride in silence. Seamus gave me his address and promised to call me when he won the Golden Glove Championship, so I could write a story on him. I've never heard from him.

He dropped Sheree and me off at a taxi station and we waited for someone to pick us up. It was two in the morning.

I put on my hawk feathers for protection while we were waiting for a cab to come along. About twenty-five minutes later, one stopped and we asked the cabby to drive us around Greenwich Village. He was very black and slight. He must have thought we were lesbians because on the way to Greenwich Village he pointed out every lesbian bar we passed. He stopped in front of a building with a giant plaster head of the Statue of Liberty and said, "Largest lesbian club in New York. Men not allowed there. You like?"

When we told him we didn't want to stop, he gave up. I asked him where he was from and he said Nigeria.

"I been in America seese months."

He looked at me with my feathers and asked where I was from. I told him I was born here, that I was an American Indian. He pulled the cab over to the corner and stopped.

"Oh, how much would I like to talk to you. You are the real Americans. This was all your home before we started coming here. I am learning about you in my classes. Right now, you are having a lot of problems with the government discriminating against you. To me, it's so sad. I want to do something."

I was stunned and a little ashamed. For a moment I couldn't decide whether to say something flippant or believe his sincerity. I believed he meant what he was saying, even if it was just a temporary state of naiveté. I answered lamely that there was always hope or something stupid like that. Here was this black Nigerian who barely spoke English, guiding us around New York City in the early morning hours, trying to comfort me about the problems of the American Indian.

He again said he wished he could talk to us but he must go home to his family. We were his last fare. We asked him to drop us off at the Staten Island Ferry. As he drove away, I thought about my ambivalence toward newcomers. Ambivalence at best; racism at worst.

After all, the flood of white people is responsible for my being alive. (I am part white.) And yet, according to the melting-pot theorists, turning "us" into "them" has not been easy. Even after two hundred and ten years of world-wide immigration into the United States, Indians still exist, numbering two million people in some eight hundred and forty-six tribes. About the same number of new immigrants living in New York City.

We took the ferry to see the Statue of Liberty. The Nigerian had made my feelings toward immigrants soften. Maybe more newcomers was a good thing. In a way, newcomers have forced us, at least some of us, to be stronger.

I've always believed that mixing white and Indian blood makes first-generation half-breeds unpredictably mean, and often confused. Confused by their misdirected anger, confused by their choices, confused by their inherited instincts which the scientists say don't exist.

> Man is a thinking animal therefore he suppresses any instincts
> and he learns from his environment. Take an Indian child

from a reservation and put him with a white family in Boston and chances are that he'll become a Bostonian and a working member of society. Eventually the Indian child will forget about his home and ancestry.

That's the theory I learned from a behavioral psychologist at the University of Oklahoma. But that was ten years ago. Now a recent university study, completed in 1986, says that your genes determine whether or not you can do mathematics. I believe if your genes can help you find the answer to a trigonometry problem, then they can likewise make you crazy.

John Stuart says it more directly: "You never know what you're gonna get when you breed two different kinds of dogs. Most of the time, the dog is smarter than its parents, but then there are those times when the dog is born a complete idiot. You just never know when it comes to breeding."

Half-breeds live on the edge of both races. You feel like you're split down the middle. Your right arm wants to unbutton your shirt while your left arm is trying to keep your shirt on. You're torn between wanting to kill everyone in the room, or buying 'em all another round of drinks.

Our erratic behavior is often explained away by friends and family as "trying to be." If you're around Indians, you're trying to be white. If you're around white friends, you're trying to be Indian. Sometimes I feel like the blood in my veins is a deadly mixture of Rh positive and Rh negative and every cell in my body is on a slow nuclear melt-down.

As we approached America's statue of freedom, the only sound on the ferryboat was the muffled churning of its engines.

I thought about all the Indians huddled on reservations, the tired women-whores bound to their pimps, the Irish boxer, the poor Nigerian cab driver. I thought about our relationship to each other. Now almost two years have passed and still the images of those people have stayed with me through all the July Fourth hoopla and one-hundredth birthday celebration of the Statue of Liberty. Even though not one word was mentioned about America's natives, only about the immigrants who've been coming here because they believed our country was better than theirs, I've decided Emma Lazarus, who wrote the Statue's welcoming inscription, was really an Indian: "Give me your tired, your poor, your huddled masses yearning to breathe free. . . ."

You did. Now where do we go from here?

Misha Gallagher
STORIES DON'T HAVE ENDINGS

V V V V
V

In the early 1980s, Mary TallMountain published a book of poems called "There Is No Word for Goodbye," and later in that decade LeAnne Howe published a short story called "Indians Never Say Goodbye." Ending this storytelling session with Misha Gallagher's "Stories Don't Have Endings" reminds us that our stories, like our relationships, and like the traditions they nest within, go on and on.

Primarily a poet, Gallagher gives evidence in "Stories Don't Have Endings" of her poet's relationship to language. Its tone of loss and haunting sense of loveliness intensify her feeling that she's in an unfinished dialogue with her mother and with the past, and move us beyond the particular details of a lesbian Indian's relationship with her own mother to a recognition that the story is about human women's relationship to their Mother Earth.

STORIES DON'T HAVE ENDINGS. That's the problem for me. When I look on my life, the things that have happened, I can't find any way to wrap things up. I was too lonely. I lived in an absence of relationship. When I got tired of a place I moved on. And I brought everything with me, all my hope and despair, packed neatly into my guitar case and sung out again through the strings. Songs I refuse to sing anymore.

Even my mom's death, there's no ending there. I'm waiting to resume something with her, an unfinished dialogue. Things weren't always so good in the past as they might be one day out among the new stars of our universe. I want to see my mom again, sitting on some big flat granite slab in a meadow, warm sun, blue of the noon sky, and my sisters there too. And a cold, clear river running by, shallow enough to wade in, yellow sandy bottom. It might be that way.

And where will my dad be? I don't know. I leave him in his pink negligee and blond wig, standing in the kitchen warming his coffee. Even if I knew I wanted to, I can't bring him into our circle. He is too complicated and I still have a child's fear of the abnormal.

Don't tell me I can't use that word! I know all about it.

I can accept him for the ways he came through for my mom at the end. It sounds mean for me to say, but it must have taken him a load of courage to lie down with my mother after she received Extreme Unction, and hold her hand. How many years had it been since he lay with her on the same bed? My mom held her own for a day and a half after that. We bathed her, my older sister and I, turning her gently, and water streamed away from the hot mass of tumor that had erupted beneath her skin. Maidu skin, creamy brown, soft as velvet.

Like I say, things weren't always good between my mom and me. There were years of intense struggle. Struggle for what? For control on my mom's part, for autonomy on mine. I suppose autonomy. I never achieved it. I gave in to her always. I was alert to her, even I guess when I imagined I wasn't. These days, I find myself hoping mama isn't watching from on high. But then I figure, well, it's time she knew the truth. So I strut around in my levis and black t-shirt, wearing my leather jacket. I don't turn her photo to the wall when I take my woman to bed and make love to her until she's crying out.

My mom knew she had a butch daughter. But it is a fine balance, a fine balance I had to maintain. When I slipped off into the butch side, boy, my mom would be mad. "Why are you carrying that girl's suitcases?" she'd ask indignantly. "She's big enough to carry her own. What are you trying to do, be the man? It looks ridiculous!"

Probably it did look ridiculous. There's a little door beneath my heart that opens on the word shame, and every shameful moment of my life crawls over that doorway and down into that dark place.

She didn't want me to be my dad. I mean what I say. She didn't want me to be like him, dressing up in clothes of the opposite sex and pretending to be that sex, that gender. "It looks ridiculous!"

But when I wasn't trying to look like a boy I still looked like a boy in my brown cords and white shirt and cook's apron. That woman who came in the deli where I worked, she was after me, flirting. She thought I was a teenage boy, a Greek. My friends laugh when I tell that story. "An Adonis," they say. And I laugh too. But that woman saw what she wanted to see. She bought baklava from me, no wonder she thought I was Greek. And in those days I'd say to Rachel, "Come here and dance with me!" and we'd practice some steps to a hora, or some Greek dance, around the tables, me humming the melody. And Rachel was a beautiful girl with long thick black hair. That woman admired what a pretty couple we were.

"What is that boy's name?" she asked my boss, Mrs. Goldstein.

"Which boy?"

"That Greek boy."

"What Greek boy? We have no Greek boy."

The woman was looking confused. And I was standing behind them, realizing, "Yeah, that lady thinks I'm a boy."

And was she ever ashamed when Mrs. Goldstein looked at her in astonishment and said, "She's no boy!" That woman never came back in the deli after that.

But hell, maybe she was only disappointed because she couldn't introduce me to her sixteen-year-old niece, Susie. Who knows?

Which reminds me that I did "rob the cradle" once with a sixteen-year-old married girl. And she knew I was a woman. But that's another story. I stole her heart, her husband stole money from me. So everything is equal.

But those aren't the stories I was planning to tell. I was thinking about Hood River, the farm, the factories where I worked. I was remembering the long days in the fields, baling hay. That was the summer. And autumn, there were rain showers in September clearing off to puffy clouds above the river, in a turquoise sky, autumn planting before supper, before the moon rose, full as a pumpkin.

I was anorexic in those days, slip-sliding on the factory floor in my proud boots, me on the second-to-last peeler on row six, the fast row where they put the youngest or the hardest-working women.

Hell, we all worked hard. Seven and a half hours a day, loading the peeler with six pears every ten seconds. Speed up, slow down, breaktime, lunch time, off work. In hairnets and plastic aprons. I never once looked at myself in the mirror in the ladies' room. A matter of principle with me, a matter of superstition. The lunch buckets on shelves, last names printed on adhesive tape: Gray, Turner, Rideout, Springer. And my last name, Gallagher.

We'd go into the company cafeteria. Chili stew. And rain coming down hard outside, sound of wet gravel being crunched by truck tires, and truck engines churning, the hydraulic whirring of forklifts. Men's voices, hollering. After lunch I'd always go outside and walk around, rain or sun.

And as Fall time came on, more rain, cold winds, and finally snow. Lights coming on around four in the afternoon as we were driving home from the cannery.

Sometimes on Friday nights I'd go down to Stevenson with my friend Sharon. She was a half-breed like myself, but a Yakima. I was in love with her. She had five kids, was about ten years older than me.

And I had it bad for that woman. I guess everybody did. Still, her husband was always going off to the bar, or going out hunting on the weekends. I seldom saw him.

It's not much of a story. In short, a lot of time getting drunk, a lot of time talking with her, a lot of time singing. The kids would get tired and put blankets and pillows down on the living room floor and go to sleep. I guess they wanted to be near their mom, in the dark snowlit living room, that one yellow kitchen light over the sink, the coffee pot making an occasional blip.

Finish off a six-pack of beer, drink a pot of coffee, go pee every half hour, sober drunks. Two, three o'clock in the morning, me, my clitoris pounding against the tight crotch of my jeans and Sharon saying, "You should always do whatever you want to do." Lady, if you only knew what I want to do. And I reach out to touch her long, Indian hair, just brushed.

She doesn't say a word, just looks at me.

But another time she says, "If you aren't comfortable sleeping on that settee, you can sleep with me. Jim won't be home tonight."

She is wearing nothing but a long yellow t-shirt. It must be near one in the morning. There is cold light on the snow, blue shadows of spruce and douglas fir, a black, glistening night of stars and half moon. I go to her room.

She is lying on her side, but her black hair is spread up over her pillow. I get in under the covers with my jeans and shirt on. I'm shivering. She is only a few inches from me.

And I lie there frozen, feeling her body heat, wanting to touch her, to take her in my arms, to put my lips to her lips, to feel her legs wrap around my legs. I want to hear her say my name. I want to tell her I love her.

I imagine how she'll recoil from me. "You queer! Get out of my bed!" And then that iciness, that look of disgust or amusement on her face whenever she looks at me and sees me looking at her.

"What are you, one of those lesbians? I better never catch you with my daughter."

So I lie there hating myself for feeling as I do, too much a coward to touch her, too much a coward to go away. Lonely. My hand nearly touching her hair.

"Sharon." My voice is less than a whisper. "Sharon!"

"Hmm?"

I don't say anything. I wait.

"Mom? Mommy?" It's her youngest daughter.

"What is it, baby?"

"Can I get in bed with you?"

"Sure, honey." She moves over toward me and lifts the sheets. Emily crawls in and curls up next to her.

"Hello, sweet lamb," whispers Sharon. "Were you scared?"

She goes on talking to Emily in a soft, warm voice. "Nothing's gonna hurt you. I love you. Do you know that?"

I hear her breathing into Emily's hair. I know her arm is around her small body, closing Emily into her heart and belly warmth.

Later I was ashamed of how jealous I felt, how I inched my body away from the two of them and cried.

But at 4:30 A.M. Sharon was up. "I'll make some breakfast for you." And she made me a sandwich of Elk meat and a thermos of coffee for me to take to work.

And after that? I guess I never did go back. I quit my job at the cannery and got another job at a factory making fishing lures and "Li'l Chief Smokers." You know, for smoking salmon, elk, deer, wild burros. Whatever.

And I didn't see her again, though once I heard she was working, selling Christmas trees at The Dalles. I drove up there in a snowstorm, like a fool. Drove everywhere, looking for Christmas tree lots. She and the kids were probably holed up in a motel room with one double bed and a kitchenette. I can imagine the kids watching TV, and her smoking, looking out the window with a far-off look on her face.

Stories. No endings. I dream of the river canyon, the Columbia River, riding our horses out by the bluffs, the northwest wind. In Spring, misty rain, dogwood blossoming in a narrow cut of the canyon cliffs. And the smell of wet asphalt, two-lane highway. Smell of pine and oak.

The day I came home, back to California, it was so cold I got the sleeping bag out of my car and curled up in it on the front porch, waiting for my mom to come home. I didn't have a key to the house.

They were surprised to see me, my mom and my younger sister. I don't think I even hugged them. Probably not. I never gave anything with my body in those days. I was always stiff with people who tried to hug me.

We made coffee. We sat at the table, as always. Somehow I knew my mom was mad at me.

"So, what do you plan to do now," asked my mom, "now that you're home?" She looked impatient. She had fourteen years left.

I lied and told her my plans. School, job, a way to support myself, my own apartment, eventually. But I really didn't know. I didn't know.

I didn't know until those fourteen years were finished, and she had moved on to the next phase, wherever, whatever that is.

I keep feeling that I want to phone home and talk to her. That unfinished dialogue. A way to explain those things I hope she now knows.

NOTES

INTRODUCTION

1. One thinks of such American mythic figures as Paul Bunyan, Captain Ahab, Sergeant York, the Lone Ranger, Horatio Alger, Luke Skywalker, Mike Hammer, Conan the Barbarian, Superman, and Rambo.

2. By *contact* I mean the point when a given Native community came in contact with Anglo-European civilization. The time of contact differs for various regions and groups within regions, ranging from 1492 to the mid nineteenth century. The Caribbean, Mexico, Central America, parts of South America, the Atlantic coast of North America, and the American Southwest came into contact the earliest, having been exploited and victimized by Anglo-Europeans at least since the end of the eighteenth century. Large parts of the Pacific coast, especially its northern regions, along with Alaska, the West, and the Great Plains, were largely untouched, at least directly, by Anglo-European conquest and colonization until well into the nineteenth century, though many tribes had experienced indirect effects of European presence for some time.

3. Ella Cara Deloria, *Speaking of Indians* (1944), quoted in the "Publisher's Preface" to her novel *Waterlily* (Lincoln: University of Nebraska Press, 1988), x.

4. As all the bands of that nation were referred to by ethnographers in her day. The Dakotas were located geographically between the more easterly Santee Sioux and the Teton Dakota (Lakota) who lived in the westernmost areas of the Sioux territory.

5. See Braulio Muñoz, *Sons of the Wind: The Search for Identity in Spanish American Indian Literature* (New Brunswick, N.J.: Rutgers University Press, 1982) for an intriguing discussion of contemporary revolutionary movements in Central America. Muñoz argues that they are led and "manned" by well-educated young people who aspire to ruling-class status but are prevented from attaining it by any other means than the overthrow of the existing power structure. To this end they enlist *los pobres*, and use the plight of the impoverished and oppressed as their main line of appeal in their recruitment effort. His analysis seems horrifyingly familiar.

6. William Brandon, *The Last Americans: Indians in American Culture* (New York: McGraw-Hill, 1974), 428. See pp. 420–49 for a good discussion of the "reservation" era up to the late 1960s.

7. Nor does it differ notably from Han policy with respect to non-Han peoples in the People's Republic of China.

A WARRIOR'S DAUGHTER / Zitkala-Ša

1. See Dexter Fisher's fascinating biographical notes on Zitkala-Ša in her introduction to Zitkala-Ša's *American Indian Stories* (Lincoln: University of Nebraska Press, 1985), from which this story is drawn.

Notes

AMERICAN HORSE / Louise Erdrich

1. See Heart Warrior Chosa's *Heart of Turtle Island* trilogy, book 1: *Seven Chalk Hills*, pp. 1–11. The book can be purchased by writing Heart Warrior Chosa, P.O. Box 355, Ely, Minnesota 55731.

AS IT WAS IN THE BEGINNING / E. Pauline Johnson

1. In 1987 the University of Arizona Press reissued *The Moccasin Maker* in an edition with notes and an introduction by A. LaVonne Ruoff, thus making E. Pauline Johnson's fiction available to a new audience.

THE CLEARING IN THE VALLEY / Soge Track

1. "The Clearing in the Valley" first appeared in *The American Indian Speaks*, published by Dakota Press in 1969, one of the earliest publications to devote all its pages to contemporary writing and art by American Indians.

EVIL KACHINA STEALS YELLOW WOMAN / Cochiti Pueblo Traditional

1. For more information about Yellow Woman, Grandmother Spider, and Keres or other traditional narratives, see Paula Gunn Allen, "Grandmother of the Sun: Ritual Gynocracy in Native America," "The Sacred Hoop: A Contemporary Perspective," "Kochinnenako in America: Three Approaches to Interpreting a Keres Indian Tale," and "Something Sacred Going On Out There: Myth and Vision in American Indian Literature," in *The Sacred Hoop: Recovering the Feminine in American Indian Traditions* (Boston: Beacon Press, 1986).

ABOUT THE AUTHORS

Paula Gunn Allen / Laguna Pueblo (b. 1939): Professor of Native American Studies/Ethnic Studies, University of California, Berkeley. Most recent publications include *Skins and Bones, WYRDS* (poetry), *The Sacred Hoop: Recovering the Feminine in American Indian Traditions* (essays and criticism), and *The Woman Who Owned the Shadows* (novel). She lives in Oakland, California, where she writes, keeps house, and tends her family.

Elizabeth Cook-Lynn / Crow-Creek Sioux (b. 1930): Associate professor of English and Indian Studies at Eastern Washington University. Publications include *Then Badger Said This* (stories and poems) and *Seek the House Relatives* (poetry). She lives in western Washington where she edits *Wicazo Sa Review*, a journal dedicated to issues in Indian education, and enjoys grandmotherhood.

Ella Cara Deloria / Yankton Sioux (b. 1889): Linguist and novelist. Publications include *Dakota Texts, Dakota Grammar* (with Franz Boas), and *Speaking of Indians*, among others. For accounts of her life and work see "Afterword" to *Waterlily* and "Ella Deloria: A Biographical Sketch and Literary Analysis" by Janette K. Murray (Ph.D. dissertation, University of North Dakota, 1974).

Louise Erdrich / Turtle Mountain Chippewa. Publications include *Love Medicine, Beet Queen, Tracks* (novels), and *Jacklight* (poetry), among others. She won a National Book Award for *Love Medicine*. She lives in Cornish, New Hampshire.

Misha Gallagher / Maidu (b. 1949): A poet and linguist, Gallagher lives in Albuquerque, New Mexico.

Linda Hogan / Chickasaw (b. 1947): Publications include *Calling Myself Home, Daughters, I Love You, Seeing through the Sun* (poetry), and *That Horse* (fiction), among others. She lives in Idledale, Colorado, in the mountains above Denver, where she writes and leads workshops.

LeAnne Howe / Chocktaw (b. 1951): Primarily a print journalist working for the *Dallas Morning News* and *USA Today*, her other publications include *Coyote Papers* and *A Stand Up Reader*. She has had her play *Big PowWow* (with Roxy Gordon) produced in Fort Worth. She lives in Arlington, Texas.

Humishima (Mourning Dove) / Okanogan (1888–1936): Her white name was Cristal Galler. With around four years of formal American education, Humishima worked mostly as a migrant food worker. She worked on her writing after long hours in the field. She published two books, *Cogewea, the Half-Blood* (novel) and *Coyote Tales* (traditional Okanogan collection). The Okanogans now reside on the

Coleville Federated Tribes Reservation in Washington. For biographical information, see Dexter Fisher's Introduction to the University of Nebraska Press's reprint of *Cogewea, the Half-Blood.*

E. Pauline Johnson / Mohawk (Iroquois) (1861–1913): Long known as the poet laureate of Canada in Canadian literary circles, her earliest poems date from 1892. She published *The White Wampum, Canadian Born, Flint and Feather* (poetry), *The Legends of Vancouver* (Chinook stories she gathered and reworked), and *The Moccasin Maker* (short stories). For more about her, see A. LaVonne Brown Ruoff's Introduction to *The Moccasin Maker* (reissued by the University of Arizona Press, 1987).

Delia Oshogay / Chippewa: Details about her life remain unknown, other than that she narrated the story "Oshkikwe's Baby" collected by Ernestine Friedl at Court Oreilles in 1942. (This is not uncommon. Usually little is said about the women and men who tell stories that find their way into published collections.)

Vickie L. Sears / Cherokee (b. 1941): Her stories have appeared in *The Things that Divide Us, Hear the Silence, Gathering Ground,* and *Gathering of Spirit,* among others. She lives in Seattle where she practices her professions of storyteller and psychotherapist.

Pretty Shield / Crow (b. ca. 1858): "I told Sign-talker [Linderman] the things that are in this book, and have signed the paper with my thumb." Pretty Shield was a wise woman of her people, a member of the Sore-lips clan and of a prominent Crow family.

Leslie Marmon Silko / Laguna Pueblo (b. 1942): Publications include *Ceremony* (novel), *Storyteller* (stories and poetry), and *Laguna Woman* (poetry). She lives on a ranch outside Tucson, Arizona, where she is writing a new novel.

Mary TallMountain / Koyukan (b. 1918): Publications include *There Is No Word for Goodbye, Matrilineal Cycle* (poetry), and *Green March Moons* (fiction). Recently her poems appeared on public transit systems in eleven cities. She lives in San Francisco, where she participates in many poetry and story readings and writes a column, "Meditation for Wayfarers," for the Franciscan (Catholic) magazine *Way of St. Francis.*

Soge Track / Taos-Sioux (b. ca. 1949): Her story was written and published while she attended IAIA (Institute for American Indian Arts) in Santa Fe, New Mexico, in 1969.

Anna Lee Walters / Pawnee/Otoe (b. 1946): Publications include *The Sacred: Ways of Knowledge, Sources of Life* (with Peggy V. Beck; nonfiction), and *The Sun Is Not Merciful* (short stories). She lives on the Navajo Reservation in Arizona, where she works as editor for the Navajo Community College Press, writes, and takes care of her family.

About the Authors

Zitkala-Ša / Yankton Sioux (1876–1938): Her American name was Gertrude Bonnin. Publications include *American Indian Stories* (essays and short stories) and *Old Indian Legends* (traditional stories). She was a passionate advocate of Indian rights.

FOR FURTHER READING

OLD-WAY STORIES

Barnouw, Victor, ed. *Wisconsin Chippewa Myths and Tales and Their Relation to Chippewa Life*. Madison: University of Wisconsin Press, 1977.

Benedict, Ruth, ed. *Tales of the Cochiti Indians*. Introduction by Alfonso Ortiz. Albuquerque: University of New Mexico Press, 1981.

Clark, Ella, ed. *Indian Legends of the Pacific Northwest*. Los Angeles: University of California Press, 1953.

Erdoes, Richard, and Alfonso Ortiz, eds. *American Indian Myths and Legends*. New York: Pantheon, 1984.

Linderman, Frank B. *Pretty-Shield, Medicine Woman of the Crows*. Lincoln: University of Nebraska Press, 1972.

NEW-WAY STORIES

Allen, Paula Gunn. *The Woman Who Owned the Shadows*. San Francisco: Spinsters ink, 1984.

Cook, Lynn. *Seek the House of Relatives*. Marvin, S.D.: Blue Cloud Quarterly, 1983.

———. *Then Badger Said This*. New York: Vintage, 1978.

Deloria, Ella Cara. *Waterlily*. Lincoln: University of Nebraska Press, 1988.

Erdrich, Louise. *Beet Queen*. New York: Holt, Rhinehart & Winston, 1986.

———. *Love Medicine*. New York: Holt, Rhinehart & Winston, 1984.

Hale, Janet Campbell. *The Jailing of Cecilia Capture*. Albuquerque: University of New Mexico Press, 1987.

Howe, LeAnne. *Coyote Papers*. Dallas: Wowopi Press, 1985.

———. *A Stand Up Reader*. Dallas: Into View Press, 1987.

Green, Reyna, ed. *The Remembered Earth*. Albuquerque: University of New Mexico Press, 1981.

Johnson, E. Pauline. *The Moccasin Maker*. Introduction, annotation, and bibliography by A. LaVonne Brown. Tucson: University of Arizona Press, 1987.

Mourning Dove (Humishima). *Cogewea, the Half-Blood*. Notes and biographical sketch by Lucullus Virgil McWhorter; introduction by Dexter Fisher. Lincoln: University of Nebraska Press, 1981.

Ortiz, Simon J., ed. *Earth Power Coming: Short Fiction in Native American Literature*. Tsaile, Ariz.: Navajo Community College Press, 1983.

Ortiz, Simon J., and Kenneth Rosen, eds. *The Man to Send Rain Clouds: Contemporary Stories by American Indians*. New York: Viking, 1974.

Silko, Leslie Marmon. *Ceremony*. New York: Viking, 1978.

———. *Storyteller*. New York: Seaver Books, 1984.

Walters, Anna Lee. *The Sun Is Not Merciful*. Ithaca, N.Y.: Firebrand Books, 1985.

Zitkala-Ša. *American Indian Stories*. Lincoln: University of Nebraska Press, 1985.

———. *Old Indian Legends*. Lincoln: University of Nebraska Press, 1985.

BIOGRAPHY AND LITERARY CRITICISM

Allen, Paula Gunn. *The Sacred Hoop: Recovering the Feminine in American Indian Traditions*. Boston: Beacon Press, 1986.

———, ed. *Studies in American Indian Literature*. New York: The Modern Language Association, 1983.

Bruchac, Joseph, ed. *Survival This Way: Interviews with American Indian Poets*. Tucson: University of Arizona Press, 1987.

———. *Native American Renaissance*. San Francisco: Harper & Row, 1985.

Swann, Brian, and Arnold Krupat, eds. *I Tell You Now: Autobiographical Essays by Native American Writers*. Lincoln: University of Nebraska Press, 1987.

HISTORY AND REFERENCE

Brandon, William. *The Last Americans: The Indian in American Culture*. New York: McGraw-Hill, 1974.

Jennings, Francis. *The Invasion of America: Indians, Colonialism, and the Cant of Conquest*. New York: W. W. Norton, 1975.

Thornton, Russell. *American Indian Holocaust and Survival: A Population History Since 1492*. Norman: University of Oklahoma Press, 1987.

Waldman, Carl. *Atlas of the North American Indian*. Maps and illustrations by Molly Brown. New York: Facts on File Publications, 1985.

GLOSSARY

Adobe: A pueblo house, made of a certain kind of clay and straw. Sometimes pueblo houses are made of adobe bricks. More often they are stone, plastered inside and out with adobe mud, then painted with a special kind of fine white clay or calcimine. Adobe houses are roofed with vigas, logs that span the width of a room or the entire dwelling. The vigas support closely packed small branches that are topped with a layer of clay-dirt a few inches thick. Adobes are the major architectural style of the Southwest. The houses made of stone are indigenous to the Southwest (primarily Arizona and New Mexico). Those made of adobe bricks are Spanish in origin.

Allotment Act: Also known as the Dawnes Severalty Act. Passed in 1887. Compelled commonly held tribal lands to be broken up and allotted to individual nuclear families.

Anishinabeg: The name by which Chippewa/Ojibwa people refer to themselves in their own language.

Aszoon (Athapascan): Fire.

Band: Certain tribes, such as the many Sioux groups, are divided into what white ethnographers have called bands. The band is composed of loosely related families who share a language, social organization, and spiritual system. Bands can have a fairly large number of members, not all of whom live in the same campgrounds or pursue the same hunt. In summer, bands would come together for socializing, politicking, and romantic trysts. It was a prime time for young people to socialize and choose mates.

Beadwork: Originally women worked with dyed porcupine quills, applying them in patterns to dressed skin for dresses, breeches, shoes, and decorative apparel. After contact with Europeans, Italian glass beads were used, and today many Indian women and men produce beautiful beadwork from glass or plastic beads that is either done on a small loom or stitched directly onto cloth to be applied to skin garments, moccasins, headpieces, armbands, purses and the like. Quillwork is also still done.

BIA (Bureau of Indian Affairs) ("Indian affairs are the best!" — that's an Indian joke): Established in 1824 as part of the Department of War. It was officially recognized by Congress in 1832 and later moved to the Department of the Interior.

Blackcoat: This man (in E. Pauline Johnson's story "As It Was in the Beginning") seems to be a Protestant version of the blackrobe.

Blackrobe: Jesuit priests acting as agents of culture change in North America.

Blood: Indian.

Breed: See **Half-breed.**

Cache: A stash of something, usually food. An English word fallen into disuse.

Camp, camp circle: Arrangement of lodges among greater or smaller groups, common in the Great Plains. From before contact up until the end of the nineteenth century, Midwestern Indians moved around seasonally, coming together in large numbers for a time in the summer, living in more scattered camps during the rest of the year, often breaking down into camps of several families in the long winter months so the food supply — mostly small game — would meet needs. Lodges were set up in a circle around a central dance ground. The positions of lodges were governed by relationship, family status, and seniority in status categories.

Carlisle Indian School: Located in Carlisle, Pennsylvania, alongside Dickinson College, and founded by Colonel Richard Pratt Carlisle in 1879. Carlisle was intended to educate Indianness out of Indian people in accordance with the colonel's liberal policy. He believed that his methods would save Indians from white abuse and destruction.

Chief: An English word for leader or spokesperson. Used to connote respect, derision, or the perceived social position of the Indian man so designated.

Chieftain: A lesser chief.

Contact: The point at which a given tribe or band came into contact with Anglo-Europeans.

Counting coup: A man of the Plains was equipped with a stick about two or three feet long and maybe a couple of inches in diameter. Armed with only this stick, called a coup stick (from the French), the combatant would leap into the fray and tag his enemy with it. The idea was to humiliate or shame the opponent by being able to get close enough to tap him. In early periods this alone constituted Plains warfare. It was not until the battles with whites that warfare that involved killing your opponent came into vogue, and for the most part this style of war was limited to conflicts between tribal and white combatants.

Dakota: See **Lakota.**

Do-eent'a (Athapascan): How are you?

Dha'wa'eh (Keres): Thank you.

Ecomienda (Spanish): A feudalistic system under which Indian lands and labor were handed over to Spanish colonists (*ecomenderos*).

Gisakk (Athapascan): White man.

Great Spirit: Post-contact, post-Christian way of referring to or addressing the Mysterious Powers of the planet and universe. Probably an anglicized version of pidgin Indian, derived from the Anishinabeg Kitchi Manido, or Big Spirit Person. This entity was not the same as the Christian concept of God, but one of a variety of manidoos who was known as the Big Manido. Many contemporary Indian people address the Great Spirit with true sincerity within their own tribal spiritual framework and outside of Christian circles.

Half-blood: Earlier term for half-breed.

Half-breed: A person of both Indian and non-Indian parentage, usually a person who is Indian and Anglo-European, though many breeds are Indian and Afro-American or Indian and Asian-American.

Haskell Institute: Opened in 1885 outside of Lawrence, Kansas, on the site of summer meeting grounds for dozens of Plains tribes, Haskell Institute is at present an institution of higher education for Indians from all over the United States.

Hochen, pl. **hocheni** (Keres Pueblos): War captain or country leader. A man who organizes social and spiritual events, such as rabbit hunts, ditch cleaning, and walking outside the village limits with a corn mother (iarriku).

IAIA (Institute for American Indian Arts): Located in Santa Fe and formerly the Santa Fe Indian School, the IAIA has graduated many fine artists and writers in the past three or four decades.

Iarriku (Keres Pueblos): A Corn Mother, i.e., a perfect ear of corn that is dressed in a particular way, kept respectfully, and fed daily. People receive them in early infancy but others are in the keeping of clan mothers for religious and ceremonial purposes.

Ite, missa est (Latin): Go, it is finished. Said at the end of Roman Catholic masses in the pre-Vatican II rite. (See Mary TallMountain, "The Disposal of Mary Joe's Children.")

J. C. Penney blanket: Cotton blankets that are thin but large so they can be folded into layers good for insulation against heat or cold. Many times they are pastel and white plaid. Taos men wear them wrapped around their bodies and heads in a way that reminds me of Bedouin men's way of wrapping themselves.

Kiva: An underground chamber reached by means of two ladders, used for religious services and men's socializing and weaving among the Pueblo Indians of the Southwest. Usually restricted to members of a given religious organization, many Pueblos have several kivas in use.

Lakota/Lacota (also called Dakota): One of the Siouan groups residing in the Great Plains from the late eighteenth century to the present.

Lodge: What is popularly known as a tepee or wigwam. Pretty Shield's play lodge was the Crow version of an American girl's dollhouse.

Mass: The ceremonial religious ritual of Roman Catholicism. It centers on the ritual transformation of bread and wine into the mystical flesh and blood of the human-supernatural Jesus Christ.

Medicine bag: The pouch, wrappings, or other container used to store medicine objects.

Medicine society: An organization for practitioners of a given spiritual discipline within a particular tribe.

Medicine: An English term that is widely used to refer to healing and other paranormal competencies that spiritual adepts have developed throughout Native America.

Meriam Survey: A report officially entitled *The Problem of Indian Administration*, published in 1929 by a private investigation agency, the Institute for Government Research. The survey, which assessed the condition of Indian people in the United States in the mid 1920s, criticized much of the government's policy toward its legally defined dependent populations, which had resulted in the deaths of hundreds of thousands and left the survivors in poverty, dangerously poor health, and with meager educational opportunities. It also criticized the land allotment policy of the federal government and recommended changes in policy at all levels toward Indian communities.

Métis (sometimes pronounced "michif"): A mixed-breed community of people who reside mostly in Canada and the northern United States.

Michif: See **Métis.**

Midewiwin: The main spiritual and religious system of the Ojibwa and Chippewa (Anishinabeg). It features a variety of rituals (dances, prayers, and ritual actions) and training in spiritual disciplines. Practitioners of the higher grades of the Midewiwin (known as *mide* priests, but who may be male or female) are able to perform a variety of paranormal feats. Their prayers are particularly powerful. Certain experiences, such as near-death experiences, are signs that a Chippewa or Ojibwa is called to the Midewiwin. It is a protective as well as a spiritual development system.

Mission system: A prominent tool of Spanish conquest and colonization, the mission system indulged in terrorism, hostage-taking, brainwashing ("re-education"), incarceration, starvation, and reprogramming. Rape of Indian women by priests and army personnel was common, as were beatings, hangings, and other kinds of spiritual, physical, mental, and emotional abuse. The great mastermind of the California mission system, Fray Junipero Serra, is a candidate for sainthood at present. The Roman Church expects to confer its signal mark of honor on him before the 1990s.

Mixed-breed/mixed blood: A term used to apply to people descended from more than one tribe, for example, Laguna-Lakota.

Parfleche: A container made from skin or bark. Exquisitely beautiful examples can be seen in museums, where they have been stored after they were stolen, found, or perhaps even purchased for a tiny sum.

Piñon (Spanish): Pinenuts that are borne bountifully by the western mountain pine trees; also the trees themselves.

Poles: The skinned logs or straight branches used to form the skeletal structure of a lodge.

Pony-drag (travois): Two long poles harnessed to a pony (or, in pre-contact times, to a dog), with the farther ends left to drag on the ground behind. Skins were stretched between the poles and the device was used to carry household goods or the infirm, elderly, or very young children.

Relocation: Under the termination push of the 1950s and 1960s, federal authorities mounted a massive effort to relocate reservation and rural Indians into the cities through offers of job training, housing, orientation help, and jobs. The effort succeeded in its main aim — getting Indians out of the countryside. However, it didn't improve Indian unemployment, life expectancy, health, or education. In fact, it may be a major factor in the teen suicide rate among Indians and in the other severe psychological damage Indians sustain. It created a vast generation of urban Indians; today about two-thirds of all Indians live most of the year in urban areas. Cities with large Indian populations include Chicago, New York, Los Angeles, the Bay Area, Denver, Dallas-Fort Worth, Tucson, Phoenix, and Albuquerque.

Removal Act: Passed by the United States Congress in 1830 during the Jackson administration, this act enabled the United States to force tribes into exile in distant locations.

Shota: A special or wondrous horse, touched or gifted with supernatural powers. (See Elizabeth Cook-Lynn, "The Power of Horses.")

Shoyapee (Okanogan): White man.

Skin: An urban Indian slang term for Native American.

ACKNOWLEDGMENTS

Thanks to the Ford Foundation and the staffs of the National Research Council and of the Native American Studies program, University of California, Berkeley, especially Janie B. White, Dorothy Thomas, and Christine O'Brien, for research funds and staff support that aided the completion of this book. Thanks also to the storytellers of all Red Nations who keep our spirits and our truths alive. I am particularly grateful to the women whose work appears in *Spider Woman's Grand-daughters* who opened their hearts to the page and made this collection possible. Their generosity empowers us all to remember and to keep on.
Dha'wa'eh.

Grateful acknowledgment is made to the following for permission to reprint the selections in this volume: Pretty Shield, "A Woman's Fight": reprinted from *Pretty Shield: Medicine Woman of the Crows* by Frank B. Linderman; copyright © 1932 by Frank B. Linderman; reprinted by permission of Harper & Row Publishers, Inc. Zitkala-Ša, "A Warrior's Daughter": reprinted from *American Indian Stories* by Zitkala-Ša (Lincoln and London: University of Nebraska Press, 1987). Delia Oshogay, "Oshkikwe's Baby": reprinted from *Wisconsin Chippewa Myths and Tales and Their Relation to Chippewa Life*, ed. Victor Barnouw; © 1977 (Madison: University of Wisconsin Press). Louise Erdrich, "American Horse": reprinted by permission from *Earth Power Coming: Short Fiction in Native American Literature*, ed. Simon J. Ortiz (Tsaile, Ariz.: Navajo Community College Press, 1983); © 1983 by Louise Erdrich. "The Warrior Maiden": reprinted from *American Indian Myths and Legends*, ed. Alfonso Ortiz and Richard Erdoes (New York: Pantheon, 1984). "The Woman Who Fell from the Sky": reprinted from *The Woman Who Owned the Shadows* by Paula Gunn Allen (San Francisco: Spinsters Ink, 1983); © 1983 by Paula Gunn Allen. E. Pauline Johnson, "As It Was in the Beginning": reprinted from *The Moccasin Maker* by E. Pauline Johnson (Tucson: University of Arizona Press; reprint 1987). Soge Track, "The Clearing in the Valley": reprinted from *The American Indian Speaks*, ed. John R. Milton (University of South Dakota Press, 1969); © 1969 by Soge Track. Ella Cara Deloria, "Blue Bird's Offering": reprinted from *Waterlily* by Ella Cara Deloria by permission of University of Nebraska Press; copyright © 1987 by the University of Nebraska Press. Anna Lee Walters, "The Warriors": reprinted with permission from *The Sun Is Not Merciful* by Anna Lee Walters (1985); published by Firebrand Books, 141 The Commons, Ithaca, N.Y., 14850; © 1985 by Anna Lee Walters. "The Beginning and the End of the World": reprinted from *Indian Legends of the Pacific Northwest* by Ella E. Clark, © 1953 by The Regents of the University of California; © renewed 1981 by Ella Clark. "Coyote Kills Owl Woman": reprinted from *Coyote Tales* by McGee. Humishima, "The Story of Green-blanket Feet": reprinted from *Cogewea, the Half-Blood* by Mourning Dove (Humishima), 1927 (Lincoln and London: University of Nebraska Press, 1981 [reprint]). Mary TallMountain, "The Disposal of

Acknowledgments

Mary Joe's Children": reprinted by permission of the author; © 1989 by Mary TallMountain. Vickie L. Sears, "Grace": reprinted by permission of the author, who expresses her thanks to Linda Luster for her listening clarity; © 1989 by Vickie L. Sears. Linda Hogan, "Making Do": reprinted from "The Grace of Wooden Birds" in *The New Native American Novel: Works in Progress*, ed. Mary Dougherty Bartlett (Albuquerque: University of New Mexico Press, 1986); © 1986 by Linda Hogan. Elizabeth Cook-Lynn, "The Power of Horses": reprinted from *The New Native American Novel: Works in Progress*, ed. Mary Dougherty Bartlett (Albuquerque: University of New Mexico Press, 1986); © 1986 by Elizabeth Cook-Lynn. "Evil Kachina Steals Yellow Woman" and "Sun Steals Yellow Woman": reprinted from Franz Boas, *Bureau of American Ethnology Bulletin* 98 (1936). "Whirlwind Man Steals Yellow Woman": reprinted from *The Woman Who Owned the Shadows* by Paula Gunn Allen (San Francisco: Spinsters Ink, 1983); © 1983 by Paula Gunn Allen. Leslie Marmon Silko, "Yellow Woman": reprinted from *Storyteller* by Leslie Marmon Silko, published by Deaver Books, New York, N.Y., 1981; copyright © 1981 by Leslie Marmon Silko. Paula Gunn Allen, "Deep Purple": © 1989 by Paula Gunn Allen. LeAnne Howe, "An American in New York": reprinted from *A Stand Up Reader* by LeAnne Howe (Into View Press, 1987); © 1987 by LeAnne Howe. Misha Gallagher, "Stories Don't Have Endings": reprinted by permission of the author; © 1989.